WORKAWAY

The Human Costs of Europe's Common Labour Market

Jonathon W. Moses

BRISTOL
UNIVERSITY
PRESS

First published in Great Britain in 2023 by

Bristol University Press
University of Bristol
1–9 Old Park Hill
Bristol
BS2 8BB
UK
t: +44 (0)117 374 6645
e: bup-info@bristol.ac.uk

Details of international sales and distribution partners are available at bristoluniversitypress.co.uk

British Library Cataloguing in Publication Data
A catalogue record for this book is available from the British Library

ISBN 978-1-5292-1101-6 hardcover
ISBN 978-1-5292-1102-3 paperback
ISBN 978-1-5292-1104-7 ePub
ISBN 978-1-5292-1103-0 ePdf

Cover design: blu inc, Bristol
Front cover image: Lerone Pieters/unsplash

Bristol University Press uses environmentally responsible print partners.

Printed in Great Britain by CPI Group (UK) Ltd, Croydon, CR0 4YY

Two dignitaries sat in the bleachers, watching a military parade. For nearly an hour, the two watched a long progression of jets, artillery, missiles, heavy machinery, military bands and rows upon rows of marching soldiers. Bringing up the tail end of the procession was an open-air convertible, filled with a handful of slouching and bespectacled middle-aged men. Puzzled, the one dignitary turned to the other to ask, 'Who in the world is that motley gang?' The other dignitary responded knowingly: 'They are the economists. You cannot imagine the damage they can unleash'.

Contents

List of Figures, Tables and Boxes

Figures

Tables

Boxes

List of Abbreviations

CAP	Common Agricultural Policy
CEDEFOP	European Centre for the Development of Vocational Training
CF	Cohesion Fund
COVID-19	coronavirus
EAFRD	European Agricultural Fund for Rural Development
EAGGF	European Agricultural Guidance and Guarantee Fund
EC	European Community
ECB	European Central Bank
ECFTUC	European Consortium of Free Trade Unions in the Community
ECJ	European Court of Justice
ECSC	European Coal and Steel Community
EEC	European Economic Community
EES	European Employment Strategy
EFSF	European Financial Stability Facility
EFSM	European Financial Stabilization Mechanism
EFTA	European Free Trade Area
EGF	Pan-European Guarantee Fund
EIB	European Investment Bank
EMU	Economic and Monetary Union
EPP	Euro Plus Pact
ERDF	European Regional Development Fund
ESF	European Social Fund
ESM	European Stability Mechanism
ETUC	European Trade Union Confederation
ETUF	European Trade Union Federation
ETUI	European Trade Union Institute
EU	European Union
EU11	Bulgaria, Croatia, Czechia, Estonia, Hungary,

	Latvia, Lithuania, Poland, Romania, Slovakia and Slovenia
EU15	Austria, Belgium, Denmark, Finland, France, Germany, Greece, Ireland, Italy, Luxembourg, Netherlands, Portugal, Spain, Sweden and the UK
EU17	Austria, Belgium, Cyprus, Denmark, Finland, France, Germany, Greece, Ireland, Italy, Luxembourg, Malta, the Netherlands, Portugal, Spain, Sweden and the UK
EU27	Austria, Bulgaria, Belgium, Croatia, Cyprus, Czechia, Denmark, Estonia, Finland, France, Germany, Greece, Hungary, Ireland, Italy, Latvia, Lithuania, Luxembourg, Malta, the Netherlands, Poland, Portugal, Romania, Slovakia, Slovenia, Spain and Sweden
EU28	Austria, Bulgaria, Belgium, Croatia, Cyprus, Czechia, Denmark, Estonia, Finland, France, Germany, Greece, Hungary, Ireland, Italy, Latvia, Lithuania, Luxembourg, Malta, the Netherlands, Poland, Portugal, Romania, Slovakia, Slovenia, Spain, Sweden and the UK
EU LFS	EU Labour Force Survey
EURS	European Unemployment Reinsurance Scheme
EWC	European Works Council
FDI	foreign direct investment
GDP	gross domestic product
GNI	gross national income
GoE	Group of Experts
ICFTU	International Confederation of Free Trade Unions
IIP	international investment position
ILO	International Labour Organization
IMF	International Monetary Fund
ITO	International Trade Organization
ITWF	International Transport Workers Federation
MFF	Multiannual Financial Framework
MIP	Macroeconomic Imbalance Procedure
MaT	Maastricht Treaty
NCLM	Nordic Common Labour Market
NGEU	Next Generation EU
NUTS	*nomenclature des unités territoriales statistiques*

	(nomenclature of territorial units for statistics)
OCA	optimum currency area
OECD	Organisation for Economic Co-operation and Development
OLA	optimum labour area
OMC	open method of coordination
PCS	Pandemic Crisis Support
PD-A1	Portable Document A1
PEPP	Pandemic Emergency Purchase Programme
SEA	Single European Act
SGP	Stability and Growth Pact
SME	small and medium-sized enterprise
SURE	Support to mitigate Unemployment Risks in an Emergency
TARGET2	Trans-European Automated Real-time Gross settlement Express Transfer
TEC	Treaty establishing the European Community
TEU	Treaty on European Union (Maastricht Treaty)
TFEU	Treaty of the Functioning of the European Union
TIG	tungsten inert gas
ToA	Treaty of Amsterdam
ToP	Treaty of Paris
ToR	Treaty of Rome
TSCG	Treaty on Stability, Coordination and Governance
UNICE	*Union des Industries de la Communauté européenne* (Union of Industries of the European Community)
USCLM	US Common Labour Market
VAT	value added tax

List of Country Abbreviations

AT	Austria
BE	Belgium
BG	Bulgaria
CY	Cyprus
CZ	Czech Republic (Czechia)
DE	Germany
DK	Denmark
EE	Estonia

ES	Spain
FI	Finland
FR	France
GR	Greece
HR	Croatia
HU	Hungary
IE	Ireland
IT	Italy
LT	Lithuania
LU	Luxembourg
LV	Latvia
MT	Malta
NL	The Netherlands
PL	Poland
PT	Portugal
RO	Romania
SE	Sweden
SI	Slovenia
SK	Slovakia

Preface and Acknowledgements

I do not expect that the average reader in political economy or European studies will be familiar with the word I chose for the title: Workaway. A workaway is an itinerant sailor: someone who catches a ride on a ship by swapping their labour in exchange for passage. Wages and benefits are excluded from that exchange. At an earlier time, when insurance policies were less intrusive, shipping companies less oligopolistic, and the world was a lot bigger, any person could wander down to the local port, ask for the ship's captain and negotiate a workaway position to wherever that ship might be heading.

This sounds very exotic and adventurous. But workaway is a lot of work, most of which is unpleasant. Maritime workaways chip away rust, bathe in puddles of red lead, oil/grease machinery, swab decks … you name it. They do this work in exchange for board, a bunk (that would otherwise lie vacant) and the potential wrath of the captain (to whom they have already surrendered their passport, pocketknife and a 'working' deposit). Working away might fuel a short-term adventure, but it is not sustainable over a lifetime.

I have chosen this title, because European workers are increasingly expected to behave like workaways. Labour markets have become like ports of call: each beckoning with the promise of better wages and employment. Instead of protecting local labour markets from the whims of economic change, we have chosen to leverage the opportunities provided by more distant markets. Consequently, when local labour markets are hit by economic storms, their workers are cast adrift to find employment in some far-away labour market – often located on another side of the continent. Like the mariner, this labour is often vulnerable, desperate and exploited.

This new labour market is not limited to Europe. In each of the world's continental economies, workers are increasingly asked to behave as if they were mobile factors of production. This book began as a larger comparative project. Over the past two decades I have studied the different ways that large (continental-wide) economies have integrated their labour markets, while sharing a common currency. India, China, the US and the EU have shared common challenges in this regard, and each has experimented with policies that encourage/deter interstate labour mobility, regulatory harmonization and interstate transfers (among other things). Remarkably, we have little idea of what lessons can be learned from these varied experiments. Which of these economies have been most successful in integrating their vast and varied labour markets? Who has benefited from these attempts at integration? Which policies were pursued and how effective have they been? What should be the measure of success when referring to labour market integration?

In search of answers to these types of questions, I spent months in the field, accumulating piles of data from each of these vast markets. In so doing, I incurred numerous intellectual and personal debts. Although the current book is limited to the European experience, I could not have developed its argument without studying how other large economies are dealing with the same sorts of challenges. This study has been a joint effort, as I have leaned heavily on local experts for access and insight. While it is not possible for me to thank all the people who have helped me in each of these markets, over all these years, I am especially grateful for the assistance and guidance received from Moushumi Basu, Fang Cai, Kam Wing Chan, Kang Liu, S. Irudaya Rajan, Rakhee Thimothy, Krishna Vadlamannati and Zhanxin Zhang.

I believe there is a great deal we can learn from comparing how China, the US, India and Europe have tried to unify labour markets across huge territories, sharing a common currency. I find it astonishing that such a comparative study has not yet been launched, but I have been overwhelmed by the sheer amount of information that is generated by such a comparison, and the difficulty of keeping abreast of so many concurrent developments in a rapidly changing field of research.

Just when I was ready to give up, I was fortunate to cross paths with Stephen Wenham, my acquisitions editor at Bristol University Press. Stephen convinced me to narrow my focus on European developments, and coaxed this book out of a mire of frustration. By sidelining my research on the US, China and India, and focusing on Europe, I could salvage much of my earlier work. I'm very grateful for his support and guidance along the way.

While focusing this work on Europe has made the project manageable, it has also made it more normative. I suspect there are two reasons for this. The first is that I look at Europe as an outsider, from a national perspective (in Norway) that remains critical of the EU's constant demands on its sovereign authority. I'm sure that Europe appears differently to those who are perched in Brussels, Frankfurt or Florence.

I present a different view of Europe, a less flattering one than usual. I recognize this is awkward, but the picture I draw is neither fanciful nor inaccurate: the book that follows is filled with empirical evidence that supports this picture. But the evidence is gathered to underscore a normative argument: that Europe has prioritized the needs of its markets over those of its citizens for too long, and the accumulated costs are becoming unbearable. In short, this project aims to show that the EU has been heading down the wrong path, and it is time to change direction.

I realize that this sort of normative framing can make some readers uncomfortable. But if politics is the art of the possible, then the job of the political scientist cannot and should not be limited to describing events – especially when these developments inhibit or restrict democratic voice. One central task of political science should be to provide alternative visions for the political community and to show how they can be achieved. A democratic vision is about securing political authority that respects and reflects the values of its constituents. Markets and the drive for greater efficiency should play an important role in this vision of politics, but it is a supporting role.

Because of this framing, it is especially important that I shield my readers/reviewers from any association to, or responsibility for, the normative argument that follows. Like every author, I have benefited from the help of readers – especially those readers who don't share my normative concerns. I owe my greatest debt of gratitude to those friends and colleagues who have read the entire manuscript in its many varied forms. In particular, I would like to thank Michael Alvarez, Ibrahima Amadou Dia, Peo Hansen, Jo Jakobsen and two anonymous reviewers for their useful suggestions, comments and criticisms. While it should be obvious, it still needs to be said: the work that follows has benefited greatly from their comments and criticisms, but I alone remain responsible for the final product.

Trondheim, Norway
December 2020

PART I

A New Approach

1

Belaboured Europe

Freedom. For over sixty years, a group of states has fought to secure greater freedom of movement for Europe's workers: their 'fourth freedom'. The Treaty of Rome (ToR) trumpeted the 'Freedom of movement for workers shall be secured within the Community by the end of the transitional period at the latest' (ToR, 1957: Art. 48). Countless treaties, directives and court decisions have ploughed a path to make it easier for workers to find employment away from home. The focus of this effort has been on reducing the regulatory and administrative barriers that are held to inhibit the free movement of workers.

This effort at removing barriers is unique, important and popular. Although migrant workers continue to struggle with different languages and cultures, they face fewer formal barriers to mobility. Public opinion surveys have consistently showed that Europeans consider the free movement of people, goods and services within the European Union (EU) as the most positive result of European integration (see, for example, Eurobarometer, 2007: 94, and 2010). While there has been some critical discussion within Europe about the political cost of this fourth freedom (witness Brexit and the growing xenophobia across Europe), most policymakers and analysts continue to embrace the right to free migration in Europe, as do I.

If we can agree about the desirability of freer labour mobility, it is more difficult to agree about why, how, and even if, we should integrate Europe's sundry national labour markets. Indeed, we have never asked ourselves some of the most pressing questions related to labour market integration:

- Does 'labour mobility' require a 'common market for labour'?
- What do we hope to achieve in creating a common labour market?
- What (or who?) is a common labour market meant to serve?

3

I hope to spark a discussion about the benefits and costs of economic integration, especially labour market integration. I do this because I believe it is a mistake to create one common market for labour in Europe. A continent-size market for labour is simply not suitable for workers, who would prefer to find secure and well-paid jobs closer to home. If our objective is freedom (as I think it should be!), we can and should encourage labour mobility, while still providing stable, secure and well-paid jobs for workers where they live.

Seeing like a market

I focus attention on these important questions, because I believe Europe has lost its way. We have forgotten that markets should be means to achieve greater ends; not ends in themselves. In short, we have succumbed to Karl Polanyi's (2001 [1944]) 'economistic fallacy'.[1] This economistic fallacy is particularly evident in Europe's approach to labour market integration, but it is prevalent in other policy spaces as well. Europe is changing its political institutions to meet the needs of an idealized market, rather than subordinating the market to the needs of its democratic community.

The careful reader may have noticed that I am playing with the title (and subject matter) of James Scott's (1999) magisterial *Seeing like a State*, which shows how centrally managed social plans misfire when they impose schematic visions that do violence to complex interdependencies that are not – and cannot – be fully understood. I will argue that the attempt to create a common labour market in Europe is a similarly flawed and dystopic vision: it ignores the real needs of those who will occupy the market being created.

The purpose of European market integration should be to improve the lives of Europeans. In considering labour market integration, Europe's goal should be to improve the lives of workers. To do this, we need to understand how labour is *not* like all the other commodities for sale in the market. We need to consider what workers need, and respond to those needs. In short, we need to create labour markets that work for labour.

As I demonstrate in Chapter 4, our reasons for establishing a common labour market have shifted over the years, and the current form of that market would appear alien to its original architects (see, for example, Hansen and Hager, 2010). In the early years of European integration there was an explicit recognition of the need to defend local labour markets and the relative power of labour. The freedom of labour was indeed prioritized over the freedom of commodities, services or capital.

To secure worker protection and welfare across member states, the scope of economic integration was circumscribed.

Over time, and as the nature of European economic integration expanded to include a shared currency area (in particular), strong welfare state provisions were seen to inhibit further integration. After all, Europe cannot enjoy strong welfare states that decommodify workers *and* still encourage the sort of price flexibility and factor mobility that a common currency area requires.

This tension is usually explained with reference to the inefficiencies of European labour markets and the need for dramatic reforms. But the tension is just as much the result of a poorly designed Europe – one that prioritizes the needs of its markets over the needs of its people. Today, the argument for a common market in Europe leans less on 'freedom' and more on 'economic utility': we encourage labour mobility as an instrument of economic policy, and as a locomotive for growth.[2]

For example, in part of its effort to meet the goals of Europe 2020 (and to create a 'job-rich recovery'), the European Commission emphasizes the potential role that worker mobility can play in encouraging economic growth and adjustment:

> Intra EU labour mobility can simultaneously increase economic activity and employment levels by helping overcome mismatches and imbalances on the labour market and making them function dynamically and more efficiently. Geographic mobility is also a potential source of economic growth that helps improve the (re)allocation of resources by acting as an adjustment mechanism for distorted labour markets whilst also enabling economies to better cope with sudden shocks. (European Commission, 2012a: 1)

Of course, economic growth is a good thing, especially when its benefits can be distributed fairly among those who have helped to produce it (more on this later). The problem with Europe's current approach to market integration is that its policymakers are (implicitly) abdicating their own responsibility for local economic management. Rather than allowing policymakers to create better conditions for employment at home, workers are increasingly expected to go out and find jobs wherever they may be found. This tendency increased significantly during and after the 2008–09 Great Recession.[3] Hence my title: *Workaway* (see Box 1.1).

This book offers an alternative approach to labour market integration, which begins by recognizing the way that labour is different from other

Box 1.1: Workaway

This term originates on the docks, where a workaway is an itinerant sailor: someone who catches a ride on a ship by swapping their labour in exchange for passage to a distant port. Additional wages and benefits are excluded from that exchange.

This sounds rather exotic, and migration is often framed in exotic terms. But a workaway is a sort of indentured servant, albeit for a relatively limited period of time. Workaways are stuck with an often-distasteful job, far away from familiar legal, cultural and institutional settings, and at the mercy (and potential wrath) of the ship's captain. Before the journey, workaways surrender their passports, any personal weapons and a small 'working' deposit – as a guarantee that the promised labour will be forthcoming. They are only free on departure from the ship.

I am borrowing this term and using it to describe Europe's labour migrants. As we shall see, Europe's approach to market integration increasingly requires that workers are forced to seek work in distant markets, when local labour markets fail. I use 'workaway' to describe this type of *market-forced migration*. A new term is necessary, as it cannot be freedom, even a fourth freedom, to be forced by poverty, desperation and a lack of local opportunities to migrate to a distant and unfamiliar market, seeking work from a position of increased vulnerability.

commodities; considers a type of market that is more appropriate to the special needs of labour; and then contrasts that alternative approach with the current state of European affairs. In doing so, this book takes an uncommon form, in that it combines normative and economic analyses. This is not to ignore questions of efficiency, or to imply that justice and efficiency cannot coexist, but to remind the reader that efficiency is not (and should not be!) the sole criterion for evaluating public policy.

Before entertaining a new argument, we should examine the failures of the status quo. That is my objective in this introductory chapter. I begin by laying out the schematic vision of Europe's market reformers, or the current 'state of opinion'. I then conduct a simple test, a survey of the 'state of the (labour) union', to show how little progress we have made in achieving the reformers' promised gains. In light of these failures, I suggest that we return to the drawing board, rethink our approach to labour market integration, and consider a new approach to 'moving forward'. The remainder of the book presents this new path forward.

State of opinion

Europe's approach to market integration rests on several disparate contributions. Indeed, there is a phenomenal amount of work done by both policymakers and analysts on the integration of European markets. To simplify, and to capture the breadth of this consensus, I offer a stylized synthesis, drawing on the contributions from two complementary groups of analysts: one political, the other economic. Both groups tend to be supportive of the effort to create a common labour market in Europe.[4] While no single author can be captured by this synthesis, I believe it is representative of the whole, and it is meant to be an accurate and uncontroversial representation.

On the one hand, there is a broad-based recognition of the importance of free mobility as a political, even a moral, objective. From this *political* perspective, free mobility is depicted as Europe's fourth freedom (alongside the free movement of capital, trade and services) – loudly (and rightly!) heralded as an important goal in its own right.

Much of the work done by political scientists conceives of labour market integration in negative terms:[5] it focuses on removing constraints to the movement of citizens, and calls this freedom.[6] Here, we find many of the nuts and bolts of the integration literature, as political scientists document the need for (and progress towards) the removal of regulatory and administrative barriers, or the need to confront the challenge of language, culture or information asymmetries in deterring migration.[7] For these political scientists, a successfully integrated labour market is one that enjoys broad public support, low/few barriers/restrictions to entry, and/or exhibits a high degree of interstate labour mobility.

A second, but related, group includes those who advocate for increased market integration on the grounds that it can secure 'efficiency gains' and greater economic growth (for example, Cacciatore and Fiori, 2016). This *economic* approach offers an umbrella argument that extends over all types of market integration – be it labour, capital, goods or services – but it collects around a shared logic, a product of neo-Ricardian trade theory. Gathered under this umbrella are those who believe that the integration of markets will generate economies of scale, prompting a reduction in prices, thereby delivering welfare gains for the community as a whole.

Box 1.2: Eurosclerosis

The term 'Eurosclerosis' was popularized by German economist Herbert Giersch in a 1985 paper of the same name. He used it to refer to the economic stagnation that can result from *excessive regulation, labor market rigidities, and overly generous welfare policies*. Eurosclerosis (which stems from the medical term *sclerosis*, meaning the hardening of tissue) describes countries experiencing high rates of unemployment, even during periods of economic growth, due to inflexible market conditions. Although originally used to refer to the European Community (EC), it is now used more broadly as a term for countries experiencing similar conditions. (*Investopedia*, 2019, emphasis added)

In this literature, labour is assumed to behave like any other commodity/service, and there is an implicit belief that the market for labour should act like any other market. (For an elaboration, see Chapter 2.) As a result, efficiency arguments are easily transferred from one type of market to another (in covering-law style, as per Hempel). Hence, more general arguments about the benefits of economic integration are often refitted to study the integration of national labour markets.

Better yet, from the economist's perspective, labour markets provide very fertile ground for the transplant of these arguments, as European markets are often seen to be in desperate need of reform. These markets have become the poster child for Eurosclerosis (see Box 1.2), and are often depicted as lethargic, overregulated, hobbled by restrictive traditions and captured by strong labour unions. In integrating these sluggish national markets, policymakers hope to introduce a series of reforms that can make the European market for labour more efficient. From this perspective, integrating Europe's labour markets provides an opportunity to create a new, more competitive, flexible and mobile working stock in Europe. While this objective may be more controversial than the first (freedom of movement), it enjoys widespread support, especially within policy circles and among research communities.

Among economists, a successfully integrated labour market is one characterized by a convergence of wages for comparable jobs.[8] In this view, the price of labour follows the *law of one price* (that is, wage convergence), after internal barriers to mobility and exchange fall by the wayside. To be frank, markets per se don't really appear in this type of work: labour is a factor of production, the supply (and price) of which shifts uneventfully in response to a changing demand curve.

Similarly, the literature on optimum currency areas (OCAs) recognizes the utility (and economic benefit) of an integrated labour market, but there is little focus on the actual processes, institutions and incentives used to bring about that integration.[9] Here, the integration of national labour markets plays a central role in the functioning of any large, shared currency area. Labour migration across regional economies is seen as an important supplement to federal fiscal transfers, flexible prices (wages) and capital mobility; but *in the absence of these alternative adjustment mechanisms*, labour mobility is expected to bear the brunt of the adjustment. Unemployed workers are encouraged to seek work in other regional economies (out of state), and the process of migration will help to equalize regional economic variation across the shared area. In so doing, migrant workers dampen the economic boom in the host region (increasing the local labour supply, decreasing its wages), and stimulate economic activity in the recessed (sending) region – by shrinking the local supply of labour and hence raising its wages, and by the remittances sent home by the migrating workers. From the perspective of an OCA, like the economic perspective in general, a successfully integrated labour market will deliver increased wage convergence and mobility over time.

Both the political and economic literatures tend to assume the utility of (and mutual benefit from) integrated markets, but neither has focused much attention on the actual means by which integration might be achieved, other than removing barriers to mobility. Each of these literatures assumes that the integration of labour markets is much like that of other markets and that an integrated labour market is beneficial for all participants: a promised 'integration dividend' (Offe, 2015: 4). The focus of this work is on improving economic efficiency and creating 'a more perfect market'. When these two literatures are combined, the resulting synthesis is liberal in nature and is remarkably influential among policymakers in Europe.

When policymakers embrace a liberal approach to market integration, *in general*, they aim to create a market that is indifferent to geography (that is, where there are no protectionist measures limiting integration), and where prices converge. They also expect that a larger market (in terms of both numbers and geography) generates greater efficiencies, lower prices and higher rewards. While policymakers recognize that individual producers may be hurt by this integration, the increased gains that result can be redistributed in a Pareto optimal manner, securing broad political support.[10] Finally, and most obviously: from a liberal perspective, an efficient market is one that clears (where Say's law rules the roost) and freedom is understood in terms of the absence of barriers to action.

When applied to labour markets, *in particular*, this approach to integration leads policymakers to focus on minimizing the barriers that hinder labour mobility and distort market prices (wages). Once this is done, policymakers expect several benefits, derived from the more efficient market that results: a common labour market should display higher levels of labour mobility, and (consequently) we should expect wages to converge and unemployment to fall (as a result of the increased competition). In short, the objective of labour market integration is to improve the nature of the market in hopes of increasing efficiencies.

As we shall see, I do not believe this is an appropriate way to think about labour market integration, because I do not think that labour acts (or should act) like any other commodity being exchanged at market. But Europe has been struggling for decades to integrate its labour markets along these lines, and it is only fair to measure its success by the terms of its advocates. After decades of effort, how much closer has Europe come to reaping the benefits of its approach to integration?

State of the (labour) union

Using the liberal approach, as described in the preceding section, we can assess Europe's effort at integrating its labour markets with reference to just four indicators. If labour market integration in Europe has been successful, we should expect to see:

- a reduction in the number and use of regulatory and administrative hindrances to mobility;
- a significant level of interstate labour mobility – as evidence of workers exercising their freedom;
- a subsequent reduction in wage disparities across Europe; and
- a reduction in unemployment levels across the European market – as evidence of a more efficient market.

I wish to avoid a technical analysis of the data and aim for a straightforward empirical snapshot. When measured by these four simple indicators, the 60-year effort to create a common labour market in Europe has been successful in only one regard: in reducing barriers to mobility. We have yet to witness any substantial benefits with regard to wage convergence, mobility or unemployment levels. This empirical summary, though simple, should not be controversial, although readers will likely differ on how to interpret the results.

In terms of the first indicator, a *reduction of protectionist barriers*, there should be little doubt that Europe has been quite successful. As noted in the opening pages, there is strong public support for reducing the sort of administrative and regulatory barriers as well as information asymmetries that can hinder mobility. This has included efforts to make public sector jobs and housing more accessible to foreigners, to make pension and entitlement transfers more portable, to facilitate the movement of family members, and to standardize professional qualifications – for example the European Qualifications Framework (CEDEFOP, 2020). Compared to the US, and across a variety of sectors (such as public procurement, services, and the regulated goods market), EU regulations are both more centralized (having a single set of coherent rules for exchange) and more liberal (that is, they adopt rules that open exchange to competition).[11]

Indeed, when Europeans are asked about the sort of practical hindrances that might deter them from migrating, the most frequently mentioned barrier is language (52%). Administrative barriers and/ or concerns about the transferability of their qualifications are not placed very high on their list of concerns: only 13% and 10%, respectively, named these as practical difficulties when working abroad (Eurobarometer, 2010: 117).

On this first indicator, then, the effort at labour market integration has been extremely successful. Indeed, the lifting of regulatory and administrative hurdles might be counted among Europe's greatest integrative successes, and it has proven to be remarkably popular. Unfortunately, the predicted rewards from this liberalization, in the form of increased market efficiencies, are more difficult to substantiate.

Despite a remarkable reduction in barriers to entry, evidence of the second indicator, *labour mobility*, is surprisingly sparse. This is surprising for at least two reasons. First, Europeans have long expressed rather positive opinions about mobility, especially as an engine of European integration. Second, as the barriers to mobility have been gradually reduced, we should expect more and more Europeans exploiting the opportunity to exercise their fourth freedom. Perhaps it is time to consider if there is something greater than formal barriers keeping Europeans closer to home?

On average, only about 3% of EU citizens – roughly 17 million people – currently live in another EU member state (Barslund and Busse, 2016: 3). When we whittle this population down to its working-age component, the 2017 number is significantly smaller: 12.4 million (European Commission, 2018a: 13). According to EU Labour Force Survey data from 2012, about 3.1% of the total working population in EU member states came from another EU member state. Not only is this number (3.1%) itself small, it is smaller than the number (at 4%) of non-EU, third-country nationals working in the EU (Eurofound, 2014: 17)!

These migrant stocks tend to congregate in the economic engines of modern Europe: 74% of them are found in just five countries (Germany, UK, Italy, France and Spain). The sending countries are also relatively concentrated in number, with 50% of the (EU) working-age migrant stocks coming from Romania, Poland, Portugal, Italy and Bulgaria (European Commission, 2018a: 13).

These 'stock' figures are not a particularly good measure of labour migration, as they cannot reflect the degree to which workers are being pushed out by (or drawn to) local business cycles (so-called 'sparrow flights'). For this, we need to rely on flow figures, which are not as reliable and more difficult to interpret. A recent Organisation for Economic Co-operation and Development report (OECD, 2012a: 64) found that cross-border flows among EU member states represented only about 0.3% of the total population in 2010. This compared rather unfavourably to the corresponding number in the US (across 50 states), where migration was significantly higher, at 2.4% (see also Eurofound, 2014: 17).

Figure 1.1 uses the same flow data as in the 2018 EU labour mobility report (European Commission, 2018a) but compares it to the active population (age 15–64), rather than the full population, to focus on labour mobility (and filter out family members and pensioners). It is still a problematic indicator, as it will include a number of mobile residents (such as students) and not all states are equally diligent in reporting inflow/outflow numbers, but it is the best we have.

Figure 1.1 displays the net migration distribution for EU28 member states, year by year (in each column), from 2008 to 2017. Here, there are three evident trends worth commenting on. First, the scale is measured in per mil (not per cent) terms: we are looking at a given number, per one thousand residents. In short, these numbers are remarkably small! Second, there is a widening distribution of net migrant flows, as a share of working-age population, after the 2008 financial crisis – and the spread is increasing on both ends of the net distribution. This is the increased tendency for workaway that motivates this study. Finally, it would appear that the freedom of mobility is not equally shared by all EU citizens, as the same countries, year after year, seem to be haemorrhaging workers: Romania (RO), Lithuania (LT), Latvia (LV), and Croatia (HR).[12] All this seems to suggest that European labour migration is increasingly driven by economic necessity:

Figure 1.1: Net mobility flows, active population, per mil

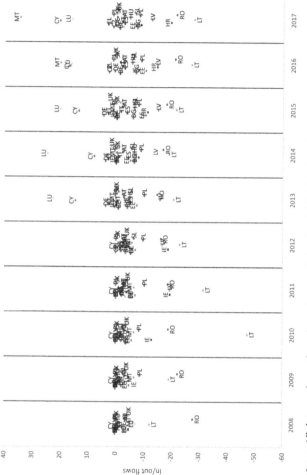

Notes: All data are drawn from the active population (aged 15–64). The inflow data combine migrant inflow (active population) from other EU and EFTA countries; the outflow data (active population) combine both national and EU citizen outflows. The flow data are then divided by the country population, in per mil terms; for example inflows–outflows)/active population*1000.

Source: Adapted from Eurostat (migr_emi1ctz; miugr_imm1ctz; and ifsi_emp_a)

Figure 1.2: Wage divergence

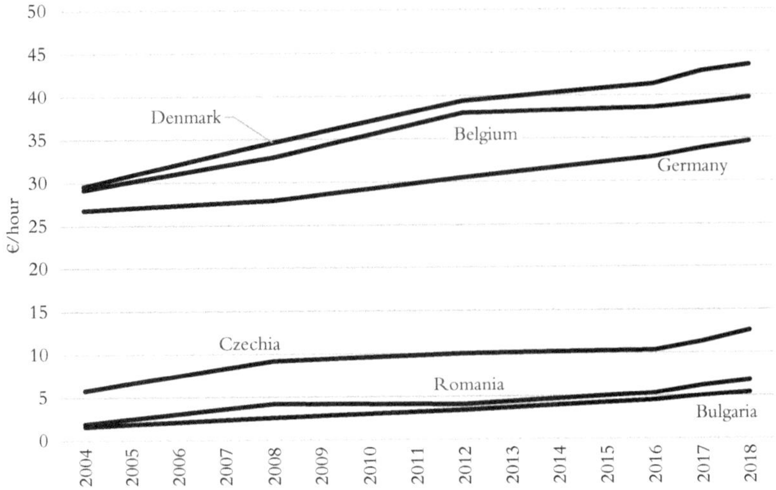

Notes: Labour cost for labour cost index (compensation of employees plus taxes, minus subsidies) in industry, construction and services sectors. Euros per hour, annual data.

Source: Adapted from Eurostat (NACE Rev.2 TPS00173)

Europe is relying more and more on workaways. We return to take a closer look at the scope of European labour mobility in Chapter 8.

All in all, the level of interstate migration in Europe is surprisingly small (even if it had been rising before the COVID-19 outbreak), given the expectations generated by the liberal approach to labour market integration. The same negative results are evident in the third indicator: *wage convergence*. Despite significant efforts to reduce regulatory barriers to entry, and a small increase in labour mobility – especially after the Great Recession – European wage levels continue to be plagued by huge disparities. These disparities, and their development over time, are easily captured by a simple comparison of labour costs, across Europe's cheapest and dearest markets, as shown in Figure 1.2.

In this figure we can clearly see that the costs of labour in Romania and Bulgaria are about half those in Czechia today, whereas these costs in Germany, Belgium and Denmark are substantially higher. When we look at the overall wage costs across Europe (not just these six examples), we see a slight convergence over time,[13] but the remaining differences (as seen in Figure 1.2) are substantial. Obviously, this is a very simple indicator, and some differences in pay will reflect different kinds of work, but the gaps shown here are enormous, even as the work tasks are relatively similar, for example teachers, bus drivers, bar staff, car assembly workers and so on.

The point is that we are not seeing the scope of wage convergence we should expect, given the substantial reduction in regulatory hindrances. This is the same conclusion reached by an exhaustive empirical study that found little evidence of wage convergence across borders in Europe:

> Although the labor force today is more mobile and fewer trade impediments exist compared with the situation in 1993, substantive differences in wages and commodity prices still prevail. Some European countries still exhibit relatively high wages, such as Denmark, France, and Spain; others are associated with relatively low wages, such as Germany. Thus, there is a need to explore the reality of the situation, especially in the labor markets of European countries. In other words, why are the disparities between lower- and higher-wage member states not declining over time, as indicated by price equalization theory? Factor price convergence, which is an outcome of this theory, is not seen among EU member states. (Naz et al, 2017: 38)

The last indicator for evaluating the success of European labour market integration, *unemployment*, is the most depressing of all. Even though the EU has made it easier for Europeans to secure work abroad, internal migration has been rising (minimally) over recent years, and the EU had experienced eight (!) consecutive years of economic expansion, prior to the COVID-19 outbreak, unemployment remains a *significant* problem in Europe.

Figure 1.3 illustrates the scope of the problem by offering a customized 'box and whisker' diagram to display the annual change in unemployment in the common EU labour market (the box), from 2008 to 2018, and the unemployment outliers (both high and low) for each year. From this figure, we see that the overall EU28 unemployment trend has hovered between 6.8% and 10.9%, and was decreasing slightly after 2013. These numbers are disconcertingly high. Worse still, individual countries experienced unemployment rates above 20% for eight of the past eleven years.

A more frightening picture develops when we look at the levels of youth unemployment in Europe, as it suggests that a generation of young Europeans is finding it very difficult to enter the labour market. In 2019, across the EU28, 15 out of every 100 young workers were out of a job. These numbers will surely grow with the effects of the COVID-19 outbreak. At the height of the Great Recession, the

Figure 1.3: Unemployment rate, EU28 and outliers, 2008–18

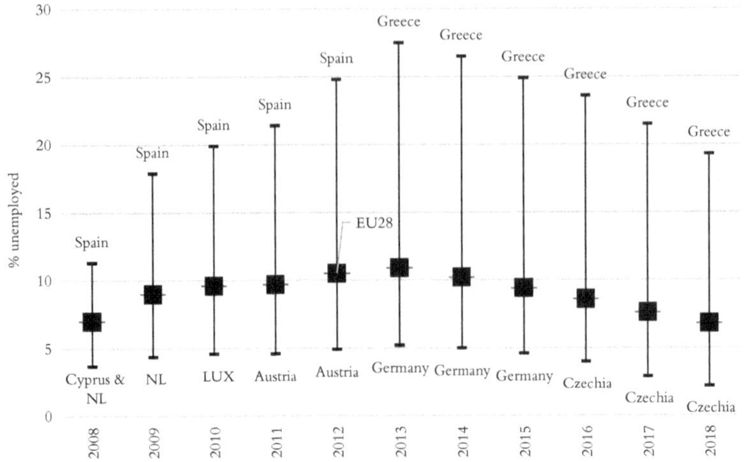

Note: Annual average, percentage of active population.

Source: Adapted from Eurostat (une_rt_a)

(EU28) youth unemployment level reached almost a quarter (23.8%). In countries like Greece and Spain, more than half of the youth labour force was out of work in 2013, and it is only marginally better today (roughly 40% and 34% respectively).[14]

There are other worrisome signs as well, even if the liberal approach to labour market integration does not direct our attention to them. Europe sustains very high levels of income inequality. Across the EU, the top 20% of the population (those with the highest income) received 5.2 times as much income as the bottom 20%. In individual members states, such as Bulgaria, the difference is over eight times as much (Eurostat, 2018)! Worse, there has been a clear deterioration of worker influence and relative power across a whole range of indicators, such as a shrinking share of national income going to labour, falling unionization levels and so on (see, for example, Bernaciak et al, 2014; Theodoropoulou, 2019). We return to these challenges in Chapter 9. Worse still, these inequalities seem to be fuelling some rather ugly and radical political movements across Europe (Henley, 2018).

Moving forward

From this brief, and admittedly simple, overview of recent economic developments we can conclude that Europe has been successful in just one thing: removing barriers to labour mobility. We also find evidence of a slight increase in labour mobility and wage convergence after the Great Recession and before the COVID-19 outbreak. By and large, however, the lifting of barriers to labour mobility has yet to reap the promised gains from increased market efficiencies, at least not to the levels we were led to expect. Why is that?

There are two possible ways to answer this simple question: we need to try harder, or we need to try something new.

Try harder

The first possible response is that the approach itself is sound, but that Europe has still not gone far enough in liberalizing its labour markets. This is, I think, the most common and usual response to the failure of markets to deliver better results. Proponents of this view will point to the continued existence of language barriers, more discrete/informal barriers to mobility, and other market hindrances (such as the influence of unions, or the existence of welfare protections that deter mobility or restrict price flexibility). Hence, the problem may be that the labour market in Europe continues to function inefficiently, despite years of reform.

There are at least three problems with this response. First, it assumes that the labour market can and should be understood like any other market. This response sees the European worker as a commodity, the European polity like a market. But labour is not a commodity like all the others (Polanyi, 2001 [1944]), even if this simple fact is often overlooked. As Robert Solow (1990: 4) noted over 30 years ago: 'Among economists, it is not obvious at all that labor as a commodity is sufficiently different from artichokes and rental apartments to require a different mode of analysis.' For the rest of us, however, labour is clearly different from artichokes, and the costs of a poorly designed labour market can extend far beyond the realm of the market. This argument is further developed in Chapter 2.

Second, this approach is methodologically suspect, especially in light of the aforementioned problem. What happens when theory and practice don't agree? There are only two options for resolving such dilemmas: we can change the theory so that it becomes more consistent with the way the world actually works (think Aristotle); or we can change the world (practice) so that it resembles more closely the theory (think Plato). Economists tend to prefer the latter approach: they imagine an ideal market, where supply and demand curves meet in equilibrium (see Chapter 2), and use this ideal market as the standard for evaluating real-world markets. When labour markets do not clear as the ideal market model would lead them to expect (and when do they ever?), then the economist works to remove all the unique characteristics that define labour, so that it becomes (in effect) more like an artichoke.[15]

In embracing this economistic view of the world, policymakers have *not* tried to create a market for labour (that is, a market for workers, rather than a market for artichokes). Instead, European policymakers work to create conditions that improve labour market efficiencies (in effect, they aim to encourage workers to act like artichokes). From this view, it makes sense for policymakers to focus attention on market reforms that improve competitiveness (read deregulation), flexibility (read falling wages) and mobility (read workaway). But it only makes sense if workers are like artichokes.

The problem is that increased competitiveness, flexibility and mobility tends to benefit one partner in the labour contract, more than the other. This brings me to my third concern. By focusing on market functionality, markets are depicted in the abstract – disembedded from their political contexts. This is a problem for at least two reasons. First, the predominant standard for evaluating market exchange is efficiency, while the standard for evaluating political exchange tends to be justice. In 'seeing like a market', policymakers focus myopically on efficiency, at the expense of justice.

Second, this approach fails to recognize that workers are more than a service for sale on the market: workers, as citizens, also enjoy rights, routines and obligations that are still attached to political domains. Because workers are citizens who enjoy rights and entitlements, the integration of labour markets entails the integration of social models across Europe. In this realm, justice – rather than efficiency – is the more appropriate standard of evaluation.

Try something new

I prefer the alternative response: to argue that the current approach is itself misguided. I believe it is a mistake to think the labour market is like other markets, and that we should measure the success of labour market integration in the same way that we measure success in the markets for artichokes or investment portfolios. I believe that the liberal approach to labour market integration is flawed in a number of ways and it deviates from the view of Europe's original designers (as I demonstrate in Chapter 4).

First of all, let me say that there is nothing wrong with removing barriers to labour mobility. To my mind, this is one of Europe's greatest successes, worthy of celebration. It is a popular measure, and free mobility can indeed be liberating. But encouraging mobility is something very different from creating a common labour market, and the freedom to migrate (the fourth freedom) is very different from being forced to workaway. After all, most workers – as family members and friends – don't want to chase down jobs on the other side of the continent. In general, people prefer to work closer to home. The best solution, for most people, is to find a well-paid and reliable job in the *local* labour market. Any labour market reform that doesn't recognize this simple fact, and which forces a significant increase in long-distance worker migration, is bound to be unpopular and ineffective. Worse, while this migration may make sense from an economic perspective, it makes for terrible (and unjust) social policy, generating significant human costs. Instead of building labour markets that can sustain local communities, we destroy local communities to sustain an idealized, continental-wide labour market. This is backward.

Second, the result of this approach to integration undermines the structural power of labour (vis-à-vis capital), and the resulting imbalance of economic and political power explains the current state of affairs (meagre wage increases, lower labour shares of income, rising inequality). This is *not* the sort of Europe many of us envisioned for the future: we hoped for a social Europe that could function as a counterweight to the laissez-faire US.

In the chapters that follow I offer an alternative approach to market integration, one that is rooted in the unique characteristics and special requirements of labour. This approach is different from most accounts of European labour markets, in at least two regards. First, my focus is trained at a deeper, more structural, level. There is remarkably little written about how large states have (or should) integrate their local labour markets.[16] Most accounts of European labour markets look extensively at detailed components of the market (for example, minimum wage laws, worker protections, workers councils, immigration levels and so on), or specific actors (for example, employers' organizations, labour unions). These studies tend to be very descriptive, scientific and detached. For years I have followed these descriptions and have tried to make sense of the stark decline in relative labour power over time.

While these accounts are important, they are only small parts of a much larger puzzle. Indeed, the authors of such reports often realize as much, and begin their studies with a contextual appetizer. For example, in their introduction to an impressive four-volume survey titled *Collective Bargaining in Europe*, the authors note that:

> The institutions of collective bargaining in Europe are under pressure from four wide-ranging developments. First, the adoption of monetarist and neo-liberal policies … Second, the dominant strand of 'negative integration' (Scharpf, 1996) with European integration comprising deregulation and measures to facilitate the 'four freedoms' within Member States … Third, further pressures for wage moderation arose from the terms of economic and monetary union … Fourth, the sub-prime and financial crisis of 2008, followed by the sovereign debt crisis, generated a series of shorter-term demands on policy that exacerbated the longer-term pressures arising from the three points mentioned above. (Waddington et al, 2019: 13)

I couldn't agree more, and this book takes the appetizer and makes it a meal: it aims to describe these broader pressures on European labour, and how they have undermined its structural and associational power.[17] It is only by looking at the effects of a common currency union, the nature and the size of the EU budget, the scope of factor mobility and so on that we can understand how workers have come to bear a larger share of the burden of economic adjustment in Europe's common market.

The second way my argument differs from most of the existing literature is that I draw attention to the injustices of reform. The book that follows is unabashedly normative. I am concerned with both efficiency and justice, but fear that the latter is consistently devalued in our embrace of the former. Denizens of Europe need to ask: 'What kind of Europe do we hope to build, and what role should the market play in that construction?' This is a political question, not an economic one: in evaluating our diverse answers to this question, the standard of evaluation should be justice, not efficiency. After all,

> no economist has a privileged insight into questions of right and wrong, and none deserve a special say in fundamental decisions about how society should operate. Economists who argue otherwise and exert undue influence in public debates about right and wrong should be exposed for what they are: frauds. (Romer, 2020: 157)

It may be that Romer is too hard on his fellow economists: quite often they are willing to avoid questions of justice all together. But even this is a problem. To the extent that economists and policymakers wilfully ignore questions of justice, and focus myopically on efficiency gains, I am tempted to do the same: to focus this study on the just effects of reforms, at the expense of efficiency. But this is not necessary. The postwar order teaches us that it is possible to design an efficient and just integrated market that protects local policy autonomy. At the same time, the efficiency gains we were promised – the so-called 'integration dividends' (Offe, 2015: 4) – have proven to be wildly exaggerated in practice.

If we prioritize democracy and recognize that the needs and desires of different communities will vary (as do their local economic conditions), then it is important that elected officials have access to the tools they need to secure popular outcomes. We want and need governments to be responsive to the needs of the people for which they stand. I believe, following Polanyi, that the best way to preserve democratic institutions is to extend their influence over economic decisions.

Chapter overview

This book comprises ten chapters. The first two chapters provide a foundation upon which the rest of the book builds. Chapter 2 starts by examining the basic component of any labour market: labour. Because labour power is different from other commodities and services being exchanged at market, it makes little sense to assume that labour markets should function in the same idealized fashion as other markets. Among other things, workers are tied to location in ways that other goods and services are not, such that labour and capital react and benefit differently when markets are expanded. Chapter 2 considers these unique characteristics so that we can rethink market integration with an eye on the special needs of labour.

Chapter 3 describes what such a market might look like. Taking a cue from the literature on optimum currency areas (OCAs), this chapter offers an alternative theory of market integration, but one that is grounded in the unique characteristics of labour, as described in Chapter 2. This *optimum labour area (OLA) approach* also generates an ideal market (like the liberal approach) but it offers an approach that prioritizes sustainable and productive employment opportunities *near home*. I hasten to emphasize that this approach is designed to show what is possible, even desirable. It is not meant to describe current events or to generate outcomes that are promptly feasible (politically). We must first agree about what future we will chose; only then can we decide how to secure it. This chapter shows why a continental-sized labour market can never be optimal for labour, because labour markets are necessarily local and unique. In recognizing this, we can use OLA theory to inform policy priorities that can help workers, employers and policymakers adjust to what is clearly a suboptimal market.

My analysis of labour market integration in Europe is spelled out in Chapters 4–9, which make up the empirical heart of the book. This argument is a rather complicated one, with many moving parts. I hope this brief overview can help the reader see how they all fit together. In a nutshell, I argue that Europe's effort to create an optimum currency area has resulted in a suboptimal labour area.

Despite a decades-long effort at greater economic integration, the European common market continues to rest upon a plethora of local and regional labour markets, each of which sings to its own economic tune. Any attempt to integrate European markets will introduce constraints on political autonomy, but the nature of these constraints will vary with the form of integration. For example, integrating capital markets will constrain political autonomy in different ways than the integration of goods markets, and the effect of integrating some goods markets (for example agriculture) will differ significantly from the integration of others (for example office equipment).

I hold that the manner in which the EU has integrated its markets (for capital, goods and services) has made it increasingly difficult for Europe's local labour markets to balance and thrive. In their effort to create a common market, especially a common capital market and currency area, member states have jettisoned many of the policy tools that elected officials once used to stabilize their local labour markets. Autonomous monetary, fiscal, regulatory and procurement policies have been sacrificed or hobbled to secure a level playing field and/or to encourage market-wide efficiency gains.

As a consequence of these integration efforts, a greater share of the burden for local labour market adjustment is now borne by workers, in the form of unemployment, falling wages and market-forced emigration – what I call 'workaway'. This reliance on workaway is still rather limited, but it grew significantly in response to the Great Recession. If the human costs of workaway are not recognized and addressed, I fear that this trend will continue in Europe's post-COVID economic recovery.

While it might not have been the intent of European policymakers to undermine the relative power of labour, it is clearly the result, as is evident in several of the aggregate figures introduced earlier in this chapter. The design of Europe's common market requires a significant amount of human suffering because national policymakers are unable to stabilize their local labour markets, for the benefit of their constituents.

The reduced capacity of elected leaders to stabilize local labour markets might even contribute to undermining democratic legitimacy (at both the member state and EU levels), as European elections matter less and less in determining how we live our lives.

To make this argument, I begin (in Chapter 4) by showing how economists and policymakers once recognized that economic integration requires political sacrifice, and that some forms of integration require greater amounts of political sacrifice. In the early years of European integration, member states prioritized democratic accountability over market integration, and chose a path to further integration, which protected sovereign authority, political accountability and the need to prioritize full employment, that is, to stabilize member state economies.

The contrast with our current arrangement is striking. Today, there is little explicit recognition of the political sacrifices required of increased economic integration: decisions are usually framed in terms of their promised (often exaggerated) efficiency gains, or for the need to offer a level playing field. I hope to reignite a discussion about the political costs of economic integration in Europe, because I think that the human costs of Europe's chosen path to integration are much too high. Of course, others may be willing to accept these costs in the belief that the benefits of market integration will eventually trickle down to/on workers. These differences are reasonable, and I hope this work can contribute to a discussion about the pros and cons associated with each strategy.

At the core of this argument lies a recognition that each European member state has its own, distinctive set of labour markets – a function of their unique histories, institutions, preferences and qualities. This is one of Europe's proudest accomplishments, and these differences should be embraced, not levelled. The German economy remains very different from the Greek, despite a decades-long effort to encourage their convergence. The continued existence of these significant differences implies that an economic policy suitable for German labour markets will vary significantly from what may be required to stabilize Greek labour markets. Chapter 5 maps this economic and political divergence to demonstrate the need for policy instruments that can address local needs. In the absence of such instruments, elected officials will be limited in how they can (and should!) respond to democratic demands and pressures at the local and national level.

Chapter 6 describes the slow erosion of member state policy autonomy in Europe. It points to the important role that national monetary, fiscal, regulatory and procurement policy can play (and have played) in stimulating and stabilizing local labour markets. But each of these policies has been gelded to serve a common market. The needs of a shared currency area are particularly demanding in this regard. In jettisoning their national currencies, member states have eliminated the most important tool for stabilizing their labour markets.[18] But the needs of Europe's common market have also required member states to abandon their autonomous procurement and regulatory authority, and to severely limit the scope of their fiscal authority.

Many of these abandoned tools could be replaced and/or complemented by reforms at the European level. The experiences of other large and/or federal economies sharing a common currency provide clear evidence of what is required to compensate for a lack of policy autonomy at the member state/local level. Unfortunately, these types of reforms have proven very difficult to institute at the European level (for a number of reasons). Chapter 7 considers what might be done to improve local labour market conditions in the EU, and then describes how the current design of the EU is unable to provide those improvements.

In the absence of significant policy autonomy at the member state level (Chapter 6) and given the limits to political authority assigned to the European level (Chapter 7), markets are left to clear by themselves. In a common currency area, this means that mobile factors of production (capital and labour) are expected to flow where they are needed, in response to market incentives. Chapter 8 examines the capacity of European capital and labour markets to fill this political void. In effect, the markets for labour and capital have become the frontline of Europe's defence in a growing series of economic battles/crises, although the distribution of burden is clearly unequal. In the wake of the Great Recession, European workers ended up bearing the biggest burden of economic adjustment – in the form of falling wages, shrinking welfare budgets, rising unemployment and workaway – whereas European capital markets became more of an encumbrance than an aid to economic recovery.

The picture I paint is a gloomy one. While European workers in some member states have managed to maintain their relative class power, their influence is largely limited to the member state level, where much of sovereign authority has already been hollowed out. As a whole, the labour movement in Europe has proven remarkably ineffective at protecting the political and economic gains that workers have secured over previous decades. Chapter 9 looks at the slow demise of labour power in Europe and suggests that Europe's approach to economic integration is an important reason for that decline. This argument is made cautiously, as falling labour power is not limited to Europe, but Europe's approach to creating a common market has made it difficult for workers to defend their position in the face of increased capital mobility.

Chapter 10 concludes by asking if this is the Community that Europeans want. Using the insights generated from the OLA approach described in Chapter 3, and the lessons gleaned from the other chapters, I offer two different strategies for integrating Europe's labour markets to secure a better balance of justice and efficiency.

Conclusion

Labour market integration in Europe today is presented as an opportunity to create a better market. By disciplining labour to behave more like a commodity, policymakers hope to create a more efficient labour market and greater economic growth, to the benefit of all. But the past 30 years have demonstrated that a rising economic tide in Europe does not lift all boats. While there have been periods of economic expansion, the resulting gains have not found their way to the workers who produced them. Worse, the purported gains from market integration were often exaggerated (and the social costs ignored). Unable to secure the promised gains, the attraction of further integration evaporates for workers, and the European project begins to take on a different nature – one that fuels protectionism, xenophobia and populism.

This book provides an alternative framework for discussing and assessing labour market integration. Such a framework recognizes the unique qualities of labour, and results in an integrated market that is sensitive to those unique traits. Chapter 2 begins with the basic building blocks for any approach to labour market integration: the unique nature of labour as a commodity for exchange.

2

The Uniqueness of Labour

What is a labour market, and how should it work? One common response to this tricky question lies in the field of logic. To understand what I mean, consider the following syllogism:

- markets balance when prices are allowed to match supply and demand (major premise);
- the labour market is a market (minor premise); and
- therefore, the labour market will balance when prices (wages) are allowed to match supply and demand (conclusion).

It is not an exaggeration to suggest that this simple syllogism lies beneath much of European policymaking as it applies to labour markets. We find it rising to the surface when policymakers use rigid wages, strong labour unions and/or excessive regulations (for example, those that benefit market insiders at the expense of outsiders) to explain Europe's unemployment levels.

The foundations for this argument are simple: we have a great deal of work in the field of economics that helps us to understand how markets function – in theory (the major premise). We assume that the labour market is like other markets (the minor premise). We can then conclude that a well-functioning labour market is one that facilitates price (wage) flexibility, so that the market can clear – that is, there will be no unemployment (the conclusion).

Syllogisms offer the strongest form of logical argument. As long as both premises are true, the conclusion must be true as well. But the strength of the conclusion in a syllogism rests critically on the truthfulness of the underlying premises, and there are very good reasons to doubt the minor premise here. In this chapter, I argue that the labour market is not like other markets. In arguing this, I take aim at the underlying conclusion in the syllogism previously described: that the market for labour will clear by encouraging greater factor mobility, expanding the market for buyers and sellers, and by encouraging price (wage) flexibility.

To begin with, let us start with the mainstream approach to economics. Traditionally (that is, in classical approaches), economists lean on Say's law to assume that full employment is the normal state of an economy: any deviation from the 'full employment' state is regarded as abnormal. In this approach, the supply of labour (workers' willingness to work) creates its own demand, so we needn't worry about problems of overproduction and unemployment. Whenever overproduction or unemployment threatens, the invisible forces of market demand and supply (and the underlying price mechanism) return us to full employment.

More formally, the demand for labour is seen as function of the real wage rate, that is,

$$D_N = f(W/P),$$

where D_N represents the demand for labour, W is the wage rate and P is the general price level (hence W/P provides us with the real wage rate). In addition, the demand for labour is understood to be a decreasing function of the real wage, in other words, that it slopes downward, as shown in Figure 2.1. In essence, the classical approach to economics suggests that we can generate more employment by simply reducing the real wage rate.

Neoclassical approaches are similar but fortified with a new layer of assumptions about individual behaviour (for example, individuals are rational, have access to full information, and will strive to maximize utility in a competitive market). In particular, neoclassical models assume perfect competition (full information, no transaction costs) and a homogeneous workforce. While neoclassical approaches are not hegemonic, they remain remarkably influential, and the underlying model has a significant influence on the way policymakers think about market reforms and failures. For this reason, we need to consider the mainstream model and its underlying assumptions, carefully.

In this approach, the aggregate labour supply is seen to be exogenous: it simply follows population growth. The actual size of the labour supply, however, is determined by individual incentives, and turns critically on the wage rate being offered (as seen in Figure 2.1). If wages rise, more people are attracted into the labour market; if wages fall, people will choose to avoid the labour market.

Figure 2.1: The labour market (ideal type)

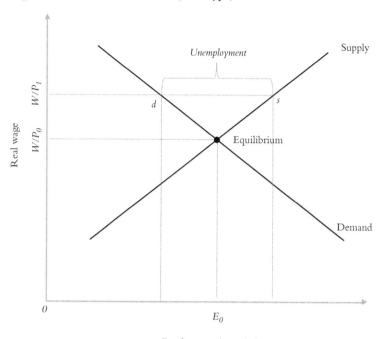

Source: Author's own

This brings us to the second, perhaps most insightful, assumption. Neoclassical approaches to the labour market assume there is an implicit trade-off between leisure and work/income. In short, this model assumes that workers look at the wage rate before entering, and they *choose whether they would prefer to work* (at the proposed wage). In other words, the wage rate reflects the 'opportunity cost of work' – that is, the worker has to decide whether it is better to work for a given hour at the proposed rate, or to spend that hour in leisure. When the wage rate is high, workers prefer work to leisure, so the supply of labour will be high. When the wage rate is low, workers prefer leisure to work, and the supply of labour shrinks accordingly.

Figure 2.1 provides us with an image of an ideal market, against which real labour markets can be compared. In the ideal market, full employment (equilibrium) depends on the capacity of wages to adjust quickly to market conditions. When wages are flexible, the supply and demand for labour power will match (as if guided by an invisible hand). If unemployment exists in the ideal market, it is because wages are inflexible, such that supply and demand are mismatched.

In Figure 2.1, if wage demands are set too high (W/P_1), the demand for labour (d) will be significantly lower than the supply of labour (s) being offered, and the difference between d and s signifies the number of unemployed. In a competitive market for labour power, workers will bid down the wage rate (from W/P_1 to W/P_0), until the labour market returns to its natural state (equilibrium), and everybody has a job (or is happily out of work, choosing to prioritize leisure).

This model of the labour market informs most policymaking on the subject – both in the EU and elsewhere. It assumes that the labour market is analogous to other markets (the minor premise, as before); and it concludes that any resulting unemployment (a market out of equilibrium) is the result of inflexible prices or barriers to the free supply/demand of labour. The problem with this argument lies in the minor premise: is it legitimate to assume that labour is like other goods and services exchange at market?

I think it is wrong to start with the assumption that the labour market is like other markets, and that its natural state is one of equilibrium (full employment). Real-life labour markets look nothing like the ones depicted in Figure 2.1 (and for good reason!). The closest living relative to the ideal market depicted before is the informal/pavement labour auctions outside almost any big box home supply store in the US (for example Home Depot), where undocumented migrants match up with informal employers for a limited period of time (usually a day, or a week). This market is devoid of labour unions, minimum wage laws, worker protection and safety laws, unemployment insurance schemes, pensions, rights to collective action, protection against overtime abuses, child labour, discrimination and so on. In these auctions, labour appears as a commodity – bought and sold, like any other.

When and where these types of labour exchanges exist, they do so illegally – in the shadows of political society. Because these workers do not enjoy the protections offered by the modern welfare state and/or labour unions, they have little legal recourse when the terms of the informal contract are breeched. Workers agree to deleterious terms because they are desperate, and the employers are there to take advantage of their desperation. The terms of any negotiated 'contract' reflect this radical imbalance of power.

This is not the type of labour market that citizens of modern states are willing to accept (even if they may allow them to exist on the margins of society). The reason such markets exist in the shadows is not because they are less efficient; it is because they expose workers to unjust treatment and exploitation. In a word, they are unfair.

There are at least three ways that the modern labour market is different from the ideal market and the pavement auctions found in Houston. First, citizens recognize that the market for labour is, in effect, a market for human life. Most workers, in the real world, do not have an opportunity to enjoy the 'opportunity costs of work' – we are forced to work, whatever the going wage, in order to survive. As a result, modern labour markets are regulated to protect workers, so they are treated *justly*. Second, in organizing, workers have managed to secure rights and protections that allow them to counterbalance the power of capital. Consequently, negotiations over wages and working conditions are determined less by the forces of competition, and more by the *relative power of labour and capital*. Most European workers have access to welfare state provisions and protections that provide a floor, under which wages and working conditions cannot fall. Finally, these worker protections and rights are linked to political territory, vary from state to state, and reflect very local balances of power between organized labour and capital. When markets are extended across political territories, it changes that balance of power to the detriment of labour. In other words, in the real world *there is a cost to distance for labour*.

It is because of these unique qualities of human labour that labour markets, in practice, tend to be the most protected and regulated forms of market. We do this because it is the right thing to do, and we pay little heed to whether these protections are cost-effective. After all, we do not ask whether it is more efficient to use slave or child labour – we simply say that is wrong, regardless of the price. As our perceptions of justice will vary from state to state and over time, so too will the nature of labour protections and regulations. This makes the integration of labour markets extremely complex. In integrating these (regulated) markets, we are in effect integrating the social models, or welfare states, that we use to protect these workers.

Human costs

Let us begin with the most important observation: labour power is part and parcel of human life. Because labour markets trade in human lives, they are placed under a number of necessary restrictions and they behave differently from other markets. In particular, communities intervene in these markets to ensure that their outcomes are just and humane. But the unique nature of labour also means that the supply, demand and the price of labour behave differently than they do for commodities in other markets.

This observation is most commonly associated with Karl Polanyi, who argued that labour was one of three fictitious commodities:

> Labour is only another name for a human activity which goes with life itself; which in turn is not produced for sale, but for entirely different reasons, nor can that activity be detached from the rest of life, be stored or mobilized. (Polanyi, 2001 [1944]: 75)

In short, we do not produce labour for the purpose of sale in a market; labour power cannot be severed from the human life that produces it, and hence labour can never be owned, stored or traded as are other (less fictitious) commodities. For these reasons, labour markets exhibit what Fred Block (1990) called 'low marketness' – they are markets in which price is only one of many factors affecting the exchange. Consequently, labour markets are remarkably 'sticky' – they do not and cannot clear as quickly or as effortlessly as economic models would lead us to expect.

Consider the issue of (re)production. A commodity is an object produced for subsequent sale on the market. Hence, Caterpillar, the company, produces bulldozers for the sole purpose of selling them. There is no other reason for Caterpillar bulldozers to come into existence. In the absence of demand for its bulldozers, Caterpillar would be forced to produce something else – perhaps tractors, or chain saws, or insurance premiums – or Caterpillar would go out of business.

Labour power is different. We do not produce children with an eye on future demand, nor do we have the luxury of going out of business should the demand for our products (children) fall precipitously. In practice, the supply of labour is completely unrelated to its demand – it is driven by other (perhaps more romantic, perhaps more xenophobic) factors. Because labour power is not produced with the intent of subsequent sale, labour makes for an awkward commodity – as it needs to be coaxed, enticed or forced into that market in order to subsist: our children become workers and must sell their labour in order to survive in a capitalist economy.

Indeed, labour supply is largely determined by demographic forces that are mostly exogenous to the market, immigration laws that limit supply, and by regulatory measures aimed at protecting workers. For example, the labour supply is severely restricted by prohibiting child labour and the work of our (post-retirement) elders. Supply is also restricted by laws that limit the number of hours we can work, the conditions under which we work, and even by the health benefits for those who are too sick or injured to work. By providing basic protections such as these, we are limiting the supply of labour, and with it improving the relative bargaining position of labour in the market (by making it scarcer). States and communities introduce these measures to protect workers from exploitative practices, because we value human life and justice more than economic gain.

This brings us to the problem of cost. When Caterpillar produces bulldozers, it assembles workers, capital investments (for example, machinery), production inputs (such as steel and paint), along with its marketing and distribution networks in the cheapest and most efficient means possible. This is necessary if Caterpillar expects to remain competitive in the international market for bulldozers. If the aggregated costs of production and distribution exceed the going price for bulldozers, Caterpillar is forced to further minimize its costs. If Caterpillar cannot reduce those costs, the remaining investments and inputs will be sold off, Caterpillar's labour will be relieved from its contract obligations, and the firm will become a memory.

Labour, once again, is different. Workers cannot become a memory: even after they are decommissioned, they still need to eat, sleep and stay warm (and in a capitalist economy these needs are paid for with wages from labour). If the going wage falls beneath the real cost of reproduction – in other words, if my job does not pay me enough to eat, feather a nest, attract a spouse, then produce, nurture and educate a child – then future labour will not be produced. If I already have children, and hope to keep them alive, I will need to cover the costs by selling additional labour (securing a second or third job). But every worker faces a limited number of hours (and energy to exert) in each working day.

In terms of supply, (re)production and cost, labour does not, cannot and should not act like other commodities for sale in the market. But labour power is also different in that the resulting labour contract does not transfer ownership rights in the same way that other (commodity) contracts do. When Caterpillar is about to make a new bulldozer, it buys sheets of heavy gauge steel, which it then cuts up into component parts. On buying the steel, Caterpillar is completely free to do with it what it wants, and it will own the resulting products/parts. After all, the owner of a commodity is usually free to decide when and where it can be offered for subsequent sale (and its asking price), how the commodity can be used or consumed, and even whether the commodity might be destroyed.

Obviously, the labour contract cannot transfer ownership in the same way. Buyers are not free to do what they wish with the labour power they acquire. Indeed, employers do not own the labour they hire – they are effectively renting time from the worker, and hoping that the worker will use this time diligently and efficiently (see, for example, Varoufakis et al, 2011: 64–5). More to the point, the labour contract is embedded in a dense network of regulations that limit what the employer can (or cannot) do with their hired hands. For the same reasons, wage levels cannot, and *should not*, become as fluid as commodity prices.[1] This sort of stickiness is a natural part of any market populated by living, breathing and empathetic human beings.

The nature of this problem is especially acute in democratic states, where the worker, as citizen, has a voice in how labour power should (or should not) be disposed; and citizens are presumed to be equal, regardless of their status or position in the labour market. Indeed, this is an essential benefit of democracy: it allows us to prioritize the needs of people over that of markets, and democratic systems of government can use the market, as an instrument, to secure what the people want. This brings us to a second unique feature of labour: the unequal nature of the resulting labour exchange.

Unequal exchange

Labour market exchanges are inherently unequal because of the initial bargaining position of the two participants (the buyers and sellers of labour). This is because the buyer's (read employer's) livelihood is seldom bound to the success of any one particular exchange involving labour; while the seller (read worker) is often under extraordinary pressure to secure a deal. As Paul Krugman (1999: 15) noted earlier in his career: 'A merchant may sell many things, but a worker usually only has one job, which supplies not only his livelihood but often much of his sense of identity. An unsold commodity is a nuisance; an unemployed worker is a tragedy.'

In effect, the employer enjoys a reserve price for labour, while the worker does not: this makes it easier for the employer to walk away from any particular deal. As the worker's livelihood (and often that of their family) depends on securing a paid job, the nature of the labour exchange is akin to an exchange between an oligopolistic producer of a specific type of medicine and a patient in desperate need of that medicine. In this light, the worker's freedom to engage in exchange, or to consider the opportunity cost of work, is more rhetorical than real.

An employer's willingness to walk away from any particular wage offer is also strengthened by another aspect of this asymmetric trade: the buyer of labour usually faces a multitude of sellers, as the number of jobs being auctioned tends to be smaller than the number of people looking for work (if you don't believe this, try to think of a place in which there is no unemployment). Indeed, the employer gains by pitting workers against one another in an effort to push down wages and working conditions. All in all, the market for labour is a buyer's market.

Of course, workers have long recognized this imbalance, and organized themselves to increase their relative power, vis-à-vis employers. In studying the power of labour, as a class, it is common to point to its two main components: structural power and associational power.[2] The *structural power* of labour is determined by the larger context, or structure, in which workers meet their employers. For example, workers in a full-employment economy enjoy greater power (relative to workers in a low-employment economy), because it is easier for them to threaten exit when they are dissatisfied with their terms of employment.

Consequently, the existence of unemployment is not simply a sign of wage rigidity, it is also an indication that policymakers prioritize the interests of capital over labour. Similarly, and as we saw in the previous section, job markets that are highly regulated (for example, they may be limited to a 36-hour work week), or located in political contexts that lessen labour's reliance on the market (that is, one that *decommodifies* workers, see Box 2.1), limit the potential supply of labour on the market, and hence increase the relative bargaining power of labour. The core of this book (Chapters 6–8) is directed at studying how market integration in Europe has undermined the structural power of labour.

Workers secure *associational power* by forming collective organizations that face-off with employers and representatives of capital to secure better conditions for workers (mostly in the workplace, but also in other regards, for example improved pensions, healthcare, or childcare provision). These organizations are designed to overcome the sort of collective action dilemmas and power imbalances that characterize the labour market and disadvantage labour. Traditionally, the most prominent labour organizations are trade unions and social democratic or labour parties. In the past, both of these economic and political organizations worked to aggregate and coordinate worker actions – for example using strikes, collective bargaining and voting – to influence decisions that affect workers and the workplace.

As a result of both types of power, complex networks of laws and regulations have been spun to decommodify workers more generally, to protect workers from unscrupulous employers, to guarantee minimum wages and so on.[3] Among other things, this regulatory latticework includes: statutory protections and benefits; collective

Box 2.1: Decommodification

Karl Polanyi (2001 [1944]: 75) recognized that land, labour and capital were all critical inputs in the production process, but that each was a 'fictitious' commodity. Land is simply nature, labour is human life, and money is socially constructed as a unit of account and a way of storing value. In addition, Polanyi demonstrated that there can be significant detrimental effects when society ignores these simple truths and treats each as if it were a commodity.

In order to safeguard their essential characteristics, each of these fictitious commodities needs to be 'decommodified'. To decommodify labour, workers need protections that will allow them to maintain a socially acceptable standard of living, independent of their participation in the labour market (see, for example, Esping-Andersen, 1985). Universal basic income, unemployment insurance, sick leave and the provision of social security are all attempts to immunize workers from market pressures. These protections ensure that workers will not be forced back to work under unfavourable circumstances or desperate need. Simply put, a worker is decommodified when their wellbeing (and that of their family) is not completely dependent upon the worker's labour market performance.

For these reasons, when policymakers encourage wage flexibility, deregulation and workaway, it is not unreasonable to refer to these efforts in terms of 'disciplining' or 'commodifying' labour, as they aim to make workers behave like commodities.

agreement protections and benefits; and a variety of social welfare obligations and benefits. This collection of benefits and obligations constitutes a regulatory framework, or a *social model*, which is tethered to political communities.[4]

This willingness to secure a more equal and just bargaining context can be seen as a modern (postwar) response to earlier political and economic crises, when markets were dislodged or disembedded from their social and political contexts (Polanyi, 2001 [1944]). In response to the excesses of the interwar period, postwar governments sought to plant market exchanges in more stable social and political terrain. With regard to the labour market, this meant recognizing that labour was more than a commodity; in other words, its reproduction served a higher purpose than just bringing a new commodity to market.

The resulting awareness led to the development of social models that protected workers from the hazards of the market and unscrupulous employers. Workers, as citizens, came to enjoy benefits and incur obligations that were linked to residency and membership in political community; so the lowest price of labour was set by the height of the underlying welfare safety net. Consequently, workers in one state came to enjoy different benefits from workers in other states – and these benefits/obligations might (or might not) be derived from their status as workers. For example, if one state passed a minimum wage law, then workers in that state could be expected to benefit from that law. Alternatively, citizens of that state might enjoy specific social security benefits – and these benefits were derived from citizenship, not from the person's status as a worker. In both cases, the state provided benefits to workers that were not universal but attached to residency in that state.[5] Seen in this light, workers are family members, neighbours and citizens – and these diverse identities influence how each worker approaches the labour market.

Modern economic theory is not blind to these developments, but a recognition of these developments tends to complicate the elegant model presented at the start of this chapter. In Figure 2.1, these sorts of political institutions drive an imagined wedge between the reservation wage[6] of the workers and the value of a job: that is, between the labour supply and labour demand schedules (see, for example, Boeri and van Ours, 2008: 14). Those very institutions needed to protect workers (for example minimum wages, trade unions, taxes and unemployment benefits) end up driving the price of labour upwards, while others (regulations on working hours, immigration policies, increase in compulsory schooling age and so on) move the price of labour in a less direct fashion, by affecting the quantity of labour available.

When we assume that labour is a commodity to be sold in a free market – one that responds quickly and effortlessly to the laws of supply and demand – then these labour market institutions become a drag on efficient exchange. Seen from a larger (more just and human) perspective, however, these institutions play a very different role. Following Polanyi, we should recognize that these sorts of regulations and social models were specifically developed to decommodify labour – to protect the person that produces the labour power:

> To argue that social legislation, factory laws, unemployment insurance, and above all, trade unions have not interfered with the mobility of labor and the flexibility of wages, as

is sometimes done, is to imply that those institutions have entirely failed in their purpose, which was exactly that of interfering with the laws of supply and demand in respect to human labor, and removing it from the orbit of the market. (Polanyi, 2001[1944]: 186)

When we recognize that labour is more than a commodity, and that the seller of labour power has social and political ties that complicate the wage bargain, then we need to expand our definition of labour markets to include these broader social and political appendages. In doing so, we recognize that there may be efficiency costs – when efficiency is understood narrowly – but these costs are worth bearing when they result in the protection of human and civil rights. More to the point, if we think about efficiency in broader terms, it is difficult to think of anything more wasteful than an unemployed worker. As Alan Blinder, a former vice chairman of the US Federal Reserve's board of governors, has noted:

High unemployment represents a waste of resources so colossal that no one truly interested in efficiency can be complacent about it. It is both ironic and tragic that, in searching out ways to improve economic efficiency, we seem to have ignored the biggest efficiency of them all. (Blinder, 1987: 33)

To balance the unequal exchange between employers and workers, we have developed nation-based protections that help decommodify labour. These protections have developed over centuries, and are rooted in the laws and practices of local and national governments, in a number of unique, nation-specific ways. As the component parts of these social models vary significantly across polities, it is difficult to establish a single comparative standard or denominator. In some polities, the social model might be secured by non-statutory agreements between representatives of employers and employees. In other polities, the social model might be grounded in law, in the form of both worker protections and citizenship rights. Some polities even combine constitutional, statutory and non-statutory frameworks. The point is that when Europe decides to create a new, continental-size labour market, we need to be sensitive to the much broader framework of regulations and laws in which the wage bargain is embedded. By focusing myopically on the wage nexus, we will miss many of the more political and social costs and consequences of labour market integration.

The cost of distance

We can now see how workers are tied to political and geographic space in a way that other commodity owners (and employers) are not: workers care about where they live and work. While there have always been, and always will be, a small fraction of people who seek out adventure and employment in strange and foreign places – whether on the other side of the country, or the other side of the globe – the vast majority of workers tend to be risk-adverse homebodies. Significant dissatisfaction and the lustre of Eldorado (so-called 'push and pull factors') are usually required to pry workers from their homes in search of employment abroad. It should go without saying, but workers have friends, family and loved ones, and the draw of these relationships often compete with the incentives and demands thrown down by the market. Consequently, we can expect that a worker's relationship to geography is neither insignificant nor neutral: *workers have strong preferences for where they will work.*

These preferences are evident when we think of workers as neighbours, fellow citizens and family members rather than factors of production. But they are also made explicit in a 2010 Eurobarometer survey, which asked about the sort of reasons that might discourage European citizens from moving abroad (see Figure 2.2). The most common response was rooted in common sense: 'My home is here.' But the list of responses includes many references to the various ways that labour is not just a commodity, but also a homeowner, a language speaker, a foreigner, someone susceptible to prejudice and so on.[7]

As workers also derive benefits from (and owe obligations to) political authorities, anchored in territory, this allegiance to territory is all the stronger. As markets stretch across political and social communities, a worker needs to balance the attraction of a distant job opportunity (and perhaps a higher wage) against the need to be near friends, family and the familiar (and how the nature of employment will affect those social relations). At the same time, any worker needs to consider how moving to another political community will affect their requisite benefits and obligations, not to mention the portability of these benefits across political communities. For workers, labour market integration involves an enormously complex, costly and, ultimately, risky calculation.

To simplify, imagine Amelie as a representative agent in an integrated European market. Amelie works as an industrial welder on the outskirts of Paris and is known for her attention to detail and skill in tungsten inert gas (TIG) welding. When Amelie is laid off from her job (for reasons completely unrelated to her performance), she will be forced

Figure 2.2: Reasons for not working abroad, EU, %

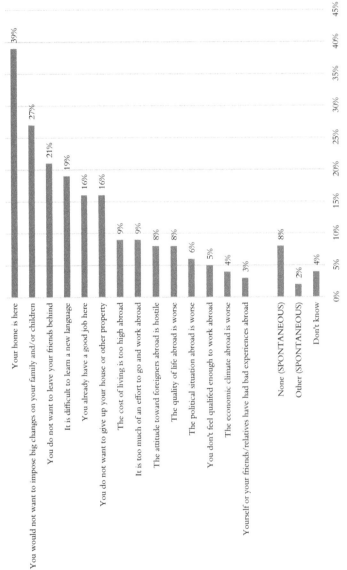

Note: The question asked was: 'And what would be the reasons which might discourage you from working abroad?'

Source: Adapted from Eurobarometer (2010: QC27, p 112)

to balance the trade-offs associated with Europe's larger, integrated labour market. We can assume that two of the most important factors influencing her decision will be the demand for her skills and language/cultural familiarity (or nearness). Figure 2.3 maps out these two dimensions across a myriad of labour markets, each represented by a small shaded circle. In this stylized depiction, labour markets are distributed in language-based 'ghettos', spread across the EU, and the demand for a given skill (for example welding) is distributed across each language ghetto. In other words, it is possible that Amelie could find a new welding job in the English-speaking ghetto, the German-speaking ghetto, the Bulgarian-speaking ghetto and so on.

In facing this array of labour markets, Amelie needs to choose between two main strategies. The first strategy (α) takes advantage of a much larger (now European) market for TIG welders. While the demand for TIG welders in Amelie's local labour market is rather limited, there may be a significant demand for those skills in, say, Germany. If Amelie is willing to move to a new country, and secure the appropriate certifications, she can continue with her trade, and maybe even earn a better wage (given heightened demand in the distant labour market). In doing so, however, Amelie has to move away from her children, parents, friends, the protections provided by her labour union and a familiar French safety net.

Alternatively, Amelie could choose the second strategy (β): she could look for work nearby, but in a job that does not require her specific skill set. In choosing strategy β, Amelie prioritizes the familiar. For example, Amelie might be able to find a job as a labourer at a construction site in her current local market, or perhaps find a job as a janitor in a nearby labour market – either in France or some other French-speaking region. These jobs don't pay as well, of course, but they allow Amelie to stay with her family and access a familiar social model and support network.

If you were Amelie, which option would you choose? From Amelie's perspective, the best alternative would be to find a secure, well-paid welding job in the environs of Paris. Absent this, and when forced to choose between strategy α and β, I think it is most likely that Amelie will prioritize her family and the familiar. When this happens, Europe loses out: it is no longer able to benefit from the (sunk) skills of Amelie the TIG welder, and Amelie ends up being less productive than she could otherwise be. It is not because of protectionist barriers that Amelie is reluctant to chase down jobs in distant markets – it is because of her human nature. For this reason, it makes much more sense to protect local jobs (and job markets) than to facilitate greater mobility.

Figure 2.3: One long-distance labour market trade-off

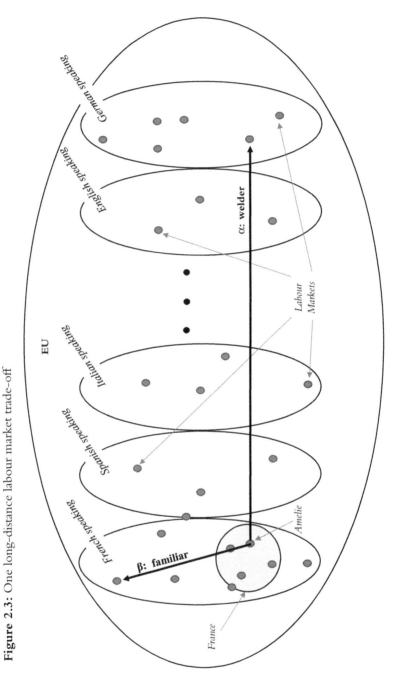

Source: Author's own

What does this tell us? Labour markets are bound to be sticky – and that it is both naive and foolhardy to try and force them to be anything else. It is better to construct a market around these very human needs than expect human workers to behave more like other commodities in economic theory.

Integration and indifference

There are good reasons why workers are reluctant to move, but this deference to location is a problem from the perspective of economic theory. The problem lies in the fact that economists usually define market integration in terms of indifference to location.[8] While there can be different stages of integration, an integrated market is one in which buyers and sellers are *completely indifferent* to where the object of purchase (or consumption) is derived. For example, an integrated market for rice would be one in which the buyers of rice are unconcerned about where the rice was actually produced, and the sellers of that rice don't care who buys it. This implies that there are no discriminatory barriers to trade (for example tariffs, taxes, quotas, passports), as these would affect the preferences of buyers and sellers.

For *most* markets, then, integration can be (and often is) measured in terms of:

1. the price spread for a good/service across a given market (the smaller the differential, the more integrated the market);
2. the absence of formal and informal barriers to trade; and
3. direct evidence of distant producers/consumers competing on equal terms.

In this light, it is not unreasonable that policymakers wish to employ similar measures to capture the degree of labour market integration in Europe.

But each of these indicators is problematic when applied to labour markets, because buyers and sellers of labour are not equally indifferent to geographic distance. Unlike commodity owners and employers, workers are inseparable from their labour power (Dow, 2003). As Marshall (1920 [1890]: *vi.iv§5*, p 326) noted: 'It matters nothing to the seller of bricks whether they are to be used in building a palace or a sewer: but it matters a great deal to the seller of labour.' The same difference in attitude could be said about whether the sewer was to be built nearby or on the other side of the continent.

Worse, expanding labour markets across space (distance) and political territory can have an adverse effect on the bargaining power of labour. Labour's sensitivity to location affects the nature of the bargains that can be secured as labour markets expand across those spaces.

Consider the effects of expanding a market across territory (within a common regulatory regime). To do this, we can examine what might be called the 'cost of distance' across three different and stylized markets: a goods/commodity market; a financial market; and a labour market. As our analytical focus is now trained on territorial distance, we will assume that these markets are already integrated and cover an expansive territory (that is, the territory is unified by a single regulatory and/or legal framework, with easy access to information):

- *Goods/commodity market:* The seller of a particular good surveys the horizons of the market in search of higher prices for that good. When there are no barriers to trade, the seller moves their goods to undercut higher prices at different places within that market. They can then exploit the price gap between the cost of production plus transport, on the one hand, and the higher prices found at different locations in the wider market, on the other. On the flip side, the buyer of this good can also shop around the market for the lowest price, and have the purchased good shipped home. In short, if transportation costs are small, then location is largely irrelevant for both buyers and sellers of goods and commodities. In this market, integration can be seen to be beneficial for both sellers and buyers (consumers).
- *Financial market:* The financial market is even less sensitive to the cost of distance, so that location matters even less in this market. Like the goods market, but where the margins are even smaller, both buyers and sellers tend to be very sensitive to price, and highly insensitive to location. As with the goods market, a financial market is integrated when the seller of a financial product (say, a share of stock in a firm) does not care about the residence of the purchaser, and the buyer of that stock is not influenced by where the headquarters of the issuing corporation happens to be located (that is, in the home polity or another). Here too, integration can be seen to increase opportunities for both sellers and consumers of financial goods and services.
- *Labour market:* This market is different. The sellers of labour are sensitive to location, in that they are bound by both political and social ties. This means that they consider the price as well as the location when deciding where to sell their labour. In most instances,

we can assume that the seller's price is inversely related to distance – the farther away the job being offered, the larger the wage required in order to entice the seller of labour (ceteris paribus – all else being equal). In effect, the seller's 'cost of distance' is significant. On the other hand, buyers of labour tend to be insensitive to location – they don't care where their workers come from (assuming they meet the requirements of the job being offered, including local language competence). Thus, labour markets can never be integrated in the same way as other markets, as it is difficult to imagine a situation (except at a high level of abstraction) in which the seller of labour does not care where the job is being offered. In this market, traditional conceptions of integration may be beneficial for buyers of labour and consumers of products that rely on labour inputs, but they are detrimental for the sellers of labour power.

From these simple examples, we can see how labour is sensitive to geographic distance, and how it is a special commodity in this regard. This comparison also illustrates how buyers and sellers of labour power will be affected in different ways than the buyers and sellers of other goods/services, when markets become larger (spatially). In the market for goods and finance, buyers and sellers are not negatively affected by the expansion of market space: relatively insignificant transportation costs mean that a larger market allows for greater opportunities for market arbitrage, to the benefit of the consumer. Buyers and sellers of labour, on the other hand, see the cost of location in very different ways: while buyers of labour are relatively indifferent to where their labour comes from, sellers of labour are not – and will be less willing to work in distant markets. In short, in expanding labour markets (across territories), policymakers can undermine the relative power of labour vis-à-vis capital.

Expanding labour markets across territories affects the underlying imbalance of power in yet another way. While a larger market offers workers more opportunities for employment (as we saw in the case of Amelie), workers must migrate in order to access those opportunities. Workaways – because they are forced to seek employment in distant locations, far from friends, family and their political support system at home – enter into employment negotiations from a position of additional vulnerability. At the same time, buyers of labour who are exploring new corners of an integrated market tend to be part of successful (expanding) enterprises; they enjoy a cushion of reserves from which to draw in the new (and distant) corner of the market. Thus, as a labour market expands across territories, the inequalities that are characteristic of the labour exchange are exacerbated when labour is forced to migrate.

Conclusion

This chapter has aimed to remind us of the obvious: that labour is not a normal commodity. Because of this, it is problematic to encourage labour market reforms on the basis of models and expectations generated from other (more general) markets. In short, I have aimed to show that the minor premise of the syllogism laid out at the start of this chapter is simply false. In our efforts to create larger and more efficient labour markets, we have lost sight of the numerous ways that labour does not, and should not, behave like other commodities for sale in the market. We have let markets rule over people, rather than letting people rule over markets. The result is a great deal of human suffering, as two recent (2019) Nobel laureates in Economics have noted:

> [Economists and policymakers] have taken it for granted that workers would be able to move jobs or places, or both, and if they were not able to do this, it was somehow their failing. This belief has colored social policy, and set up the conflict between the 'losers' and the rest that we are experiencing today. (Banerjee and Duflo, 2019: 97)

In light of the uniqueness of labour, any attempt to integrate Europe's disparate labour markets needs to address three pressing concerns.

First, wages and working conditions are too important to be left solely to competition. Because the livelihood of Europeans depends on their wages, and because human lives need protection, it is important that we take greater political responsibility for the setting of wages and working conditions. These important tasks cannot be left to some invisible hand (or benevolent god) in the hopes they will rise and fall like the price of oil. Let's be honest: labour markets are sticky, as are the politics that surround them.

This is not to say that competition cannot be useful, if properly contained. Wages are the most important price in a national economy, and should be managed accordingly: to address questions of inequality; to protect workers from underbidding one another; to ensure competitiveness (for example in the exposed sector); to stimulate an appropriate allocation of skills across the economy and so on. But when we set wages in competitive (market) settings, the result is often unjust: with men earning more than women, managers earning multitudes more than workers, and wages often falling below what it costs to live a good life (or even reproduce!).

Second, labour markets are local and embedded in political regimes. A large market, ceteris paribus, is better for employers than it is for workers. In recognizing this, any effort to extend labour markets over geographic and regulatory territories will require enormous political and economic support. Absent these supports, workers are bound to suffer. Given its human nature, labour power is drawn to local markets. Hence, local labour markets are absolutely essential, and they will continue to be so in the foreseeable future. Because citizens need paid employment to survive in a capitalist economy, and because national welfare states cannot possibly support a large unemployed population, we need to ensure that *local* markets provide living wages for everybody (or for as many as possible). Consequently, a strong labour market is a local one, where policymakers have the appropriate tools to stabilize and secure full employment.

In addition, it is important to remember that workers are also citizens, with rights, obligations and entitlements. These benefits and qualities are distributed equally among citizens, independent of market and/or purchasing power, and framed by national boundaries. Hence, we need to ensure that protections secured at the member state level are not undermined when labour markets are integrated across member state boundaries.

Finally, we need to remind policymakers that labour market reform is not just a question of efficiency. Labour market integration is primarily concerned with issues of morality, wellbeing and justice – not efficiency. In the final calculation, we should be creating labour markets that are responsive to these essential characteristics of labour. Chapter 3 provides a model, or approach, for rethinking labour market integration along these lines.

3

An Optimum Labour Area?

Europe's ambition for a unified labour market is as old as the Treaty of Rome. This ambition is arguably older and stronger than the hope to unify goods, services and capital markets in Europe. Despite this long and concerted effort, Europe still lacks an overarching approach to labour market unification. There are no comparative studies that examine labour market integration in other states and no commissioned reports focused on the costs and benefits of creating a common, continental-sized, labour market. We still lack a theory of optimum labour areas.

Europe's approach to capital market integration could not be more different. In 1999, the EU began a grand social experiment: it wanted to integrate once national money markets into a common European currency. To do so, policymakers drew from a broad-based and established literature on optimum currency areas (OCAs) and academics studied previous experiments with monetary integration (for example, in the US, the Latin Monetary Union, the Scandinavian Monetary Union) to anticipate the potential costs and benefits of jettisoning local currencies in exchange for the euro. Numerous studies were conducted by public and private research groups, with an eye to gauging the costs and benefits involved.[1] While it is possible to argue that the advice generated by this vast literature was not heeded, no one doubts that it was desirable, necessary and relevant.

This difference in approach is remarkable and difficult to understand. After all, many believe that the integration of labour markets provokes more political and social turbulence than the integration of capital markets. As we saw in Chapter 2, labour is more than a commodity exchanged at market: it is a fictitious commodity, held by family members, friends and citizens – each of which maintains social and political obligations that extend beyond the marketplace. It is because of labour's unique qualities that labour markets are the most regulated and politicized markets in modern economies. The integration of these markets affects not only the buyers and sellers of labour power, but also the larger bundle of rights and opportunities associated with national social models. For all these reasons, we might expect to find more discussion about what kind of common labour market Europe hopes to create.

This chapter provides a theoretical framework for measuring the human costs of integrating Europe's varied labour markets. This framework, in the form of an optimum labour area (OLA) model, produces its own type of ideal market, against which we can contrast actual (real) market developments. The OLA model can also generate policy proposals for building a more optimal labour area in Europe.

My motivation for this work lies in the realization that creating a common currency area privileges the interests of capital over those of labour. This realization is derived from the simple observation that labour and capital markets behave very differently (as we saw in Chapter 2). While financial asset holders are unaffected by distance, workers are bound by social, political and cultural ties that make them less willing (or able) to exploit the advantages offered by (market) size. Thus, an OCA can easily become a suboptimum labour area. Workers (and their families) are forced to make enormous sacrifices so that a common monetary union can function efficiently.

For this reason, it is both relevant and necessary to consider the design of Europe's integrated market from the perspective of labour. Rather than expecting labour to correct for the shortcomings of a poorly designed currency union, this chapter considers how capital markets and European institutions might adjust to the needs of a suboptimal labour market. To do this, we begin by taking a closer look at the literature on OCAs and the markets they create. In this review, we can see how Robert Mundell, the original architect of OCAs, thought about 'optimality' as it relates to area (domain). We then consider the sort of trade-offs that are necessary when unique, qualitatively different, economic regions share a common currency.

The remainder of this chapter takes OCA theory as its point of departure but heads off in a different direction. This alternative path prioritizes the needs of labour to consider what an optimum labour area (OLA) should look like. In short, an OLA prioritizes local/regional economic stabilization and full employment while still providing workers with the freedom to move. This OLA model generates expectations of how a shared currency area can produce significant human costs (associated with the need for internal economic adjustments). These expectations are then tested in the subsequent (empirical) chapters.

Optimum currency areas

The optimum currency area literature was launched to address the challenge of periodic balance of payments crises.[2] In an international system characterized by fixed exchange rates and rigid price (wage) levels, a country's terms of trade were no longer capable of providing the sort of adjustments needed to secure international equilibrium. In his seminal piece, Robert Mundell (1961) addressed these challenges by considering the appropriate domain (size and content) for a given currency area. In short, Mundell asked a simple question: is it better for regions (nations) to band together in a common currency area, or to maintain monetary policy autonomy and flexible exchange rates?

In comparing these two alternatives, Mundell recognized that either objective was possible and that both could be optimal; the difference depended upon our priorities, and how we chose to think about 'optimality'. For whatever reason, the finer details about what might be 'optimized' have been lost on subsequent analysts and policymakers, who saw not a choice but a fait accompli. In Mundell, however, policymakers can optimize the capacity to stabilize the component (regional/national) economies (in other words, maintain full employment in local markets); *or* they can optimize aggregate economic output, mostly by reducing transaction costs. The choice is ours.

If policymakers choose to optimize regional stability, states can maintain their monetary policy autonomy and their capacity to stabilize the regional economy (securing full employment). Defined in this way, an optimum currency area could be very small: it would be confined to the regional (not necessarily national) economic domains, which share similar economic conditions and ambitions. Variances in regional (domain-level) economic cycles are then compensated for by using independent monetary policies and flexible exchange rates, across (these smaller) currency areas. Hence, if policymakers want to secure stable economic conditions in response to popular pressures, they should embrace very small currency areas, and use flexible exchange rates across those currency areas (regions) to account for regional variances. For Mundell (1961: 660), if economic management or stabilization is the goal, then 'the optimum currency area is the region', i.e. the member state.

On the other hand, if policymakers choose to optimize the economic gains, states (regions) lose their capacity to control the regional business cycle, but economic actors no longer have to go to the trouble of exchanging currencies at the border or anticipating and responding to potential exchange rate adjustments (within the currency union). The economic gains are derived from the increased economic activity we can expect from eliminating money exchange and exchange rate uncertainty across a large market. In other words, if policymakers are interested in maximizing economic gain (here operationalized in terms of reducing 'the costs of valuation and money changing'), then Mundell recommends that the optimum currency area to be very large: 'the optimum currency area is the world, regardless of the number of regions of which it is composed' (Mundell, 1961: 662).

In short, the original architect of OCA theory believed that policymakers faced a choice as to where to place the boundaries of any future currency area: they must choose whether it is more important to stabilize regional economies (for example, secure full employment or minimize business cycle trends for its residents) or to improve the efficiency gains that can be secured by minimizing the transaction costs associated with money changing. The first objective appeals to the democrat, as it recognizes the need for democratic accountability and management of the business cycle; the second objective appeals to the economist, in that it focuses on efficiency gains.

Adjustments within a currency area

In creating the eurozone, policymakers chose to prioritize the needs of traders and money changers over the need for local stabilization policies. There are many reasons for this choice, including the desire to create a large economic counterweight to the US. In addition, it is possible that policymakers acted on faulty beliefs, in at least two important ways.

The first was a belief among policymakers that monetary policy, at the member state level, had already lost its effectiveness. After all, if regional (member state) monetary policy was no longer effective, European policymakers had little to lose in jettisoning the autonomous monetary policies (currencies) of their member states. It was only later that we realized that this belief was unfounded. Autonomous monetary policies in Europe proved remarkably effective in responding to the 2008 financial crisis (Moses, 2017a).

The second fault lies in a round of wishful thinking, otherwise known as the 'endogenous business cycle theory' (EBCT).[3] This theory proved convenient to policymakers in that it posited that increased economic integration would erode the sort of regional economic differences that necessitate local policy responses. In particular, the introduction of the euro was expected to transform member economies into an optimal currency area through the equalizing effect of market integration on interest rates, prices and wages throughout the eurozone (Issing, 2002).[4]

Rather than try to secure local economic stability, then, Europe's policymakers chose to create a large common currency area, covering several disparate regional economies (see Chapter 5). In doing so, they hoped to reduce exchange rate risk and transaction costs, sparking the sort of economic growth that sprouts from increased trade and capital flows. It is not clear to me if policymakers were aware of (or concerned about) the distributional consequences of this decision. After all, the gains from choosing this strategy are mostly pocketed by those involved in cross-national trade and financial exchanges (absent an explicit redistribution strategy), while the costs are borne mostly by workers. However, in choosing Mundell's second option, there was a clear understanding that the European currency union would be suboptimal, in the sense that it contained a number of independent economic regions, each on their own economic trajectory, and lacking adequate stabilization measures.

Once that first decision was made – concerning the scope of the currency domain – academics and policymakers pivoted the OCA literature to consider how existing currency areas compensate for the *absence* of stabilization policies. Much of this work looked to the US as an example.[5] The resulting literature pointed to the use of at least three main tools for regional (state) adjustment within a common currency area: *federal fiscal transfers, factor (capital and labour) mobility, and the reduced bargaining power of labour* – usually operationalized in terms of internal price (wage) flexibility.[6] Each of these adjustment mechanisms is the focus of subsequent empirical chapters (Chapters 7, 8 and 9, respectively).

Thinking about adjustment within a common currency area can be complicated, given our reliance on such bulky concepts (for example, 'federal fiscal transfers') and competing notions of optimality. In an attempt to clarify, I would like to introduce an example to illustrate how regional economic adjustment occurs in a common currency area. We can begin with a state in the US whose economic activity once relied heavily on the commercial aviation industry: Washington State.[7] The commercial airline industry is subject to radical business cycle swings. Thus, when the commercial aviation industry was booming, so too was Washington State's economy, and vice versa. If Washington State enjoyed its own currency, this sort of cyclical behaviour would not be such a problem: it could pursue a restrictive monetary policy when the local economy requires cooling down, and an expansionist policy (or a depreciation/devaluation) when planes are harder to sell.

But Washington State didn't (and doesn't) have its own currency – it is part of the US common currency area, and its monetary policy is decided three time zones away, in the state of New York. When deciding US monetary policy, the Federal Reserve must consider the needs of the entire federal economy – not just the local business cycle in Washington State. (The Fed tends to be more concerned about what happens in the other Washington.) It is entirely possible (and actually quite common) for some states to experience a recession, while other states experience an economic boom – as regional economies respond to different business/industry cycles. It happens, for example, that a monetary policy emanating from New York, and aimed at the economic needs of the Midwestern states, may actually exacerbate local economic conditions in Washington State. (I hasten to add that these sorts of regional differences continue to exist, despite decades of market integration in the US.)

How, then, do local/regional authorities manage to adjust their regional economy in a common currency area? The short answer is that they don't. The responsibility for regional economic adjustments has been largely taken away from local elected officials and placed with the market, which responds slowly and painfully. The main official/political response comes in the form of the first instrument: *federal fiscal transfers*. This tool works by spreading the costs of adjustment across member states in a shared currency area. For example, in the US, the federal government collects income taxes from citizens and firms from across the country. If a state is experiencing a booming (receding) economy, its residents end up sending more (less) income tax to the federal government. (Chapter 7 elaborates on how this instrument can be used in the EU.) Thus, when Washington State suffers a recession, its people send less tax to the federal government. To help Washington State climb out of that recession, the federal government takes some of the tax revenues from surplus states (those experiencing economic booms) and sends it to Washington State to help stimulate the regional economy there. It should not be surprising to learn that this sort of transfer takes time to cycle through the federal budget (all the while, workers suffer from unemployment).

But most of the regional adjustment occurs as a result of the other two instruments – price flexibility and factor mobility – and these are driven mostly by economic hardship (or the promise of better returns). Consider how these tools work in the labour market. As wages are notoriously sticky (downward), and workers are reluctant to move – for reasons discussed in Chapter 2 – it takes significant economic hardship (in the form of high and sustained levels of unemployment) to push wages downward, and to fuel workaways.

I learned this lesson, first hand, growing up in the western part of Washington State, near a large Boeing production plant north of Seattle. At the time, Boeing was the region's largest employer, and many of my friends' parents were employed at the plant. In the early 1970s, the local commercial airline industry suffered a major slump (due in large part to a cancelled contract for a new supersonic transport), what the locals still refer to as 'the Boeing Bust'. In response to the downturn, Boeing laid off most of its workforce: the employment rolls were slashed from 100,800 (in 1967) to 38,690 (in April 1971) (Lange, 1999).

What happened to the 62,110 workers who had lost their livelihood? For most of these workers, the initial reaction was to reduce spending and search for work (locally). Without a regular wage, local families modified their purchasing patterns, and local stores and businesses soon began to feel the pinch. Unemployed Boeing workers flooded the local labour market, frantically looking for any sort of work; but they were soon joined by others, as the local economy slipped further into recession (collateral damage from the Boeing Bust). With time, as the local unemployment figures grew, local wages began to drop (in other words, *price flexibility*). Absent any local stimulus measures, and with wages declining, the unemployed workers began to search for employment elsewhere (read *factor mobility*, or workaway). Many of the unemployed Boeing workers moved to California, where military aircraft production continued at pace, despite the downturn in Seattle. The exodus was massive and cruel. Indeed, the number of workaways leaving the Seattle area was so large that two local estate agents erected a billboard along the highway heading to the airport, reading: 'Will the last person leaving SEATTLE - Turn out the lights' (see Figure 3.1). Even as an adult, I still recall the pain of losing my friends to the Boeing Bust, as their families were forced to move to California, in search of employment.

In this very personal example, I have aimed to show how the labour market plays a central role in facilitating regional economic adjustments in a common currency area. Because local officials lack the requisite tools to address regional business cycles (mostly monetary policy, but also fiscal, regulatory and procurement policies), workers (and their families) are forced to bear the brunt of the adjustment: rising unemployment forces wage levels down (price flexibility), and workers are forced to workaway (factor mobility).

Figure 3.1: Boeing Bust

Note: Seattle billboard, 16 April 1971.
Source: Lange (1999) Courtesy Greg Gilbert/ *The Seattle Times*

The human costs of this adjustment are enormous, especially when compared to the alternative. After all, if Washington State had enjoyed its own currency, it could have responded to the crisis with a devaluation – immediately changing its terms of trade in a way that could help the state climb quickly out of the recession. Instead, Washington State was forced to take a lengthy and costly route out of the recession: the local unemployment level had to rocket before wages dropped (attracting new investments) and workaways increased. What makes these costs all the more difficult to accept is the realization that many of these job losses were temporary: Boeing began to hire again once the business cycle turned the corner, and many of its workers returned, sparrow-like, to their earlier jobs. To the economist, this is a sign of efficiency, with markets clearing over time; but it strikes me as horrific social policy.

From this example, we can see how the desire to create a large, continental-wide currency area in Europe – if poorly designed – can force workers to bear the burden of regional economic adjustment. The main problem is that Europe does not (and will never) constitute an optimum currency area, and that the necessary tools of adjustment are mostly absent.

The first problem concerns the small size (and make-up) of the EU's common budget. A poorly designed common budget makes it difficult for the EU to provide the sort of fiscal transfers required. As a consequence, Europe's labour markets are forced to assume a greater share of the costs of adjustment (see Chapters 7 and 8). Others have recognized these costs, but hoped that the labour market adjustments required of a common currency area can be beneficial in the long run.[8] Whatever the motivation for creating a common currency area, the burden of economic adjustment has been shifted away from elected policymakers and onto the backs of workers, as (downward) wages and workaway become the main instruments of Europe's economic adjustment strategy.

A suboptimal currency area is also costly in terms of the time required for its economic adjustments to play out. Consider the time it takes for a regional economy in a common currency area to adjust to a current account deficit. In the absence of fiscal transfers, the region's response can be characterized as an internal devaluation, where mounting unemployment generates increased workaway and downward pressure on wages. But it takes a significant amount of time before these price and mobility adjustments kick in, and the investments they are supposed to trigger follow with an even longer lag. As witnessed in Europe's response to the Great Recession, it can take some time for regional economies to adjust when the main tools for improving competitiveness are downward wages and workaway.

This is not news to policymakers or academics. Indeed, I am not aware of a single analyst of Europe's common currency who believes that the EU has developed adequate adjustment instruments. As with endogenous business cycle theory, the hope of euro-friendly academics and policymakers has been that these instruments would eventually evolve over time, most likely in response to a serious crisis (see, for example, Eichengreen, 2012). As Europe has now experienced a long string of crises, this hope hardly seems justified.

Common labour areas

In deciding to prioritize the need for reduced transaction costs over the need for local economic stabilization, European policymakers imposed a significant cost on their workers. To justify that cost, the promised efficiency gains from reduced transaction costs would have to be truly significant, and they would need to be distributed in such a way that could compensate workers for their losses. In retrospect, it is clear that these costs to labour were never repaid.

This section introduces an optimum labour area (OLA) model to generate expectations of what European labour markets might look like had policymakers chosen to prioritize the needs of workers (rather than capital). As with an optimum currency area model, an OLA approach can provide us with a measuring stick, or ideal market, against which actual economic outcomes in Europe are contrasted.

In introducing an OLA approach, we can return to Mundell's optimum currency area options, but consider how they affect the requisite labour markets. From the previous description, it should be clear that Mundell's first option (local market stabilization) is preferable, from the perspective of workers, as it shows how authorities could build a common (and optimal) market that draws together a number of smaller currency areas.[9] This option provides political authorities with the tools they need to stabilize the local labour market, so that workers can find employment close to home, in familiar regulatory contexts, with established (and protected) social models. Mundell's second option (a shared currency area) is less optimal from the perspective of workers, but perhaps more practical, given where we stand today. This option recognizes the existence of a larger currency area, and the inherent costs associated with it, but develops alternative means to protect workers from the necessary adjustments required of regional economies in a suboptimal currency area.

We should consider both options in more detail.

An optimum labour area

Let us begin with three fundamental observations. First, in a capitalist economy, material survival and reproduction (raising a family) requires paid employment or an alternative source of income. For most of us, paid employment is the only real alternative. No welfare state, not even the wealthiest social democratic welfare state, can afford to support a population suffering from a very high rate of unemployment. In short, we need jobs, and we require private employers to provide most of these jobs. In deciding how to organize an optimum labour area, we must be careful not to deter the sort of job-creating investments upon which the political community depends.

Second, a capitalist economy is chaotic – markets are characterized by boom/bust cycles, or the 'perennial gale of creative destruction' (Schumpeter, 1998 [1942]: 84). This gale slams different countries, regions and sectors at different times and in different ways. This means that jobs might be in abundance in one part of the country/continent, while being (concomitantly) in short supply elsewhere. When we recognize the existence of these asymmetric economic patterns, the question to ask is: should we expect workers to respond to local economic recessions with workaway, or should elected officials be held responsible for managing/stabilizing the local economy?

The answer to this question has both an economic and a political component. The economic component considers the type of tools that local policymakers can use to stabilize their local economies. The political component concerns the just delegation of responsibility for market failures. While the economic challenge is straightforward and easily resolved (our recent history is filled with examples of effective policy tools used to stabilize the local economy), the greater challenge lies with the political component, as it concerns questions of justice/fairness.

Here we need to ask: who is to be held accountable for local economic conditions? Policymakers prefer to abdicate their responsibility – they would rather blame a faceless market for the economic woes of their constituents. This is understandable, if not particularly admirable. Workers, by contrast, should prefer that elected officials have the capacity (and responsibility) to secure favourable *local* economic conditions. When elected officials are held accountable for managing the local economy, voters have someone to blame when the market doesn't function as promised, and a mechanism, called voting, for getting rid of the persons responsible!

As citizens of representative democratic states, workers should expect their local elected officials to be responsive to local needs, and affect local conditions (including the labour market). When elections are unable to affect important outcomes, it undermines our faith in them (and the democratic process). Workers – as citizens of democratic states – should hold locally elected officials accountable for the state of the local labour market, and these elected officials need the appropriate tools to secure these conditions. Clearly, it is not always easy to secure the sort of local economic conditions that can generate full employment, but this is what elections are for: to choose better leaders.

The third fundamental observation is a recognition that workers are more than factors of production. I have already dwelled on this point (in Chapter 2) and see no need to elaborate here. These social relationships tie us to territory in ways that make the labour market different from the market for capital, goods and services. When we recognize this fundamental need, it translates into two particular requirements with regard to the labour market. First, workers prefer to work close to home. This does not mean that workers are opposed to migration, or that they might not be tempted by better employment opportunities abroad, under varying conditions. Rather, it means that a worker's first priority will be to secure a local job, near home. Once this opportunity is assured, then workers might begin to entertain alternative (distant) opportunities.

Second, workers depend upon employment, and this makes them susceptible to exploitation. For this reason, workers prefer to find work in markets that provide suitable regulation, protection and (of course) renumeration. This means we can expect workers to prefer to live and work in a political context that is sensitive to workers' needs, and which provides the requisite protections. After all, workers are also citizens, with a voice in how the political community organizes itself (including the organization of the labour market). Through a history of democratic exercises, we have already developed networks of citizen rights and protections that allow communities to mould markets in ways that are consistent with their own local values. As citizens of such communities, we can expect workers to be in tune with those local values.

When the first (nearness) and second (protection) needs compete with one another, it should be up to the individual worker to decide which need is to be prioritized. Some workers will choose to work near home, even though they can secure better protections in a distant labour market/social model; while others may choose to prioritize the benefits of working in a better paid, and more regulated, workplace.

In light of these fundamental needs, it should be clear that an optimum labour area must meet three basic criteria:

- local officials must have sufficient policy autonomy and the tools to secure healthy local job markets;
- existing social models need to be protected and enhanced; and
- workers must enjoy the freedom to find new jobs in foreign markets, but they should do so on the basis of market strength, not weakness.

Let us consider each criterion in turn.

Policy autonomy

Given our dependence on employment, and the significant costs associated with workaway, the most important characteristic of a labour market must be the provision of local, reliable, well-paid jobs. In practice, this means that elected officials have the capacity to stabilize or manage the local (member state) economy. In the past, this sort of management capacity has drawn from a policy arsenal that includes monetary, fiscal, regulatory and procurement policies – all of which have been gutted in the name of greater efficiency and competition.[10] This is the focus of Chapter 6.

The most important tool for controlling the local business cycles has always been an autonomous monetary policy. Thus, an optimum labour market should provide local officials with the tools they need to maintain an independent monetary policy. To secure this autonomy, Europe would need to limit capital mobility across member state borders within the EU and reintroduce national currencies.[11] Then, when a member state economy suffers from a recession, the local monetary authority can stimulate investment and economic activity by lowering interest rates and/or devaluing the local currency, making their exports from that member state immediately more price competitive (relative to the competitors sold in other currencies).[12] In choosing to secure local monetary policy autonomy, workers will sacrifice the efficiency gains that are generated by sharing a common currency, but these gains have proven to be rather illusive, modest and unequally distributed. It is much more important for workers to have access to stable employment opportunities at home.

There are other tools available to policymakers for managing the local economy, even though many of them have been prohibited by European directives aimed at creating a 'level playing field' (see Chapter 6). Member states should enjoy the freedom to pursue independent fiscal policies – both on the revenue and expenditures side – to conduct countercyclical responses. They should also be able to establish their own regulations for protecting the environment and workers, and procurement policies that support local companies. By limiting capital mobility across member states, it will be possible to maintain higher tax levels (relative to competing states), and more stringent regulations, without risking capital flight. Just as significantly, investors and employers will be forced to negotiate with local authorities and labour unions, having lost their threat of exit.

Indeed, providing local authorities with the capacity to generate local economic development is one of the central lessons derived from the literature on fiscal federalism:

> Local governments [as opposed to central or overarching political authorities] are best equipped to design and administer development programs because their decisions are disciplined by market forces as well as by political pressures. Local governments must be sensitive to market considerations when designing and administering roadways, sanitation systems, public safety services and education programs. (Peterson, 1995: 18)

I realize that this is a significant change from the current way that markets are organized, and it could prove very difficult to force capital back into its national container. Economists will be concerned about the efficiency costs associated with a more managed economy. These concerns are legitimate but should not be exaggerated. Just as important is the need to create a just market – a labour market that suits the needs of Europeans.

Social models

Local policy autonomy is necessary to secure local social models, which reflect the varying needs of different communities across Europe. Local and responsive social policies are necessary to strengthen the relative power of labour, vis-à-vis capital, and to provide a social baseline of protections. In short, social models decommodify workers, so that desperation does not force us to work for substandard wages or to move away from our families.

These social models have developed, over generations, at the member state level, and reflect different means of addressing concerns and providing protections. Among the component parts to national social models are local working regulations, various unemployment benefits/schemes, different ways of supporting labour market partners, pensions, health insurance and so on. I cannot emphasize enough how different these social models are, across member state contexts (see Chapter 5 for an empirical mapping). For example, some social models rely on corporatist channels of influence to secure non-statutory – but still binding – agreements on central areas of common concern (for example local wages and the rules for acceptable action/conflict). In other states, social models are grounded in law. Sometimes the advantages of the social model are provided on account of citizenship, sometimes on account of residence, and sometimes on account of membership in a labour union. The point is that social models have developed over time, within member states, and they vary significantly as a result. This variance should be a source of celebration, not concern.

In light of this variance in social models, we need to be extremely careful about how we integrate local labour markets: we need to develop a strategy for dealing with, and protecting, this variation. Instead of using labour market integration to erode worker rights and power, we should develop an approach to integration that allows for mobility, but on the basis of strength, not desperation. To secure these protections, an OLA should require member states to treat immigrant workers from other member states as they would their own with respect to social security entitlements (and to cover the costs of such equal treatment, if necessary). In other words, immigrant workers should be provided free access to extended services in health and insurance, but also the right to unemployment benefits. In this way, migrants cannot be discriminated against on the basis of their nationality, and workers should enjoy full citizenship (and worker) rights across the common labour market. These rights should be universal, not tied to employment, nationality or fixed time limits.

Mobility

We have already seen how the need to secure local policy autonomy will require limits on capital mobility in an OLA, but the same is not required of workers. If designed correctly, workers could benefit from accessing distant labour markets, but only if they are provided with a baseline set of guarantees to deter workaway. In short, an OLA would allow workers to take advantage of foreign opportunities, but not force migration out of economic necessity.

After all, extending labour markets over larger patches of territory may benefit individual workers, but it is detrimental to workers as a group (or class). A larger market weakens the relative bargaining power of labour as a class (vis-à-vis capital), as labour bears a higher 'cost of distance' (as we saw in Chapter 2). In addition, migrant workers enter the host (distant) labour market from a position of enhanced vulnerability, as they are sheltered from the local labour movement and beyond the reach of supporting social/family/union networks. Consequently, migrant workers can easily (and often unwittingly) undermine the relative bargaining power of the local (host) labour movement.

For individual workers, however, access to a larger labour market can provide greater opportunities to find an employer willing to pay a premium price for their particular skill set (remember Amelie from Chapter 2). Likewise, individual citizens are obviously attracted to the opportunity to move freely across political territory, for example to study, retire, or fall in love. In short, the increased opportunity for individual workers to move from a low to a high productivity job results in a better utilization of labour, which should increase aggregate employment levels. However, if mobility is to be marketed as a *freedom* for workers and citizens, it needs to be driven by opportunity – not forced by necessity. For the worker, there is a world of difference between being drawn to better wages, working conditions and opportunities to growth, and being pushed away by desperation and a lack of options at home.

Indeed, from the perspective of policymakers, labour market integration is less disruptive than capital market integration, as labour market policies (or income policies) play a smaller role (relative to monetary policy) in the member state's ability to manage the macroeconomy.[13] Because of this, integrating national labour markets will have less effect on a state's capacity to pursue stabilization policies (relative to the integration of capital markets). Labour is not like capital, in that political authorities cannot increase or decrease the factor's quantity with the stroke of a pen (or the tap of a keyboard). As we saw in Chapter 2, the underlying labour supply is largely independent of market conditions.

From the perspective of workers, then, the best way to integrate Europe's sundry labour markets is to limit capital mobility, manage the trade in goods and services, increase the capacity of member states to stabilize the local labour market, maintain autonomous social models, and still allow workers the freedom to explore Europe.

A suboptimum labour area

For many, an optimum labour area appears to be too foreign or unrealistic for contemporary politics. I admit that it is difficult to conceive of a world where capital is again confined to national borders and subject to democratic control. But I believe that controlling capital is absolutely necessary to secure a more democratic and just Europe.

This section describes a more pragmatic approach. It takes as its point of departure, Mundell's second option (the one chosen by European policymakers), where the capacity to manage local business cycles has been jettisoned in hopes of securing greater efficiency gains. The European monetary union is clearly a suboptimum labour area, but is there something we can do to lighten the cost it imposes on workers?

To answer this question, we can return to the discussion of what constitutes an optimum labour area and consider how we can facilitate regional economic adjustments in the absence of autonomous monetary policies, and in a way that spreads the costs of adjustment more broadly across the community. In particular, we can consider four policy measures to strengthen European labour markets in a common currency area. The first three are derivative of the OLA and aim to take the sting out of price flexibility and factor mobility. The fourth measure strengthens Europe's capacity to employ fiscal transfers.

First, because member states have jettisoned their monetary policies, they need to develop alternative means to stabilize their regional economies and secure full employment nearby. In short, Europe needs to provide regions and member states with the resources and flexibility to distribute the costs of economic adjustment across a broader swath of the economy.

Second, Europe needs to develop a system that allows free mobility for workers, but ensures that this mobility is not driven by hardship. Europe should not be following the US example, where workaway has become the dominant adjustment mechanism (Blanchard and Katz, 1992: 52). In addition to securing adequate employment at home (the first point), Europe needs to provide its workers with a level of decommodification, such that it is possible for workers to remain at home, regardless of labour market conditions. From the perspective of workers, a successful, well-functioning market is devoid of workaway and (downward) wage flexibility. As the failure to compete in international markets is not the sole fault of workers, the cost of adjustment should not be borne mostly by workers. Employers and workers need to collaborate in adapting investments and working conditions to the needs of business *and* the needs of workers and their surrounding communities. This is best done by local economic partners (representatives of capital, labour and the community) in a context where policymakers have tools that can secure both flexibility and social security – for example through works councils (see Chapter 9).

Third, because labour markets rest upon citizenship rights that are associated with national social models, an integrated labour market requires the integration of citizenship rights. In effect, an optimum labour area is an optimum citizenship area – and policymakers need to protect local social models or establish baseline frameworks for unifying or harmonizing divergent social models. The alternative is a race to the bottom in regulatory frameworks.

Finally, to the extent that there is resistance to the first three adjustment tools, the fourth tool – fiscal transfers – needs to become all the stronger. Europe needs to commit more money to reimburse labour for the cost and burden it now bears in addressing the design shortcomings of its common currency area.

In the end, Europe has to decide how to pay for the cost of its suboptimal currency and labour areas. It cannot and should not expect workers to bear such a large share of the burden. To distribute this burden more equally, Europe can choose between several options, each of which is described in greater detail in the empirical chapters that follow. Europe can either:

- curtail capital mobility and revive local monetary policy autonomy;
- provide states with more tools to manage their local economies;
- substantially increase the EU budget, to beef up its network of fiscal transfers; or
- some combination of these options.

Conclusion

This chapter has outlined the parameters of an optimum labour area. In an OLA, policymakers enjoy the tools necessary to smooth out local business cycles, respond to asymmetric shocks, and influence the investment decisions upon which the entire community relies. The scope for securing greater autonomy is established by several policy instruments, including autonomous monetary policies (introducing capital controls, exchange rate adjustments, politicized lending tools); local procurement policies; countercyclical fiscal policies and so on. In so doing, we can again hold political authorities responsible for economic outcomes and ensure that the cost of adjustment is spread across the entire economy.

The lessons for Europe are clear:

- *Prioritize economic stability and employment* over broader efficiency gains. While the two objectives are clearly related, a myopic focus on efficiency gains can blind us to important distributional costs. In retrospect, it would seem that the efficiency gains from creating a common currency area in Europe have been dwarfed by the social costs of economic adjustment.
- Secure a *subsidiarity principle with respect to economic policy*. Member states need to be able to manage the local economy to mop up areas of unemployment. Absent autonomous monetary policies, regions will have to rely on transfers from central political authorities, so that surplus-generating regions can assist repressed regions with additional sources of economic stimuli. Ideally, member state officials should have access to incentives that allow them to prioritize local providers in response to localized needs, even if these deter broader competition. Most importantly, local authorities need the flexibility to respond to local demand in order to secure stabilization policies that exploit local sources of competitive advantage.

- By their nature, *labour markets are local*. A continent-size labour market makes little sense. Still, we can encourage mobility, and should do so during periods of economic growth, rather than in the depths of recession. To reap the efficiency gains from larger markets, while protecting vulnerable workers, Europe should develop institutions and incentives that can minimize the cost of mobility, while expanding the opportunities it provides. In short, Europe should facilitate migration that encourages upward pressure on productivity levels, wages and working conditions, while deterring the migration that is fuelled by economic need and desperation.

If supported by a baseline social model, an integrated market can secure greater opportunities for workers (as citizens), while minimizing the risk that immigrants will undermine local (host) labour conditions. In this way, market integration can generate economic growth without undermining the member states' capacity to respond quickly and effectively to asymmetric shocks.

This is the most attractive feature of an OLA: it provides elected officials with the scope of policy autonomy necessary to secure flexible responses to asymmetric shocks, while generating the efficiency gains provided by market integration. Elected officials can and should be held responsible for local economic outcomes, and these officials will wield instruments that can spread the costs of economic adjustment across a broader spectrum of the economy – so that it is not borne by its weakest members.

I have argued that all types of market integration are not created equal, and that the integration of markets across large expanses of territory generates asymmetric effects on different factor holders. For labour, the costs of distance are significant. Because of this, labour markets cannot, and should not, be integrated in the same way that the markets for goods and capital have been integrated. While this challenge is seldom recognized in contemporary debates about Europe's common market, it was a central point of discussion when Europe first began to integrate its sundry national markets. This history is the topic of Chapter 4.

PART II

Starting Points

4

From the Beginning

This chapter returns to the original discussions about market integration in Europe, to show that policymakers in the 1950s faced the same trade-off that we face today (local democratic accountability vs overall efficiency), but prioritized differently. There are several possible explanations for why Europe eventually choose a different path than the one laid out in this chapter. One explanation lies in a radically different international context in the immediate postwar period. Another explanation has to do with the declining influence of labour in Europe. The pages that follow provide a glimpse into both explanations.

Whatever the reason, it is clear that Europe, anno 2021, is a very different beast than the one imagined in the Treaty of Rome (ToR). In 1957, the common market was still being directed by a 'Community' (not a Market, or a Union), and the reason for creating a common market for labour (as well as for services and capital), was to 'promote throughout the Community a *harmonious development* of economic activities, a *continuous and balanced expansion*, an *increase in stability*, an accelerated *raising of the standard of living* and *closer relations between the States* belonging to it' (ToR, 1957: Art. 2, emphasis added).

This chapter looks back on Europe's initial motivation to build a common market, in order to show how far Europe has strayed from its original ambitions.[1] I begin by reminding the reader of the general post-war context and the plethora of new international agreements promising to build a better Europe. Although it is easy to forget today, Western policymakers in the 1950s were afraid of repeating the failures of the interwar period, which produced massive unemployment, deflation and political radicalization. Entrenched in a Cold War with their state socialist adversaries, policymakers in capitalist democratic states were committed to maintaining full employment.[2]

I then turn to focus on the debates around creating a common market in Europe, by examining three influential reports from the time: a 1953 book by James Meade; a 1956 report from the International Labour Organization (ILO); and the White Paper-like report used to inform the 1957 Treaty of Rome.[3] Each of these very different reports demonstrated an awareness of, and a concern about, the challenge of integrating national markets with varying wage and social protection levels. Each of the reports believed that market integration would lead to an *upward* harmonization of wages and social protections, although they differed on the reasons for their beliefs. More to the point, in each report, concerns about integration were tempered by a realization that states would continue to maintain policy autonomy; that labour unions would remain strong and that member state governments had the will and the capacity to protect their interests. This tempering has been mostly forgotten in subsequent analyses and debates. The third and closing section briefly considers the role of organized labour in this mix.

Our current context is remarkably different, as Europe came to embrace a more offensive integration strategy at the turn of the millennium. In the immediate postwar period – as we shall see – the plan was to integrate member state economies in a way that could encourage the growth of strong welfare states and worker protections. The scope of early economic integration was limited in recognition of the threat it could pose to workers. During this early regime, there was a concerted effort to protect migrant workers and avoid the development of a two-tier workforce in Europe. This Community in Europe was a welfare regime at its core: welfare protections were prioritized over the freedom of establishment and the freedom to provide services. Workers had the right to migrate, but most did not feel the need.

Since the turn of the millennium, the nature of economic integration and EU membership has turned this relationship upside down. The remainder of this book aims to demonstrate this simple fact. By choosing to pursue a common currency area; by jettisoning national monetary policies; by limiting the size and scope of member states' budgets; and by harmonizing regulatory regimes in an attempt to secure a level playing field (or out of fear of deterring the freedom of establishment), it has become very difficult for member states to maintain strong and autonomous labour markets. Worse, the existence of strong welfare provisions is seen as a deterrent to the sort of free movement that the currency area requires.

Concomitantly, the eastward expansion of the Community has weakened Europe's commitment to see all workers as equal (see Table 7.6). The advent and growth of 'posted workers' (see Chapters 8 and 9) has allowed employers to bypass many of Europe's legal protections and facilitated the growth of a two-tier workforce. We should be honest with ourselves: most migrant workers in Europe do *not* enjoy the same rights, privileges and remuneration as do local workers. Worse yet, in the wake of the Great Recession, these workers were forced to workaway in growing numbers (see Chapter 9). Instead of pulling together, European welfare states and the forces of economic integration are now pulling in different directions, with workers caught in the middle.

By retracing these initial steps to integration, I hope to demonstrate that we have always faced a choice over different paths to integrating European markets, and that some of these choices are better than others at protecting workers. In particular, two solutions have been with us from the start: either the member states must maintain sufficient autonomy to protect workers at the local level; or they must transfer sovereign authority upwards and harmonize European social policy at the supranational level.

Broader international context

In the aftermath of the Second World War, there was broad recognition of the need to redesign the international economic order in a way that would avoid repeating the Great Depression, and the political radicalization that led to the Second World War. In response to the extreme nationalism that had fuelled conflicts on the continent (and around the world), a plethora of new international institutions was established to cure a myriad of economic illnesses.

A new international economic order was designed to ensure that nation states could manage the threats of unemployment, deflation, protectionism and the political radicalization they leave in their wake. The Great Depression had convinced policymakers of the need to protect their citizens from the most radical and destructive cycles of capitalism, and to secure a political context capable of delivering economic and social progress. Thus, when they met in San Francisco in June 1945, to create a United Nations, the world's policymakers declared in the preamble to their Charter:

> WE THE PEOPLES OF THE UNITED NATIONS DETERMINED … to promote social progress and better standards of life in larger freedom. (UN, 1945)

At about the same time, new life was being blown into a deflated International Labour Organization (ILO). The 1944 Declaration of

Philadelphia restated the ILO's prewar objectives, but then branched out in two new directions: it focused attention on the centrality of human rights to social policy and the need for international economic planning. The declaration focused on a series of key principles to embody the work of the ILO (1944), including:

- *Labour is not a commodity* (I, a);
- poverty anywhere constitutes a danger to prosperity everywhere (I, c);
- the war against want requires ... unrelenting vigour ... (for) the promotion of the common welfare (I, d); and
- all human beings, irrespective of race, creed or sex, have the right to pursue both their material well-being and their spiritual development in conditions of freedom and dignity, of economic security and equal opportunity. (II, a) (ILO, 1944, emphasis added)

In signing the UN Charter and the Declaration of Philadelphia, states promised to maintain high levels of production *and employment*. While they recognized that free trade might bring prosperity, it also infringed on the capacity of states to fend off deflation and unemployment (after all, this was the role played by tariffs). Consequently, any effort to liberalize trade needed to be supplemented with adequate social and worker protections.

The institutional foundations to support these types of protections were secured in the same year: at the 1944 Bretton Woods conference. The interwar economic system had collapsed under the rigidity of the gold standard, the threat to stability from unregulated finance, and a deluge of protectionist measures. The Great Depression had shown people that unemployment was an inherent component of unbridled capitalism. Faced with a menacing communist threat, emanating from Moscow, Western policymakers were forced to pay more attention to the needs of their workers.

At Bretton Woods, a new international economic order was designed, based (originally) on three institutions: the International Monetary Fund (IMF), the International Bank for Reconstruction and Development (now part of the World Bank group), and the International Trade Organization (ITO), the latter of which was stillborn (and replaced by the General Agreement on Tariffs and Trade). Together, these institutions promised to deliver economic growth by encouraging international trade, while providing individual nation states with the sort of policy latitude they needed to stabilize their domestic economies.

To secure this balance, the Bretton Woods agreement limited international capital movements and instituted a fixed exchange rate system, which included political mechanisms for facilitating adjustments when required. Fixed rates of exchange would minimize exchange rate risk and encourage trade-based economic growth; national policy autonomy was secured by limiting international capital mobility. The result, a system of 'embedded liberalism' (Ruggie, 1982), encouraged international collaboration and exchange, while protecting democratic regimes from the threat associated with massive unemployment. This system provided states with the policy autonomy needed to develop more optimum labour areas. It is because of this arrangement that monetary policy became the most important tool for managing the domestic economies for most of the postwar period, and states leveraged that policy autonomy to secure full employment, high growth, economies.

The explicit aims of the (failed) ITO were laid out in its Havana Charter (ITO, 1948). Article 2, entitled 'Importance of Employment, Production and Demand in Relation to the Purpose of this Charter', underscored the necessity of integrating international trade and domestic employment policies, and Article 3, entitled 'Maintenance of Domestic Employment', made the priorities explicit:

> Each Member *shall* take action designed to achieve and maintain full and productive employment and large and steadily growing demand within its own territory through measures appropriate to its political, economic and social institutions. (ITO, 1948: Art. 3, §1, emphasis added)

While this sort of political commitment to full employment was too much for the US Senate to swallow (the US never ratified the Havana Charter), it was required by European policymakers rebuilding their war-torn economies and most exposed to the sort of political radicalization that is fuelled by economic insecurity. Full employment was the political priority, and trade was simply a means to help bring this end about.[4]

One of the central areas of concern, especially among policymakers, was the effect that increased trade would have on Europe's varying wage levels and social policies. The main issues being discussed were two in number:

- Was the harmonization of wage/social policies a necessary prerequisite of increased integration or would it come as a result of that integration?

- If harmonization comes as a result of integration, would the market facilitate upward or downward harmonization?

In effect, the question of harmonization boiled down to a question of whether the European Community should build out a common safety net and social supports, or whether member states would be allowed to maintain their sundry (and competing) systems. To these questions there were no satisfactory answers (and clearly no consensus), but they were the subject of intense discussions across the spectrum of early European integration projects.

This concern was clearly evident in the 1951 Treaty of Paris (ToP), which established the European Coal and Steel Community (ECSC). In aiming to regulate the industrial production of coal and steel in the six signatory countries (Belgium, the Federal Republic of Germany, France, Italy, Luxembourg and the Netherlands), the ToP recognized the need to do this in a way that:

a) contribute[d] to economic expansion, the development of employment and the improvement of the standard of living (ToP, 1951; Art. 2); and
b) to: promote the improvement of the living and working conditions of the labor force in each of the industries under its jurisdiction so as to *make possible the equalization of such conditions in an upward direction.* (ToP, 1951: Art. 3e, emphasis added)

While the ToP held that integration could lead to an upward levelling of living and working conditions, it lacked specifics as to how this could occur (rather than, say, a downward race to the bottom).[5] At any rate, Article 68 of the same treaty made it clear that the methods of wage fixing and systems of social benefits used by the member states were not to be affected by the ToP, except in special cases.

Three reports from the front of European integration

While the Treaty of Paris recognized the need to encourage an upward harmonization of worker conditions, it was not clear how this might come about. Luckily, the 1950s were awash with discussions about how best to achieve economic integration. This section looks at three influential views on the matter: the first offers a broader and more academic vision of the challenges of integration, while the two other reports were generated by policymakers, representing the views of the ILO and the member state governments.

Problems of Economic Union

At the time that James Meade wrote his 1953 *Problems of Economic Union,* he had already established himself as a distinguished professor of economics (first at the London School of Economics, then at Cambridge), even if his most famous works were yet to come.[6]

I begin with Meade as his approach is broader and more inquisitive than the policy reports. More importantly, Meade begins by asking the right question:

> We consider a group of countries which are coming together to form an economic union. They wish to raise their economic efficiency and so their standard of living by creating a large free-trade area and perhaps also by creating a large area within which factors of production can freely move to the most productive employments. They wish to do this in a way which is at least compatible with the avoidance of domestic booms and slumps and with the maintenance of equilibrium in their balances of payments. What are the minimum economic powers which they must surrender to the supranational or union authority? What is the maximum range of economic functions that they can properly retain for their own national governments? (Meade, 1953: 6)

This was the question on the lips of Europe's postwar governments, and it is a question worth reasking today. In response, Meade considers the costs and benefits of three different approaches for balancing the need for autonomy against the desire for greater (trade-based) integration: what he calls 'accommodating finance'; the deflation of monetary incomes; and flexible exchange rates.

The first approach, which proposes a supranational fund for transferring money from surplus to deficit states, is immediately dismissed as unrealistic. Meade argues that the second approach, which is akin to embracing a common currency solution, will not work, *because* it requires national governments to jettison their policy autonomy:

> This is important. The monetary weapon is gradually coming back into fashion after a period of disuse. I personally welcome this. But I doubt whether it is alone sufficient. I believe it should be combined with the fiscal weapon. In order to stop a depression, it may be necessary to combine

an increase in the supply of money with a reduction in taxes and an increase in government expenditure to get the new money actively spent on goods and services; and, in order to stop an inflation, it may be necessary to combine a reduction in the supply of money with an increase in taxation and a reduction in government expenditure in order to insure that the money which is destroyed comes from the active rather than from the inactive circulation. (Meade, 1953: 42)

For these reasons, Meade embraces the third approach, flexible exchange rates, even as he recognizes its many challenges (see, for example, 1953: 50–4).

The alternative to the single-currency solution is that the national governments should continue to be responsible for the issue of their national currencies and for the control of their own national supplies of coins, notes, and bank deposits, but that the rate of exchange between the national currencies should be varied in such a way as to maintain equilibrium in their balances of payments. With this system each national government would be responsible for the general monetary and fiscal policies required to stabilize its own domestic economy, expanding or contracting demand by appropriate monetary and budgetary policies in order to offset undesirable falls or rises in its own price level or levels of output and employment. (Meade, 1953: 43)

The advantages of flexible exchange rates, as opposed to the other two arrangements are two in number. First, it is easier to adjust the rates of exchange than it is the rate of wages (Meade, 1953: 44). This is an important concern, when we consider who bears the burden of adjustment (as we saw in Chapter 3). Most workers simply cannot afford a lengthy adjustment period characterized by downward falling wages. Second, a flexible exchange rate allows states to maintain their policy autonomy (Meade, 1953: 45) – and this realization was key to Meade's support.

Meade's book reminds us that there was once a clear recognition of how integration would affect policy autonomy and the capacity of democratic states to manage their capitalist economies. For these reasons, further integration needed to be pursued very carefully:

It is altogether too simple-minded to argue, as is sometimes done, that we can form a federation or other type of economic union which transfers to some supranational body just one or two precisely defined economic functions and which leaves the national governments thereafter complete freedom in the design of their own domestic economic policies, whether socialist or private enterprise, whether planned or unplanned, and whether controlled or competitive. The implications of economic union are much more far-reaching than that; and it is no accident that in the federal democratic states which really work in the modern world more and more economic power is passing from the member-states to the central union. (Meade, 1953: 83)

Unlike the reports by policymakers discussed in the sections that follow, Meade is not particularly concerned about the need to harmonize wage and social costs prior to integration. He seems to assume that these costs simply reflect varying productivity levels and he pays them little attention. He is perhaps more concerned with the effects of integration on the distribution of income, even if he does not address it directly in his book (see, for example, Meade 1953: 7). To address these issues, the previous quote seems to imply the need to harmonize social policies (as well as other political needs) and to concentrate economic power at the European level – but the reference is veiled.

The Group of Experts

Policymakers, by contrast, saw the issue of social harmonization as a central one, in need of addressing. There were substantial concerns in the broader public that integration would lead to downward pressure on wages and social protections, and these concerns could threaten plans for further integration. To investigate these concerns, the ILO commissioned a Group of Experts (GoE).[7] The subsequent report, colloquially referred to as the 'Ohlin Report' (after its chair, Bertil Ohlin), became a keystone document in subsequent discussions about European integration.

The Ohlin Report (GoE, 1956) is more pragmatic than Meade's 1953 book: it (largely) limits its view to the social implications of liberalizing commodity trade, and it doesn't consider the effects of subsequent developments (such as increased factor mobility). In particular, the Ohlin Report assumes there will be relatively limited levels of capital and labour mobility when evaluating the effects of increased trade on wages and social costs. Consequently, the report recognizes that states will experience some constraints on their autonomy, but that states will maintain recourse to autonomous monetary and fiscal policies, and are expected to use these in addressing the threat of general or cyclical unemployment (GoE, 1956: §229, §231).[8]

While the Ohlin Report assumes limited factor mobility, it often reflects on the desirability of increased labour mobility (for example, GoE, 1956: §223, §247), and it was clearly concerned about the threat of increased capital mobility (see GoE, 1956: §261). But investment capital in the immediate postwar period did not seem to be particularly interested in foreign markets, so the issue was quickly pocketed:

> Private exports of capital in Europe have been at a low level ever since the international capital market broke down in the early 1930s. This has been the result partly of a reduced inclination on the part of potential investors to lend or invest abroad and partly on their being prevented by exchange controls from exporting capital even if they wished to do so. On the one hand, political and monetary instability, together with the unpredictable nature of government intervention in economic affairs, have created a feeling of insecurity on the part of capital owners who fear, rightly or wrongly, that investments abroad may be subject to increased taxation, expropriation or nationalisation, restrictions on the right to repatriate capital or to transfer dividends, devaluation, or other risks which tend to make international investment less attractive than investment at home, especially where through protective policies domestic investment is made more secure and profitable than it otherwise would be. (GoE, 1956: §250)

A central issue of concern to the Ohlin Report was whether Europe should harmonize its varying wage and social support levels before lifting barriers to free trade; in other words, that high-wage states would have to cut their wages as a result of competition with low-wage states. On this question, their answer was a resounding 'No'. National variations in wage and social policy levels were seen to reflect differences in productivity levels, and 'there is no economic reason why the establishment of a common market should lead to a levelling down of labour standards' (GoE, 1956: §209). Indeed, the GoE (1956: §269) believed these differences were necessary to secure the efficient allocation of manpower and capital in each country, thus maximizing the output and income across all participating countries. The Ohlin Report expected that the resulting economic gains would improve working and living standards across Europe, because: a) factor mobility was limited in Europe; and, more importantly, b) of the '*strength of the trade union movement in European countries and of the sympathy of European governments for social aspirations, to ensure that labour conditions would improve and not deteriorate*' (GoE, 1956: §210, emphasis added).

These political checks on downward wage pressure depend critically on the ability of European governments to stabilize their national economies and redistribute the gains from free trade:

> We have assumed that as a general rule countries will wish to shape and carry out their social and economic policies in accordance with their national needs and preferences and that they will have recourse to international co-ordination or 'harmonisation' of such policies only if there is a clear need for such action. (GoE, 1956: §272)

To conclude, the Ohlin Report does not think it necessary for Europe to harmonize its wages or social polies prior to trade integration. Although it recognizes that there can be some downward pressures on wages and social protections in the more wealthy member states, these are not threatening because capital remained relatively immobile, labour unions remained strong, and governments were both willing and able to protect the interests of workers. The latter could be secured by the continued existence of a full array of economic policies at the member state level.

While it is seldom acknowledged, the Ohlin Report includes a very important dissent, in the form of a 'Note by Professor Maurice Byé', a GoE member and Professor of International Economic Relations at Paris University (see Byé, 1956). Byé is concerned by the fact that the committee limits itself to one of four possible scenarios – and it is the scenario that Byé believes to be least realistic of all (Byé, 1956: 134). In particular, the Ohlin Report's conclusions rest on the assumption that there will be persistent capital and labour *im*mobility in the countries of Europe, even after they are integrated. Professor Byé believed this was unlikely (he believed the more likely scenario was the one that actually comes about: where labour remains relatively immobile, while capital is highly mobile), and he argued that many of the GoE's conclusions don't hold under competing scenarios (of varying levels of factor mobility).

In particular, Byé (1956: 129) is prescient in noting that 'the threat of a flight of capital which has already been held over earlier attempts at social progress would nullify the effect of the trade unions and governments', and he is concerned that the report is overly (and unreasonably) optimistic as a result:

> The main danger of over-optimism is that it gives nations the illusion that they will both enjoy the advantages of European unification and remain fully free to make independent decisions.
>
>   Any such hope would invoke a contradiction. (Byé, 1956: 139)

Although Byé doesn't elaborate, he implies that Europe will need to adopt different forms of capital controls and a greater coordination of social policies with the advent of increased capital mobility. While Byé's analysis eventually proved to be most accurate, his dissenting comments have been largely forgotten by subsequent scholarship and policymakers.[9]

The Spaak Report and the Treaty of Rome

At the 1955 Messina Conference, the six ECSC member states celebrated the success of their integrative experiment and planned for further, subsequent, integration in the form of a European Economic Community (and Euratom). The Messina Conference appointed an Intergovernmental Committee, chaired by Paul-Henri Spaak (Belgium's foreign minister), whose report became, in effect, the White Paper for the Treaty of Rome (ToR), which established the European Economic Community (EEC).

The Spaak Report[10] is of interest to analysts because it provides some of the motivation and detail which the ToR lacks when discussing European integration. Most importantly, it provides some insight into the thinking of the member state representatives who eventually came to sign the Treaty of Rome (ToR, 1957). But the Spaak Report is clearly less interested than the GoE about the effects of trade integration on labour: labour unions are only mentioned four times in a report totalling 135 pages.

The Spaak Report (1956) recognizes significant differences in member state wage levels, working conditions and social provisions, but it does not see these as a hindrance to further integration. As with the Ohlin Report, these differences are assumed to reflect variations in productivity and general economic conditions, and there is little point in using legislation to harmonize these differences. Rather, the Spaak Report expects these differences to evaporate as a result of the common market working its magic – the invisible hand would become a helping hand for labour:

> It is therefore not possible to try to modify, as it were, by decree the fundamental conditions of an economy as they result from natural resources, the level of productivity and the size of the public sector. A part of what is usually called harmonization could therefore be the result of the very functioning of the market, the economic forces it brings into play, the contacts it brings about between the parties concerned. (Spaak Report, 1956: 61, my translation)

While labour unions are briefly mentioned as an agent for improving labour conditions in the integrated market (Spaak Report, 1956: 61), the most important means for protecting these conditions was to ensure that economic integration was limited in such a way as to not encroach on the autonomous policies of member states. What was being proposed was a *partial* integration – one that would not result in a common currency, or the erosion of member state policies. The closing sentences of the Spaak Report's review of creating a common market make this quite clear:

> It is to be stressed that, however broad, the economic integration that will be achieved by the free movement of goods, services, persons and capital is still *only a partial economic integration, since it does not involve renunciation of the autonomy of fiscal, financial or social policies, nor the creation of a single currency.* At least it has a force in itself large enough to maintain the useful degree of convergence between these policies, and to ensure that the momentum does not stop along the way. (Spaak Report, 1956: 96, my translation, emphasis added)

Because member states still wielded significant policy autonomy, the Spaak Report assumed that states would continue to protect their workers. In short, there was little need to expand the Community's social policy repertoire. Consequently, the Spaak Report advocated for the harmonization of European policy in only three, relatively limited, areas: equalization of male and female wages; conditions of overtime renumeration; and the duration of paid holidays (Spaak Report, 1956: 66).

The influence of the Spaak Report on the Treaty of Rome is clearly evident in three areas. First, as with both the Ohlin and the Spaak Reports, the ToR does not see the prior harmonization of wages and social policies as necessary, nor would these differences hinder the integration of European markets. Indeed, despite significant pressure from France (Sapir, 1996: 551–2), there are only two specific areas of harmonization that are explicitly recognized in the ToR: that men and women should receive equal pay for equal work (Art. 199) and harmonizing the duration of paid holidays (Art. 120). Note, however, that the latter only requires states to 'endeavour to maintain the existing equivalence between paid holiday schemes'.

Second, the ToR expects that economic integration will facilitate an upward harmonization of wages and working conditions, and this harmonization is secured with an expectation that members states will continue to enjoy the tools necessary to ensure stable and healthy economic conditions:

> Each Member State shall pursue the economic policy needed to ensure the equilibrium of its overall balance of payments and to maintain confidence in its currency, while taking care to ensure a high level of employment and a stable level of prices. (ToR, 1957: Art. 104)

But there is a strong (if still unexplained) belief that the market itself, and the way it is being integrated, will deliver upward harmonization of working conditions and living standards:

> Member States agree upon the need to promote improved working conditions and an improved standard of living for workers, so as to make possible their harmonisation while the improvement is being maintained.
>
> They believe that such a development will ensue not only from the functioning of the common market, which will favour the harmonisation of social systems, but also from the procedures provided for in this treaty and from the approximation of provisions laid down by law, regulation or administrative action. (ToR, 1957: Art. 117)

This brings us to the third characteristic: the Treaty of Rome provided very limited provision for direct intervention in social policy matters by the Community institutions. A short 'social provisions' chapter [Title III, Ch. 1] is used to forward a number of principles, including the promotion of improved working conditions and standards of living, and equal pay for men and women. But there is remarkably little meat placed on these skeletal provisions. The mechanism for delivering upward harmonization remains unspecified, and the Spaak Report provides precious little elaboration. For example, the 'procedures' referred to in Article 117 are limited to an effort to encourage member states to promote close collaboration in a number of fields, such as 'employment; labour law and working conditions; basic and advanced vocational training; social security; prevention of occupational accident, and diseases; occupational hygiene; and the right of association, and collective bargaining between employers and workers' (ToR, 1957: Art. 118).

There are two other potential mechanisms mentioned in the ToR, both of which are underdeveloped. Article 123 created a European Social Fund (ESF), and Article 193 created the Economic and Social Committee. At first, the ESF was considered to be the most significant social component to the treaty: it offered a 'cornerstone in the edifice of social security' (EEC, 1959: §170) and 'for the first time ... a supra-national guarantee for those living in the European Community' (EEC, 1960: §291). But the ESF never rose to expectations: its aid was mostly limited to the training and resettlement of workers who had lost their employment through structural industrial changes, and the Council only established the regulations to activate the ESF after considerable pressure was applied by European trade unions (Barnouin, 1986: 84).

Likewise, Article 193 only came about after significant pressure from trade unions in response to earlier drafts of the ToR, which lacked any provision, whatsoever, for the representation of trade unions (Dukes, 2014: 135). While the Economic and Social Committee did include representatives of trade unions, industry and other interest groups, and was responsible for advising the Commissions and Councils on specified matters, it was a remarkably weak body, without the capacity to draw up its own budget or create its own rules of procedure.

Thus, for the first decades of the postwar period, policymakers in Europe believed that it was possible to integrate national markets without harmonizing social policy at the European level. While European-wide social policy was delayed, it is an exaggeration to call it a period of 'benign neglect' (Mosley, 1990: 149f). At the time, the integration of social models was vigorously discussed and seriously considered in a series of expert reports and deemed unnecessary. Policymakers were aware of the need for upward harmonization of working and social conditions, but they believed that members states, supported by strong labour unions, had both the will and the means to bring this about. Indeed, the very nature of early European market integration was designed to ensure that these states *maintained their policy autonomy*.

As we have seen, there are subtle differences across the sundry reports in terms of where they thought the most important driver of harmonization lay: some had more faith in the power of labour unions (the GoE), while others were more mesmerized by the power of the market (ToR). There can be other reasons as well. For example, Sapir (1996: 544) argues that harmonization was simply not needed when the Community enjoyed a higher degree of economic and social homogeneity (among only six member states) and when living standards were rising across the Community. All of these things are surely important to explain the early absence of a common European social policy.

The European labour movement

Throughout the course of the 1950s, a new and bifurcated labour market was beginning to appear in Europe. At one level, there was great effort to integrate once national markets and facilitate a freer flow of labour (and capital, if originally less so). At the same time, member states retained control over their national policies so that the regulatory, and benefits, side of the European labour market remained highly segregated. This section looks at how organized labour responded to these early developments.

Labour's response was, at first, enthusiastic. Integrating Europe provided an opportunity to unify Europe's very divided and segmented labour movement. After all, when the Treaty of Paris was being written, trade unions within the six member states were already split along political, religious and industrial lines. Creating the ECSC encouraged the establishment of new, European-wide trade union bodies, unifying the socialist (non-communist) labour movement within the newly established International Confederation of Free Trade Unions (ICFTU).[11] In 1950, the ICFTU formed a 'European Regional Organisation' to represent trade unions in Western Europe, including those from both signatory and non-signatory states to the Treaty of Paris.

Not only was labour enthusiastic, its participation in the European project seemed meaningful and desirable. After all, the Treaty of Rome focused on the negative fallout from integration on workers: it contains specific social provisions involving compensation payments and re-employment schemes for workers displaced by economic integration. This is not surprising, if only because a number of trade unionists were directly involved in drafting the terms of the Treaty of Paris (Roux, 1952: 302). In addition, labour had been invited to participate in a number of bodies: three labour representatives were appointed as members of the High Authority, one of whom, Paul Finet, held the presidency for a time; and direct representation from non-communist trade unions was assured in the Consultative Committee of the ECSC, which was concerned with all the major decisions made by the High Authority (Barnouin, 1986: 5).

At the time that the Treaty of Paris was signed, there was widespread recognition by many of the principal actors of the benefits that it would bring to labour. Among them was Dr Ardenauer, the German chancellor, who justified his country's participation thus:

> I believe that every European, particularly the European worker, will reap considerable benefit from this development, for there is no doubt that he will soon be able to obtain more goods than hitherto and at lower prices, and this will raise his standard of living.[12]

By the time of the Treaty of Rome, however, European unions were increasingly sidelined from, and unimpressed with, the form of integration. Even though it was a product of the ILO, European labour was unwilling to accept the GoE's hope for a common market without a social dimension. From 1957, labour developed an alternative 'programme for Europe', aimed at *preventing* the development of a 'free' common market (Barnouin, 1986: 72–9). Labour pushed for far-reaching institutional reforms and a more transparent and democratic form of decision making in the EEC, including a directly elected European Parliament with legislative and budgetary powers, and it fought to strengthen the voice of labour in those institutions.

By this point, organized labour in Europe was less enamoured with the promise of market integration, and was concerned that the resulting market was 'too exclusively based on an unjustified confidence in the efficiency of liberalism and the permanent goodwill of the national interests concerned' (Bouvard, 1972: 72). These organizations were looking to rebuild a new market, at the European level, so that benefits and protections could be equally distributed to all workers. Along the way, they pushed for the upward harmonization of living and working conditions across the member states (as a means of achieving both improved standards and greater equality between different groups of workers), a supranational employment policy guaranteeing full employment, and the democratization of relations within the enterprise (ECFTUC, 1969). We shall return to organized labour's changing relationship to market liberalization in Chapter 9.

With the Treaty of Rome, we can already see the dwindling influence of labour on the blueprint of European integration. While the European Community was heading away from a common European social policy, organized labour was increasingly arguing for it. Labour was more sceptical of the member states' capacity to protect labour in an integrated market, and worried about the direction that integration was heading.

Conclusion

By the end of the 1950s, a new vision of European labour markets was beginning to settle at two distinct levels. At the EEC level, barriers to trade and mobility were increasingly removed, and the rhetoric of free trade was ramped up. At the same time, labour markets remained highly segmented at the member state level – largely unaffected by the creation of the common market. Different, and competing, wages, working conditions and standards were allowed to exist, side by side, and there was little explicit concern about any threat of a 'race to the bottom'. Quite the opposite was the case: policymakers believed that competition, *supported by governments and unions*, would lead to an upward mobilization of conditions.

I have retraced these earlier discussions to remind us that the decisions we face are not new: Europe has long struggled with the need to balance political autonomy and full employment (on the one hand) with economic integration and economic efficiency (on the other). By looking at how this balance was achieved in the early years, we are reminded of something that gets very little attention today: the need to prioritize democratic accountability, and to try and integrate our economies in a way that can protect this democratic accountability. In revisiting this history, I do not mean to suggest that we need to repeat it. Rather, my hope is to encourage reflection over the significant social, political and human costs of prioritizing efficiency and integration.

The market architects of the 1950s were able to see the threat to labour from increased integration, but they believed it could be boxed in. While organized labour was sceptical, policymakers believed that member states would be able to maintain sufficient policy autonomy to stabilize the local economy and channel competition in a more socially progressive direction. In effect, policymakers at the time believed that economic integration would be beneficial when (and if) states maintained their capacity to steer the economy and respond to the needs of their local labour markets.

This belief proved unjustified, for at least two reasons. First and foremost, member states slowly jettisoned the very tools that were critical to protecting labour. This process of policy surrender was driven not only by global economic trends, but also by the design of subsequent architects of European integration. These developments are described in Chapter 6. At the same time, the relative power of labour in the community, as a whole, has fallen precipitously (see Chapter 9). Europe has been unable to protect national policy autonomy and the relative strength of labour unions, even though several of the expert reports identified these protections as absolutely necessary to secure the fair distribution of the gains of trade liberalization. These threats were foreseeable, as evidenced in the more critical reports by Meade and Byé, but downplayed.

As member state policy autonomy has receded, the EU has not been able to fill the political void. This is the second reason why the original architects were mistaken to believe they could box in the threat of market integration. The challenges of providing this European response are complicated and described in Chapters 7 and 8.

What *was* justified in the conclusions of these reports was their recognition of the very different economic needs of individual member states. In this regard, very little has changed. This continued economic variance, at the member state level, is the subject of Chapter 5.

5

A Multitude of Labour Markets

In the early years of European integration, there was a broad recognition of the need to integrate economies in a way that allowed policymakers to stabilize their home markets. As we saw in Chapter 4, this was done to ensure that market integration didn't drive labour conditions and wages downward in a competitive race to the bottom. Over the decades, this lesson has been lost on policymakers, as member states have jettisoned many of the tools necessary for local economic stabilization.

Today, European integration is animated by a belief that bigger markets are better than smaller ones; that integration propels harmonization; and that markets can be self-correcting. Policymakers and academics have come to believe that socioeconomic imbalances across Europe's various regions and countries can (and will) adjust automatically on their own accord. This belief lies implicitly behind the pursuit of a *common* currency and the need for *standardized* (read common) rules for member state fiscal, regulatory and procurement policies (among others). Such efforts have been justified by reference to the needs of a level playing field and with the promise of increased efficiencies. As a result of these pursuits, however, there is less room remaining for local policy autonomy at the member state level.

The problem is that European labour markets remain remarkably segregated and unique. The goal of this chapter is to describe that heterogeneity. The continued existence of a multitude of *local* labour markets – each following their own economic path – remains a significant challenge for Europe.

In the absence of unique policy instruments that can address these local challenges, such local economic asymmetries can prove very costly. If European labour markets actually behaved in a similar manner, and actually shared similar ambitions/hopes, then it would make sense to share a unified (single) policy regime (whether it was monetary, fiscal, regulatory, whatever). But this chapter demonstrates that this is absolutely *not* the case. Europe is not one common labour market, but hundreds – perhaps thousands – of small, unique and local labour markets, many of which are heading in very different directions.

Some marketable differences

Despite the committed and diligent efforts of policymakers, European labour markets remain stubbornly varied and idiosyncratic. Europe's regional differences are substantial and borne of deep historical, cultural and political roots (see, for example, Delamaide, 1994; Berend, 2020). Consider, briefly, some of the more significant differences that, at the time of writing, dissect the EU:

- The EU comprises *27 member states*, home to about 450 million people, covering a combined area of 4,233,255.3 km^2 (1,634,469 square miles).
- These member states can be (and have been) divided into a myriad of regions, now classified as statistical units, or NUTS: *nomenclature des unités territoriales statistiques* (Eurostat, n.d.). In particular, Europe consists of *104 major socioeconomic regions* (NUTS1), 283 basic policy-based regions (NUTS2) and 1,345 small regions (NUTS3).
- Europe draws on *24 official languages*, stretching across three different language families – Indo-European, Uralic and AfroAsiatic – and including eight dominant subfamilies – Balto-Slavic, Celtic, Italic, Germanic, Hellenic, Ugric, Finno-Permic and Semitic.
- The EU has *nine official currencies*. Besides the euro, European workers can be paid with the Bulgarian lev, the Croatian kuna, the Czech coruna, the Danish krone, the Hungarian forint, the Polish złoty, the Swedish krona and/or the Swiss franc (which is used in Campione d'Italia – a part of Italy – and Büsingen am Hochrhein – a part of Germany).

While differences of nationality, language and currency are significant and important, there are three types of local economic characteristics that are especially critical from the perspective of labour: the home market's level of development; the home market's susceptibility to instability or shocks; and the nature of the home market's social model. The first difference consists of long-standing and deep-seated levels of variance, while the second type is more short term and can be either single shot or cyclical in nature. The third type of variation, in terms of social models, is the result of long-standing political, social and economic struggles. These three local market characteristics structure the discussion that follows.

Development needs

This section takes a closer look at the variance in wealth across the EU, measured at both the member state and the regional (NUTS2) level. These overall levels of wealth remain fairly stable over time and prove difficult to change – and they have a significant impact on the nature of the local labour markets.

We know that most countries exhibit large and persistent geographical differences in wages, income and unemployment rates. These variations in labour market outcomes can continue for decades (Barro et al, 1991; Blanchard and Katz, 1992) and across generations (Chetty et al, 2014). It is unthinkable that such variations don't also exist in the EU. Even in the US, the unemployment rate can vary significantly from one state or region to another. For example, in December 2019 – before the onslaught of COVID-19 – the unemployment rate in the state of Mississippi was 5.6%, while it was just 2.9% in the neighbouring state of Alabama (US Bureau of Labor Statistics, 2020).

In the EU, at the member state level, we find a significant variance in wealth, as measured in terms of per capita gross domestic product (GDP, €). This variance, in 2018, is shown in Figure 5.1. Using this indicator, the wealthiest state in the EU is Luxembourg, where per capita GDP was a remarkable €98,640. To the extent that such a figure includes so-called 'phantom FDI flows', with little substance and/or links to the local economy (see, for example, Damgaard et al, 2019), this indicator is problematic. As a result, countries such as Ireland and Luxembourg (which attract this type of foreign direct investment – FDI) appear much richer than they actually are. For this reason, it is more reasonable to list Denmark, Sweden and the Netherlands as Europe's wealthiest (per capita) states. Applying this (more conservative) ranking, the per capita GDP of the richest states in the EU (Denmark, Sweden, the Netherlands) is about *four times* the per capita GDP of the poorest countries (Bulgaria, Romania and Croatia).

These differences matter, as they reflect the relative abundance (or scarcity) of capital across member states in Europe. It should be obvious that a country's overall level of wealth is a significant determinant for the size and nature of its labour markets, and the type of investments and economic activity they can attract. By definition, a wealthy country is relatively abundant in capital (and relatively scarce in labour). Investors in capital-rich countries may be more likely to invest in

Figure 5.1: GDP/capita (€), member states, 2018

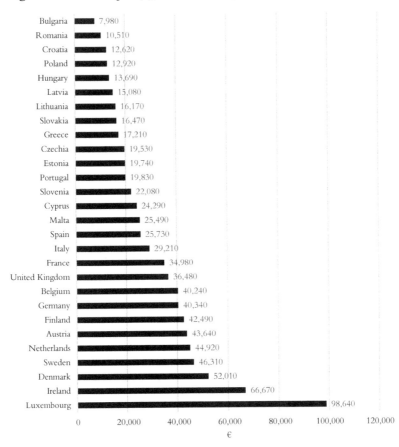

Source: Adapted from Eurostat (nama_10_pc)

productivity-enhancing measures and equipment so as to minimize their hiring costs of (more expensive) labour. These investments, in turn, justify higher wages for the impacted workers (given the higher productivity that results). In addition, wealthy countries provide workers and investors with better infrastructural and educational opportunities, which, in turn, also impact the nature of the local labour market.

This variation in wealth pervades the EU and can be found at many different levels of aggregation. When we compare per capita wealth levels at the regional (subnational) level, as is done in Figure 5.2, an interesting pattern reveals itself. Figure 5.2 uses NUTS2-level regional data from Eurostat to display regional wealth levels, as a percentage of the EU average (EU28 = 100), using purchasing power standards in

Figure 5.2: GDP/inhabitant, member states, NUTS2 level, 2017

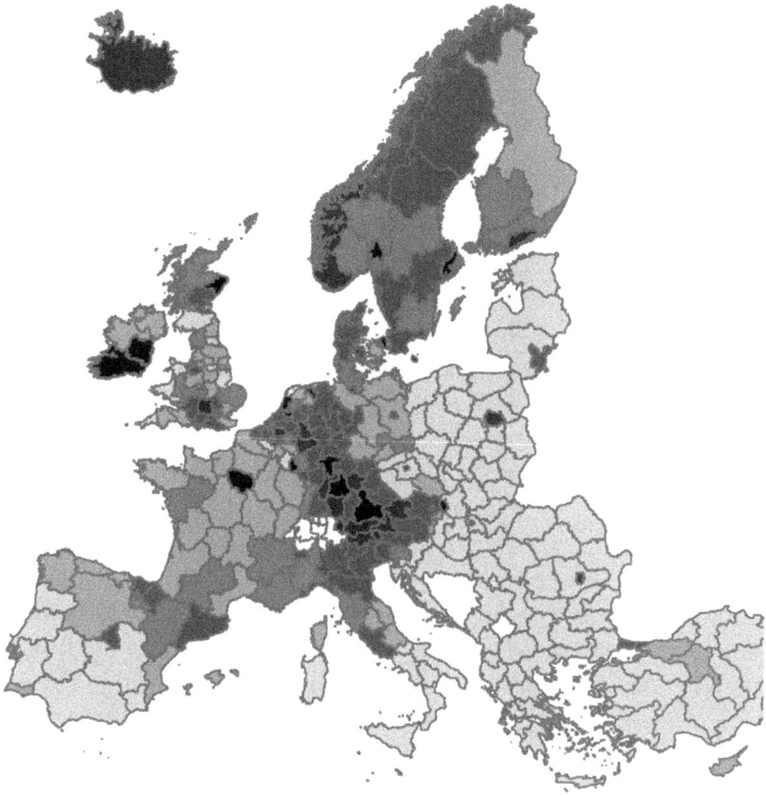

Notes: EU28 = 100; index based on GDP in purchasing power standards in relation to the EU28 average, by NUTS2 regions. The darker the unit, the higher the GDP/inhabitant level.

Source: Adapted from Eurostat (2017). Underlying data are Eurostat (nama_10r_2gdp; nama_10r_3popgdp; 8nama_10_gdp9; and nama_10_pe)

2017. In this map, we see the EU split down the middle by a thin strip made up of its most wealthy regions, stretching from northern Sweden, through Denmark, western Germany and Austria to the tip of northern Italy. The poorest regions of Europe, located predominantly in Eastern Europe, are located to the right of this strip. To the west, we find more average levels of wealth (in, for example, France and northern Spain). There are, of course, outliers to this pattern, with pockets of poverty in Portugal and southern Spain, and more wealthy pockets surrounding the French and Finnish capital cities. As at the national level, we can expect that variations in local levels of development will have a significant impact on the nature and health of local labour markets.

Of course, the EU recognizes these differences in wealth, and directs its policies in an effort to help. Indeed, I have chosen to use these indicators (GDP per capita volume indices), because they are used to allocate Structural Funds within the EU. Regions where the real GDP per capita is less than 75% of the EU average (taken over a period of three years) are eligible for support from the Structural Funds. We shall return to these funds, and Europe's Cohesion Policy, in Chapter 7.

Stabilization needs

In addition to a country's (or region's) general level of economic development, local labour markets are likely to behave differently in response to unique shocks or cycles associated with industries that cluster in their home market. These underlying disturbances can be one-time reactions to a unique specific shock (such as a global Coronavirus outbreak, or the introduction of a common currency), or familiar, repeating events connected to a business cycle. As a result, workers in one region can experience a local recession/boom, while workers in another region or labour market will not. These cycles/shocks vary across markets, depending on the unique composition of the local markets. This section examines the degree to which different regions in Europe are economically unique. In other words, we need to find out where local markets in Europe specialize in particular economic activities, and hence are susceptible to different economic trajectories and patterns.

It is not news to recognize that industries tend towards geographic concentration. The most obvious example of this is access to raw materials or production inputs. For example, it is not an accident that the Norwegian economy leans heavily on the petroleum sector: it was lucky to discover significant petroleum resources under its continental shelf. Consequently, the Norwegian labour market is very sensitive to the global price of oil and gas. When the price of oil goes up, it tends to be a good thing for the Norwegian economy (as a producer country), while a rise in oil prices tend to be damaging to the rest of Europe, which mostly consumes (not produces) petroleum products. The same thing might be said for Norway's knack at exporting salmon: investors are drawn to the attractive aquaculture conditions along Norway's coastline. Other investors, in the textile industry for example, would not be drawn to Norway, but would seek out local market regions with an abundance of (read cheap) labour – as labour is an important input factor in the making of clothes.

Other explanations for why industries tend towards geographic concentration ('agglomeration' in the unwieldy language of economists) return us to the 'cost of distance', as introduced in Chapter 2. As with the link between resource allocation and economic activity, this is not a new argument: Alfred Marshall (1920 [1890]) argued that industries concentrated in particular areas to minimize the costs of three different types of transport costs – the costs of moving goods (shipping costs), people (labour market pooling), and ideas (intellectual spillovers). Today, we often associate this approach with new economic geography, and the early work of economist Paul Krugman (1991a, 1991b), where industries are shown to be tightly clustered in specific cities and regions (rather than spread evenly around the country or globe), based largely on economies of scale, trade costs and factor price differences. The recent work of Elisson et al (2010) continues this tradition.

Although much of this work has been done in the US, these clustering tendencies are also found in Europe, and can be easily seen when we look at variations in employment specialization, as is done in Figure 5.3. This map displays the degree to which certain industries tend to concentrate in regional pockets, across Europe. In particular, Figure 5.3 maps the type of economic activity whose employment share exceeded the EU28 average by the largest margin in 2016. When we look for more general patterns in the map, it is possible to discern four different economies spread across Europe, concentrated in different geographic areas:

- *Financial Europe:* Workers in finance, insurance, property and the like tend to be concentrated in Northern Europe, just south of the North Sea: in the Netherlands, Belgium, Luxembourg (and a handful of European capitals).
- *Administrative Europe:* Public administration workers, in sectors such as defence, education, health and social work, are concentrated in the other Nordic regions, such as northern Germany and France.
- *Industrial Europe:* Europe's industrial workers are spread out across the middle part of the continent: Germany, Poland, the Czech Republic, Slovakia, Croatia and northern Italy.
- *Rural Europe:* The primary sector still dominates on the margins of Europe: Greece, southern Italy, Ireland, Romania, Bulgaria and parts of Portugal and Spain.

Given these different sources of economic activity scattered across Europe, we should not be surprised to find that Europe's sundry regional economies experience significantly different business cycles. In other words, to the extent that different regions rely on

Figure 5.3: The five economies of Europe

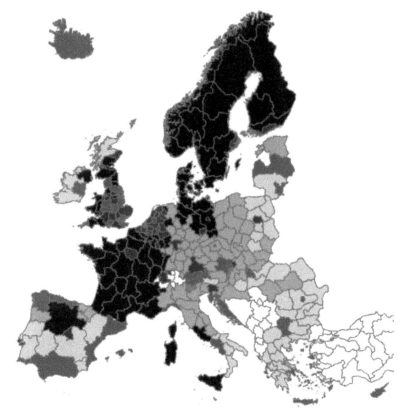

Notes: Employment specialization, 2016. Percentage points, based on difference compared with EU28 average, by NUTS2 regions. Sectors go from light to dark, from: no data (white); agriculture, forestry and fishing; industry; construction; wholesale and retail trade; finance and insurance; and public administration (darkest). The Norwegian data are national.

Source: Adapted from Eurostat (2019). Underlying data are Eurostat (nama_10r_3empers; nama_10_a10_e)

different types of economies, we cannot expect them to behave in the same way. If a region is dependent on a particular industry/ sector, and that industry goes into a slump – for whatever reason – then the local labour market will be negatively affected and local unemployment levels will rise. (Recall the 'Boeing Bust' example described in Chapter 3.) Alternatively, and concomitantly, another industry, located in another part of Europe, may be experiencing a booming labour market. This is not a single, extraordinary event we

Figure 5.4: Business Cycle Clock

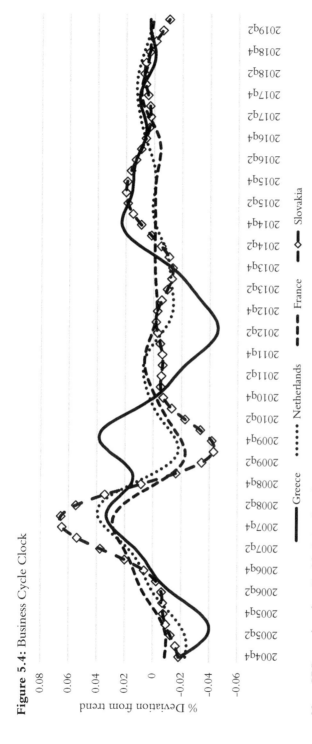

Note: GDP growth cycle as % of deviation from the trend.

Source: Adapted from Eurostat (2020)

are talking about here, but a normal and reoccurring characteristic of capitalist economies.

One of the easiest ways to map business cycle trends in Europe is with Eurostat's 'Business Cycle Clock'.[1] I suggest that readers visit the site and compare their country's business cycle trends with that of its main trading partners and the EU average. Figure 5.4 takes data from that site to compare the business cycle in four European states: the Netherlands, France, Slovakia and Greece over the past 15 years. As the Eurostat Business Cycle Clock does not include data from all member states, I have chosen these states to represent the four different economies noted previously: financial Europe; administrative Europe; industrial Europe and rural Europe, respectively.

As we now know that Europe's economy is divided into concentrated economic clusters, which vary across countries, we should expect business cycles to vary across regions and states. Indeed, in Figure 5.4 we can clearly see how the amplitude and recovery paths vary significantly across the cases, and the Greek business cycle is behaving very differently than the others.

Over the years, there have been numerous studies of business cycles and their harmonization across eurozone member states, and the exposure of eurozone economies to a variety of asymmetric shocks. The motivation for many of these studies can be found in Chapter 3, as analysts are looking to ascertain the degree to which Europe constitutes something like an optimum currency area.[2] For example, a 2013 IMF study on the promise of a common fiscal policy among eurozone states began with a telling figure of the scope of country-specific growth shocks in the eurozone (reproduced here as Figure 5.5). In a simple figure, we can clearly see the significant economic variation that continues to separate EU member states.

Most studies have focused on the synchronization of short-term fluctuations in economic activity, using relatively simple methodologies. One of the more sophisticated studies, both conceptually and methodologically, is Bandrés et al (2017), which conducts its research at both the national and regional levels. Bandrés et al (2017: 9) begin by examining the member state-level data and find evidence of a growing, single cluster: what appears to be a common European monetary cycle. When measured at the national level, then, there seems to be some evidence of business cycle convergence going on in Europe.

But when they employ regional-level data, Bandrés et al uncover a number of different business cycles in Europe, attributed to five different regions, of very different sizes:

Figure 5.5: Country-specific growth shocks in the eurozone, %

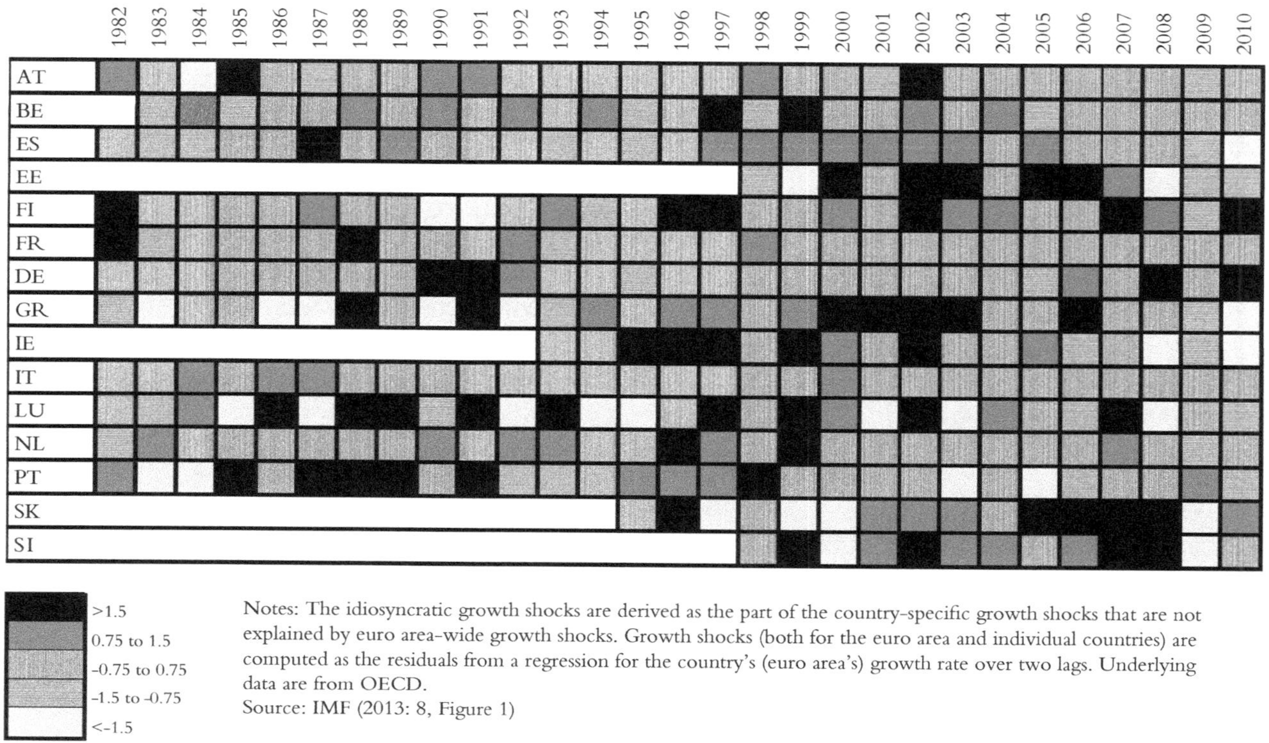

Notes: The idiosyncratic growth shocks are derived as the part of the country-specific growth shocks that are not explained by euro area-wide growth shocks. Growth shocks (both for the euro area and individual countries) are computed as the residuals from a regression for the country's (euro area's) growth rate over two lags. Underlying data are from OECD.

Source: IMF (2013: 8, Figure 1)

five different groups of European regions which share different business cycle characteristics. Group one contains most of the *Greek regions* (5.6% over the total number of regions). Groups two and three include, mainly, *German regions*, plus a couple of regions from southern European countries in group two (6.1% over total number of regions) and some regions of *the core countries* in group three (7% over the total number of regions). Group four is, mainly, composed of regions belonging to *northern European countries* (18.8% over the total number of regions). Finally, group five is the largest and is composed of *the other European regions* (62% over the total). (Bandrés et al, 2017: 9, emphasis added)

Although the Bandrés et al study doesn't look at the type of underlying economic activity that could be generating these different (regional) business cycles, the variation they reveal does not appear to be all that different from the patterns we saw in Figure 5.3, where four distinct economies were evident in Eurostat's employment share data. Once again, we find evidence of significant regional diversity in Europe's member state economies.

External sensitivities

To the extent that Europe's regional economies are characterized by specialized economic activities, it leaves them more exposed to any number of different types of shocks emanating from abroad, whether they are political, economic, social, viral, or whatever. One of the most prominent shocks in recent times is the dramatic rise of China as the world's manufacturer. After all, if you are working in a company that produces top-shelf widgets, and China begins to produce very similar widgets for the same global market, only at a much lower price, then your job, and the community in which it is located, is bound to be severely (and negatively) affected by the Chinese competition. This is the starting point of a fascinating new research agenda that looks at the impact of trade adjustment on local economic regions.

David Autor and his colleagues (2013a, 2013b, 2014, 2016) have been examining the effects on US local labour markets from Chinese imports. What makes their approach particularly interesting is that it recognizes that labour markets are, in practice, constrained to a 'commuting zone'; in other words, a cluster of neighbouring counties,

---

Box 5.1: Commuting zones

I am not aware of any 'commuting zone' tallies in the EU context, but we can get a hint of what they might look like by taking a closer look at the underlying Tolbert and Sizer (1996) study. Their study calculated that the US had 741 commuting zones in 1990, at a time when the US population was roughly 250 million. They then estimated that these 741 commuting zones could be further boiled down into 394 distinct labour markets. Briefly, their labour market was based on a commuting zone, but included an additional population criterion (over a certain population threshold). In 1990, the average population size of a US labour market was said to be 630,000 people, and the largest single labour market was in Southern California (Tolbert and Sizer, 1996: 18–19).

In the EU today, there are almost twice as many people (450 million) than in the US in 1990. If we assume that European labour markets should be roughly the same size as US labour markets in 1990 (in other words, 630,000 people on average), and we ignore cultural/language/national boundaries that still divide Europe, then we might expect to find around 700 unique labour markets in today's Europe. This number lies somewhere between the 283 NUTS2 regions (the level at which European policy tools are found) and the 1,345 regions that constitute NUTS3.

---

to which workers are able to commute in search of a new job (see, for example, Tolbert and Sizer, 1996). Box 5.1 provides a brief description. Autor et al examine whether commuting zones that compete with Chinese imports are being harder hit than other commuting zones in the US, or whether the effects of trade competition are more spread out across the country (as economists have traditionally held). Their reasoning is simple and can be illustrated with a straightforward thought experiment.

Imagine that Europe consists of just two types of economic activity: the production of olive oil and electric garage door openers. The global market for electric garage door openers can change rather quickly as new, more efficient producers enter the market (say, from China). Those job markets where electric garage door opener producers tend to concentrate will be strongly affected by the new competition, and local producers may go out of business – with rising unemployment in the local job market as a result. None of this competitive pressure affects the olive growing parts of Europe, except that consumers in these parts can now buy cheaper (imported) garage door openers. The market for olive oil, by contrast, is unlikely to be quickly undermined by a new competitor in the same way. However, the global supply of olives could be negatively affected by some strange new plant illness in California. Should this happen, European olive growers can expect record margins, affording strong local labour markets. This is good for those regions producing olive oil, but it will hurt the rest of the EU, which will end up having to pay more for its olive oil (due to the global fall in supply).

This is the logic behind Autor et al's studies. But, in contrast to much of the work done on European labour markets, they *do not* assume that electric garage door opener workers will pack up their vans and move to find work in Europe's olive groves. Autor and his colleagues are aware of the human limits to labour migration (beyond these commuter zones) as they document how adjustments in local labour markets are remarkably slow, with wages and labour force participation rates remaining depressed (and unemployment rates remaining high) for at least a full *decade* after the China trade shock hits. Not only that, but they find that affected commuter zones also experienced significant increases in transfer payments to the displaced workers, in the form of unemployment insurance, Trade Adjustment Assistance, means-tested entitlements, disability benefits and so on:

> Individuals who ... worked in manufacturing industries that experienced high subsequent import growth garner lower cumulative earnings, face elevated risk of obtaining public disability benefits, and spend less time working for their initial employers, less time in their initial two-digit manufacturing industries, and more time working elsewhere in manufacturing and outside of manufacturing. (Autor et al 2014: 1799; see also Autor et al, 2016: 230; and Autor and Duggan, 2003)

I am not aware of any comparable research being conducted at the EU level, but similar studies have been done in a handful of European states, showing significant wage declines in response to import competition in Norway (Balsvik et al, 2015) and Spain (Donoso et al, 2014), and an insignificant wage reduction in Germany (Dauth et al, 2014). Population responses (read migration) to local trade shocks are also limited in other countries. Analyses from Germany (Dauth et al, 2014) and Spain (Donoso et al, 2014) both find weak and statistically insignificant spatial mobility in local labour markets that are exposed to import competition from low-wage countries. In short, and as is evident in the US, there is every reason to expect that local labour markets in Europe are exposed to shocks whose affects will differ from other labour markets.

We can expect the same sort of variation to external shocks that are broader in nature, such as what we saw in response to the Great Recession. After all, member states' exposure to foreign markets (for both goods and capital) varies significantly. Thus, when the next global financial crisis hits, it is going to affect Europe's debtor countries much differently than its creditor countries. Similarly, when a global olive tree fungus or leaf spot disease hits California, it will affect Greece differently than Finland, as Finland doesn't grow any olives. A similar shock can be delivered by the next renegade US president who decides, Trump-like, to slap a tariff on European automakers with a midnight Tweet: this action will affect auto-producing regions differently than other regions.

One simple way to anticipate these varied effects of global shocks is to consider the exposure of each member state to trade and capital flows from beyond Europe. Figure 5.6 shows the export exposure of member states, measured as the percentage of total exports going to non-EU countries in 2018. To simplify the presentation, the countries in this figure have been clustered into four different groups. The darkest group captures a small group of countries, in which more than 50% of their 2018 exports went abroad (UK, Ireland, Malta and Cyprus). The lightest shaded group includes countries where less than 25% of their total exports went to markets beyond the EU (Estonia, Austria, Luxembourg, Romania, Slovenia, Poland, Hungary, Czechia and Slovakia). The remainder of the countries lie somewhere in between these two groups (in terms of both shading and trade exposure), while the Spanish case lacks data.

Figure 5.7 does the same thing, but looks at the share of a country's imports in 2018 that come from non-EU countries. Here, too, the countries can be clustered into four groups, not terribly different from the four clusters we found in Figure 5.6. The darkest group in Figure 5.7 represent countries in which more than 50% of their imports came from outside the EU (Ireland and Malta). The lightest shaded countries are those in which less than 25% of their total imports come from beyond the EU (Latvia, Austria, Portugal, Hungary, Romania, Slovenia and Estonia); and the remaining countries are in between these two groups (in both shading and trade exposure). Once again, Eurostat provides no comparable data for Spain.

Because of differences in the composition of their GDP and differences in their natural trading partners, we can be certain that any

Figure 5.6: Share of total exports to non-EU markets, 2018

Notes: Darker shades convey greater export dependence. Data from Spain are lacking. See text for further clarification.

Source: Adapted from Eurostat (nama_10_exi)

number and kind of different exogenous shocks will impact member states and regions in different ways. These types of differential impacts may be even stronger and more debilitating when we consider the variation in member state relationships to international financial markets. Given the proven volatility of financial markets, member state exposure to them should be an especially tender subject.

I have chosen two different measures to reveal the extent of member state exposure to international financial markets: a country's net international investment position (IIP) and its level of net external debt. A country's net IIP captures the net value of its external assets and liabilities with the rest of the world. These assets (liabilities) are simply the total value of funds that a country's residents lends to (borrows from) non–residents. When a country's external assets are greater than its liabilities, then its net IIP is positive. It is probably not

Figure 5.7: Share of total imports from non-EU countries, 2018

Notes: Darker shades convey greater import dependence. Data from Spain are lacking. See text for further clarification.

Source: Adapted from Eurostat (nama_10_exi)

surprising that Germany is by far the largest net lender in the EU, with a surplus IIP of €2,073.4 billion! The difference separating the size of this surplus, when compared to the most indebted countries in Europe – Spain (€–.966 billion), Ireland (€–.535 billion) and France (€–.385 billion) – is very evident in Figure 5.8.

If we begin with the IIP figures and then take out the equity and investment share components, as well as any financial derivatives and gold bullion (not to mention the sign convention), we are left with a country's net external debt (IMF, 2014: §7.51). The net external debt level provides us with a fair indicator of how exposed a state is to international capital markets, and the figure can be made comparable by converting it to a share of GDP, as is done in the top panel of Figure 5.9. (I have also inverted the debt figures to make more intuitive sense.) Here, we can clearly see that three EU countries are in the business

Figure 5.8: Total net IIP with rest of the world, member states, 2018

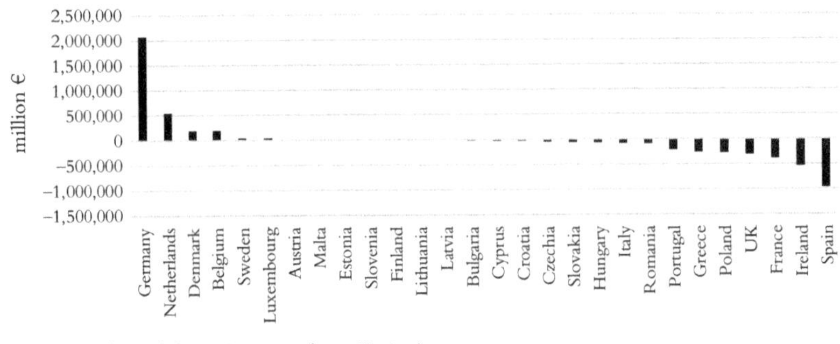

Source: Adapted from Eurostat (bop_iip6_q)

of attracting foreign capital and have accumulated remarkably large surpluses (negative debt): Luxembourg (1,941.4% of GDP!), Ireland (398.9% of GDP) and Malta (205.3% of GDP). Consider how different Ireland now looks, when we compare its standings in the net external debt category (second biggest surplus), relative to its IIP standing (the second most indebted).

I have excluded these three surplus countries from the bottom panel in Figure 5.9, so as to better see the scale of the debt being held by European states. Cyprus is the most indebted country in the EU28, with a net borrowing position that assumed 144.3% of its GDP. When the next financial crisis hits Europe, the needs of Germany, Luxembourg and the Netherlands will vary significantly from the needs of Cyprus, Spain and Ireland. These differences have been, and remain, substantial.

From this section we see how different member states are exposed to foreign trade and financial markets. Any number of shocks will hit these markets in the future and they will affect these local labour markets in very different ways. These effects might be positive or negative, but they will not be similarly distributed across the multitude of labour markets in Europe.

Social models

From the perspective of workers, surveying these different markets in Europe, there is at least one other type of relevant cross-national variation: the way nations structure their industrial relations and provide social protection (social security, public expenditures, wage supports and so on) when market conditions turn sour. After all, an ironworker

Figure 5.9: Net external debt, member states, 2017

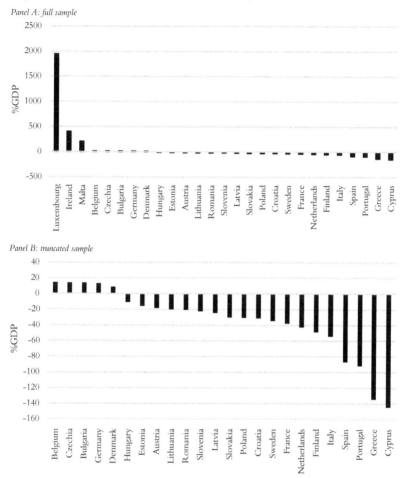

Notes: Truncated sample excludes Luxembourg, Ireland and Malta. I have inverted the debt figures so as to make more intuitive sense. Hence, Cyprus is the most indebted country in the EU28, with a net borrowing position that assumed 144.3% of its GDP.

Source: Adapted from Eurostat (bop_iip6_q)

in Sweden surely experiences the European labour market to be very different than their Latvian counterpart. Even one of Europe's headline measures, the use of works councils, varies significantly across the EU, with 19 of the EU27 employing some form of 'co-determination', but with radically varying content (*The Economist*, 2020a). (We return to this subject in Chapter 9.)

For lack of a better term, I have been referring to these differences in terms of social models, and member states continue to maintain their national, path-dependent, social models. This variation continues to exist, despite decades of effort to try and streamline member state policies/regulations. For example, some European labour markets are embedded in social models that rely on corporatist channels of influence to secure non-statutory – but still binding – agreements on central areas of common concern (for example local wages and the ground rules for acceptable action/conflict). In other states, where industrial relations are less hierarchal and organized, these conditions may be set by laws (such as a minimum wage law), and their social models are less inclusive. André Sapir (2006: 370) makes this point quite compellingly: 'the notion of the "European social model" is misleading. There are in reality different European social models, with different features and different performance in terms of efficiency and equity.'

There are a number of ways that we might map these different social models. The most famous of these look to variations in welfare state provisions and/or the broader structure of industrial relations. It is no secret that European states embrace different approaches to the role of the market and the private sector in providing welfare and distributing wealth for workers and citizens. For example, Europe includes prominent examples of all three types of Gösta Esping-Andersen's (1990) *Three Worlds of Welfare Capitalism*: liberal, conservative and social democratic. Subsequently, it has become standard practice to include a fourth, distinctly Southern European social model, as well (see, among others, Leibfried, 2002; Ferrera, 1996; Aiginger and Leoni, 2009).

The EU also includes both *Varieties of Capitalism* (Hall and Soskice, 2001): Ireland is a prime example of a liberal market economy, whereas Germany, Sweden and Austria are typical of coordinated market economies. As with the different types of welfare states in Europe, systems of corporate governance, industrial relations, access to finance, interfirm relations and patterns and modes of state intervention differ significantly across member states of the EU (Hall and Soskice, 2001; Iversen and Soskice, 2013). For example, Bob Hancké (2013) lays out the variety of social pacts (p 27) and wage-setting systems (p 34) distributed across the older EU member states.

As a means of summarizing these differences, Sapir (2006: 375–6) draws on Esping-Andersen's work to distinguish between four European social models, which overlap substantially with the four worlds of welfare capitalism described previously:

• The *Nordic model* is found in Denmark, Finland, Sweden and the Netherlands and builds on strong labour unions and highly compressed wage structures. It provides the highest levels of social protection expenditures and universal welfare provision, with extensive fiscal intervention in labour markets based on a variety of 'active' policy instruments.

- Ireland represents the *Anglo-Saxon model*, which is characterized by a mixture of weak unions, relatively wide and increasing wage dispersion and a comparatively high incidence of low-pay employment. Countries with this model feature relatively large social assistance programmes (as a last resort), but cash transfers are primarily oriented towards the working-age population.
- In the *Continental model*, unions remain strong, although their membership is on the decline, as regulations stretch coverage of collective bargaining to non-union contexts. This model is found in Austria, Belgium, France, Germany and Luxembourg, countries that rely extensively on insurance-based, non-employment benefits and old-age pensions.
- In the *Mediterranean model*, the wage structure is covered by collective bargaining and is strongly compressed, at least in the formal sector. These countries (Greece, Italy, Portugal and Spain) focus their social spending on old-age pensions and provide for a high segmentation of entitlements and status. Their social welfare systems tend to draw on employment protections and early retirement provisions, and these are used to keep certain segments of the working-age population from participating in the labour market.

These four models are in no way monolithic, and Sapir (2006: 376) recognizes that there 'are not only wide differences between these four models but also within each of them'. Like the variances we saw in local economic structures, this variance in social models means that very different regions and states in Europe will respond very differently in the face of even similar economic events/shocks or cycles. We saw this clearly in the varied responses to the most recent financial crisis:[3]

> High and unevenly distributed unemployment in Europe is not only the consequence of asymmetric shocks. It is true that shocks were of varying intensity and nature across countries, but even after controlling for these differences, the labour market responses appear to have been different across countries. Some countries used the intensive margin of labour market adjustment more, while others concentrated their response on the extensive margin. Some countries had bargaining structures that allowed for nominal wage cuts preventing mass lay-offs, while others could not

use wage reductions as an alternative to dismissals. These institutional differences, in a context where the inactivity margin was not used – the labour supply of older workers was increasing, unlike in previous recessions – turned out to be very important in the differential rise in unemployment. Another important factor was labour market segmentation between temporary and permanent contracts, allowing wage increases to coexist with large employment losses, even within the same sector. (Boeri and Jimeno, 2015: 22)

Just as importantly, these differences in social models will be influenced, changed, even undermined by the common policies and laws emanating from the EU, leaving the different social models 'asymmetrically exposed to the encroachment of EU law as it may catch institutions in one state doing a parallel task to those not caught by it in another' (Chalmers et al, 2016: 12).

One way to think about this 'asymmetric exposure' is to consider how these unique and complex institutional arrangements are part of development strategies that were (themselves) intricately linked to national monetary systems. In the past, Southern Europe employed economic development strategies that relied on strong domestic demand, fuelled by inflation, a large public sector and widespread job security. These countries pursued a weak currency policy, they were less concerned about export competitiveness, and they were willing (and able) to accept higher levels of inflation, government debt and currency devaluations. In Northern Europe, by contrast, the economic development strategy was export-driven, requiring a tighter lid on inflation and the development of national institutional arrangements (such as negotiated incomes policies) that could limit inflation and wage growth in the exposed sector. In this strategy, inflation, debt and devaluation needed to be shunned (see, for example, Streeck, 2015: 13–14; Hancké, 2013). My point is that these unique national systems developed over time and are intricately linked to different types of monetary policy. When these unique institutional arrangements are forced to adopt a common monetary policy, the supporting institutions will not, and cannot, play the same role as before.

Conclusion

Despite the hopes, ambitions and efforts of European policymakers, Europe remains a continent characterized by many, very different, local labour markets. Rather than try to erase these differences as hindrances to a more efficient market, we should protect and celebrate these unique characteristics as artefacts of European history, culture, tradition and political self-determination.

This chapter documents the degree to which national and regional variations continue to exist in Europe. As long as these differences continue to exist, we need to provide policymakers with the tools they need to respond in ways that can stabilize and grow their local economies. A single monetary policy, or a standardized (one-size-fits-all) approach to fiscal, regulatory and procurement policies cannot possibly address the uniqueness of these very different economic regions. Instead, EU member states require a more substantial toolbox, filled with a number of different tools.

The chapters that follow show how Europe does not have the tools it needs to address this variation. In the same way that a single fire hose, even a large one, cannot extinguish a myriad of local and widely dispersed fires, a shared policy regime (such as a common monetary policy and the constraints it imposes on other policy instruments) cannot possibly address the local and variable economic needs of member states. This lack of policy autonomy at the member state level – their access to a nearby fire hose – is the subject of Chapter 6. In the absence of these important tools for stabilizing their local labour markets, the burden of economic adjustment will need to shift upwards (to the EU level – see Chapter 7), or downwards (on market participants – see Chapter 8).

PART III

Adjustment Mechanisms

6

The Demise of Member State Policy Autonomy

In Chapter 5 we saw how Europe's labour markets remain remarkably segmented: they continue to reflect unique national and regional characteristics, despite a concerted political effort – stretching over decades – to reduce barriers to mobility. We have one common market, but a plethora of local labour markets, each reacting differently to external stimuli. Unfortunately, Europe's approach to market integration has made it more difficult to address these local needs. It is now the market, more than political authority, which must respond to the needs of regional economic adjustment. In clearing a level playing field for that market, Europe has undermined the economic resilience of its member states. Consequently, local labour markets are increasingly unable to withstand, recover from, and/or reorganize in the face of market, competitive and environmental shocks. The evidence of this incapacity lies in Europe's frightfully high unemployment figures, as presented in Chapter 1.

Chapter 5 endeavoured to show that local labour market variance can be the result of several different factors. Some regions may be overly dependent upon a particular employer, industry or sector, as we saw in the case of Washington State and Boeing (in Chapter 3). Other regions will have local markets that are precariously exposed to pressure from third-country competitors, such as China. Still others may be more or less susceptible to broader external shocks, as was evident in the varied responses to the 2008 financial crisis and the COVID-19 outbreak. Local differences of these sort require localized policy responses in the face of changing conditions.

One of the most significant differences separating markets is their level of economic wealth and development. Minimizing these differences has long been the aim of European policymakers, and has become a staple argument for increasing the fiscal power of the EU. We will examine some of these European-wide efforts in Chapter 7. Claus Offe, for example, discusses the promise for European-wide institutions as 'the only adequate scope of managing European-wide problems':

> A metaphor is that if you need to fight a fire on the upper floors of a high-rise building, you need a *long* ladder. 'National' means of intervention are simply far too 'short'.
> (Offe, 2016: 65)

Offe's metaphor reveals more than he seems to realize. The problem with fires, like economic conditions, is that they often vary in type. Some fires can be doused with water, others require fire-retardant chemicals. It matters little if firefighters have access to a long enough ladder, if they use it to bring water to a greasy kitchen fire. In matters of economic policy, one size doesn't fit all, and a single fire hose or ladder (even a long one) will not suffice to douse local economic hotspots.

Europe's many and varied labour markets resemble such hotspots, each of which can be fuelled by a different source; for example business cycle downturns, global supply challenges, financial crises. To address these local and unique demands, elected officials need access to local and unique policy tools. In the past, the policymaker's toolbox has included (among other things) autonomy in monetary, fiscal, regulatory and procurement policies. Europe's current dilemma lies in the fact that its member state policymakers no longer have access to these tools – at least not to the extent required. In pursuing its current path to market integration – one that prioritizes the lowering of barriers, level playing fields and standardized (common) policies – the EU has left national policymakers with remarkably little capacity to manage their home labour markets.

Before documenting this slow erosion of member state policy autonomy, I hasten to note three important caveats. First, the push towards harmonization was originally driven by good intentions, but it has been pursued in excess and with insufficient critical reflection. After all, *some* harmonization/levelling is necessary to facilitate interstate exchange. In these cases, the efficiency gains from greater integration might suffice to pay for the reduced policy autonomy that it produces.[1] The trick is for policymakers to balance the political and moral costs of these decisions against the promised economic reward (Moses, 2021).

Second, in describing the atrophy of member state capacity, I do not mean to suggest that all, or even most, of the policies I discuss need (or should) be restored to member states. My intent is to describe the loss of this policy autonomy and to remind readers of its continued utility. In so doing, I do no mean to suggest that any or all of these tools should be returned to democratically accountable officials, or that some of these tools do not suffer from significant downsides.

Finally, it is important to point out that there is more flexibility in the system than most member states have been willing to recognize (or leverage). This flexibility lies in the incredible complexity of Europe's regulatory patchwork (as we shall see). Member state governments continue to maintain some scope for effective policy choice at the national level. My point is to show how this scope has diminished, not that it has disappeared entirely. I am hoping that a discussion about the need for flexibility will draw some attention to this simple fact. The forced response to COVID-19 – where some of Europe's binding fiscal rules were abandoned (European Commission, 2020b), its rules about state aid to local businesses were loosened (European Commission, 2020a), and the European Commission (2020g) proposed a significant economic recovery plan – demonstrates what is possible in Europe, given sufficient political will. I return to the COVID-19 response in Chapter 7.

The remainder of this chapter is structured to address the two most important economic needs separating EU member states, as described in Chapter 5: the need for autonomous development policies and the need for autonomous stabilization policies. Beneath each of these rubrics, we can see how the push for a single market in Europe has sidelined or eviscerated most of the specific policy instruments that member states once used to manage their local labour markets.

Development

As we saw in Figure 5.1, the EU includes a variety of member state economies that stretch across the wealth–poverty continuum. Some states, such as Germany, have a proven capacity to compete on the international stage and have spent generations building up a highly skilled workforce, with access to very deep investment pools and sophisticated production technologies. As a result, the German economy is one of the most productive and competitive in the world.

It was, of course, not always this way. Germany, like most of Europe's developed economies, climbed up the economic ladder by eschewing free-market policies. These countries grew their economies behind the protection and support provided by high tariff barriers, sectoral industrial policies, infant industry protections, state-sponsored industrial projects, politically responsive central banks, autonomous monetary and fiscal policies, supportive procurement and regulatory policies and repurposed industrial technologies.[2]

When the European Community was a small group of relatively homogeneous and similarly developed economies, there was little need to consider the role of different development strategies. At its first juncture, as is evident in the Spaak Report (*Political and Economic Planning*, 1957: 225–6), Europe's nascent economic community had to choose between creating a free trade area or a customs union. A free trade area would have allowed individual states to maintain their own tariff policies vis-à-vis the outside world, and hence could have allowed for a higher degree of industrial protection in each member state. But officials decided on a customs union, even if meant greater constraints on member state policy autonomy. The reason for this choice seems to be a recognition of the difficulty and complexity of trying to align the foreign tariff policies of six signatory states.

More to the point, in the early stages of European market integration, significant scope for national policy autonomy remained with member states, and each member recognized the need to maintain that autonomy (as seen in Chapter 4). Over time, however, the EU has expanded to include a number of new member states with remarkably varying levels of economic development, while limiting the policy options that these states need to address their specific and unique economic and political needs.

Today, member states are expected to develop their economies by embracing free-market policies that look good on paper but are far less impressive in practice. It is hypocritical to suggest that Europe's least developed economies should embrace policies that were *un*acceptable to Germany and the others (during their economic ascendency). As Friedrich List verily noted when considering which path was appropriate for Germany:

> It is a very common clever device that when anyone has attained the summit of greatness, he kicks away the ladder by which he has climbed up, in order to deprive the others of the means of climbing up after him. In this lies the secret of the cosmopolitan doctrines of Adam Smith ... and all of his successors in the British government. (List, 1916 [1841]: 295)

The list of policy tools that Europe's less developed member states might use to 'catch up' to the more wealthy member states is a long one, but

I will draw attention to the demise of member state policies in three areas that are particularly relevant for developing economies: infant industry protection; procurement policy; and regulatory policy.

Infant industry protections

In his book *Bad Samaritans*, Ha-Joon Chang (2010) argues that it is both immoral and imprudent to force his six-year-old son into a job market that would require him to compete directly with adults. Chang reasons that it is better for his boy to attend school and develop his skills while shielded from the labour market, before forcing him to compete with adults who have spent years developing their skills. The same sort of logic can and has been employed to protect infant industries from free trade. If a country hopes to develop a new industry that can compete in international markets, it must first protect and nurture domestic producers (for a limited time) before exposing them to competition with more mature and established producers.

Less developed economies suffer from a great many shortcomings, relative to more developed economies, and these shortcomings undermine any promise for fair competition. Among other things, developing countries struggle with poor infrastructure, insufficient private capacities and underdeveloped markets (that are easily manipulated). Because of these shortcomings, the production costs for newly established industries within a country will be higher (initially) than for well-established, more efficient foreign producers of the same product, who benefit from greater experience, more knowledge and higher skill levels. To level the playing field, states have embraced a number of temporary measures, including trade protection, producer subsidies and reduced competition, for example through allowing mergers and/or state ownership. But these are exactly the sorts of policies that are curtailed by the complex networks of rules and laws that constitute European competition policy, as described in Box 6.1.

In short, member states are forbidden from using import-restricting policies to help develop their domestic industries. This is a clear and obvious cost of joining a customs union, and new member states should be aware of it. But the EU also restricts the use of a number of other tools that could be used to protect infant industries, including non-tariff barriers, financing instruments, public supports in market access, and indirect instruments that can strengthen export activities, such as research and development and training supports, export processing zones and so on. These tools have been sidelined along Europe's level playing field – even when it is clear that this field benefits mature

Box 6.1: The complexity of EU competition policy

EU competition policy is a dense bramble of laws, regulations and treaty obligations. In this legal bramble, the market's invisible hand becomes very visible (and heavy). To get an idea of the complexity, we can turn to the European Commission's (2012b) summary of EU competition law, which is divided into four subgroups, each of which is linked to a substantial supportive literature:

1. anticompetitive agreements (including cartels) and abuses by companies of dominant market positions;
2. mergers and acquisitions;
3. government support; and
4. international cooperation in the field of competition.

When we dive deeper into the third category 'government support' (European Commission, 2014a), we learn that this category can be further divided into ten different types of rules securing a level playing field in the realm of government support:

1. treaty provisions on state aid;
2. general procedural rules;
3. enabling regulation and general block exemption regulation;
4. temporary rules established in response to the economic and financial crisis;
5. horizontal rules;
6. sector-specific rules;
7. specific aid instruments;
8. reference/discount rates and recovery interest rates;
9. transparency of financial relations between member states and public undertakings; and
10. services of general economic interest.

To overcome the complexity of this regulatory maze, the European Commission (2014b) has created a single document containing all the EU 'state aid' rules currently in force, as they apply to the manufacturing industry and services. I hasten to note that this description is quite limited, in that it does *not* extend to the specific rules applicable to agriculture, fisheries, transport and coal. Still, this document, *Rules Applicable to State Aid*, totals 1,002 pages! And this is just one of the four main areas of the EU's competition policy noted before.

over infant producers. The EU also favours international investments and capital flows, enhanced private intellectual property rights, and has reduced many forms of national regulation and labour protections (see Chapters 7 and 9, but also Landesmann, 2015). While exceptions are sometimes allowed, Europe's institutional and policy guidelines are explicitly aimed at levelling opportunities that allow officials to prioritize local producers.

Procurement policy

Another way in which sovereign states have traditionally protected and nurtured local competences is by way of their procurement policies. After all, the state is a major purchaser of goods and services, and it can use its buying power to support local labour markets and industries. As with broader infant industry protections, this avenue of state influence has been closed to EU member states, starting in the mid-1980s, when public purchasing was first identified as a barrier to the completion of the Single European Market (see Martin et al, 1997). Believing that increased competition in procurement markets would bring substantial savings, the Commission pushed to prohibit public preferential purchasing and introduced a series of EU procurement directives.

These directives stand in support of several articles in the EU's consolidated version of the Treaty on the Functioning of the European Union (TFEU, 2012), which explicitly prohibit member states from discriminating on the basis of nationality (TFEU, 2012: Art. 18); require that member states grant the freedom of establishment (TFEU, 2012: Art. 49); establishes the freedom to provide services (TFEU, 2012: Art. 56); and prohibits state aid in most forms (TFEU, 2012: Art. 107). The relevant texts from these four articles are listed in Table 6.1.

Subsequent EU directives have been aimed at establishing a non-discriminatory procurement process, where 'contracting entities shall treat economic operators equally and non-discriminatorily and shall act in a transparent way'.[3] These include:

- The *Concession Directives* (1994, 2014). These directives disallow preferential treatment to domestic suppliers. The 1994 directive was subsequently renewed and sharpened by Directive 2014/23/EU on the award of concession contracts. Directive 2014/23/EU was seen as necessary, as public contracts were regulated by Directives 2004/17/EC and 2004/18/EC, and public works concessions were partially covered by Directive 2004/18/EC, but

Table 6.1: Sample of treaty obligations restricting autonomy

Article 18 TFEU (ex Article 12 TEC) on *Non-Discrimination*

'Within the scope of application of the Treaties, and without prejudice to any special provisions contained therein, any discrimination on grounds of nationality shall be prohibited.'

Article 49 TFEU (ex Article 43 TEC) on the *Right of Establishment*

'Within the framework of the provisions set out below, restrictions on the freedom of establishment of nationals of a Member State in the territory of another Member State shall be prohibited. Such prohibition shall also apply to restrictions on the setting-up of agencies, branches or subsidiaries by nationals of any Member State established in the territory of any Member State.'

Article 56 TFEU (ex Article 49 TEC) on *Services*

'Within the framework of the provisions set out below, restrictions on freedom to provide services within the Union shall be prohibited in respect of nationals of Member States who are established in a Member State other than that of the person for whom the services are intended.'

Article 107 TFEU (ex Article 87 TEC) on *State Aid*

'Save as otherwise provided in this Treaty, any aid granted by a Member State or through State resources in any form whatsoever which distorts or threatens to distort competition by favouring certain undertakings or the production of certain goods shall, insofar as it affects trade between Member States, be incompatible with the common market.'

Source: TFEU (2012)

the award of service concessions had remained within the realm of sovereign authority.

- The *Utilities Procurement Directive*. Directive 2004/17/EC coordinates the procurement procedures of entities operating in the water, energy, transport and postal services sector (OJ L134, 30.4.2004).
- The *Procurement Directive*. Directive 2004/18/EC coordinates procedures for the awards of public works contracts, public supply contracts and public service contracts (OJ L134, 30.4.2004).

As is the case with infant industry protections, the design of Europe's single market prohibits the use of state procurement policies as instruments of local economic development. Local officials and policymakers are required to award procurement contracts on the basis of transparency and 'best value for money'. In short, governments cannot prioritize local employers, but must choose on the basis of price/value. In this legal context, it does not matter that the successful bidder may be a multinational enterprise, largely indifferent to local providers, and planning to abscond with the resulting profits (rather than reinvest them in the local economy).

Regulatory policy

Finally, I would be remiss if I didn't mention the way that the EU, and especially the European Court of Justice (ECJ), has worked diligently to ensure that the national regulation of labour markets does not interfere with the right to free establishment. A series of high-profile ECJ decisions, as listed in Table 6.2, have prioritized these sorts of vague economic freedoms (such as 'the right of establishment') over fundamental workers' rights, secured over centuries of national struggle.

As with treaty obligations that limit a state's capacity to protect infant industries, and procurement directives that limit the state's ability to promote local content, these court cases have clearly restricted the scope of actions available to member state governments, national trade unions and employers' organizations.[4] The Viking and Laval decisions imposed restrictions on the strike activity of trade unions (when they get in the way of a free market), even when they were protected by collective labour law at the national level. The Rüffert decision concerned the use of collective agreement clauses in (national) public procurement laws, and the Luxembourg decision was about interpreting the national scope of implementing legislation on the Posted Workers Directive. Each example of national regulatory autonomy was judged to be illegal from the perspective of community law.

As a result of these controversial decisions, it was increasingly clear that governments and trade unions had been severely limited as to what kind of rules they can use to protect workers and/or to regulate labour market relations – if these rules were seen to interfere with fundamental market liberties, such as 'the right of establishment' or 'the freedom to provide services'. This ominous constraint was implicitly recognized in a 2018 revision (Directive 2018/957) of Directive 96/71/EC on posting of workers, which sought to ensure that posted workers were held to terms and conditions of employment that were as close as possible to those offered to host-state employees. Although this directive was immediately challenged by the Polish and Hungarian governments, their challenge was dismissed by the European Court of Justice on 8 December 2020 (ECJ 2020). This provides some grounds for hope.

Nevertheless, EU membership entails a significant constraint on member state sovereignty and the capacity of these states to develop their local economies. While we have witnessed growing interest in,

Table 6.2: Sample of ECJ decisions restricting autonomy

Case	Description
Viking	*International Transport Workers Federation* v. *Viking Line ABP* (2007) The Viking line operated ships that sailed between Estonia and Finland. These ships sailed under a Finnish flag with Finnish workers, organized under the International Transport Workers Federation (ITWF). Viking wanted to reflag, from a Finnish to an Estonian flag, in order to pay (lower) Estonian wages. The Finnish workers struck and got the ITWF to ask non-Finnish members to boycott Viking. In response, Viking sought an injunction in the English courts, claiming the union's action infringed on its right to freedom of establishment (TFEU, 2012: Art. 49). The (English) High Court of Justice granted the injunction, but it was overturned so it could be heard before the ECJ. Although the ECJ thought it was for the national court to ultimately resolve the issue, it decided that the ITWF's activities were incompatible with EU law. In effect, the ECJ acknowledged (for the first time) the right to take collection action and the right to strike as fundamental rights, but gave priority to the fundamental (economic) freedom of business owners over those fundamental workers' rights. ECJ, Case C-438/05 Viking (2007), ECR I-10779–10840
Laval	*Laval un Partneri Ltd* v. *Svenska Byggnadsarbetareförbundet* (2007) Laval was a Latvian construction company that had contracted to renovate a school in Vaxholm, Sweden. In Sweden, labour market partners negotiate collective agreements on wages and other working conditions on a case-by-case basis. Byggnads, the Swedish construction workers union, tried to get Laval to sign its collective agreement, but the company refused and signed a collective agreement with a Latvian trade union (at much lower wages) instead. Byggnads responded with a blockade, and received support in solidarity from the Swedish electricians trade union. While the Swedish Labour Court recognized the action to be legal, the case was referred to the ECJ, which decided that the collective action violated the freedom of services articulated in Article 56 of the TFEU. In short, the ECJ recognized the Swedish workers had a positive right to strike, but it also ruled that the right to strike must be exercised proportionately and was subject to justification in cases where it might infringe upon the freedom to provide services. ECJ, Case C-341/05 Laval (2007), ECR I-11767–118904

Table 6.2: Sample of ECJ decisions restricting autonomy (continued)

Case	Description
Rüffert	*Dirk Rüffert v. Land Niedersachsen* (2008) This case considers a procurement law from the German state of Lower Saxony (Land Niedersachsen) on the award of a public contract. This law limited the granting of public contracts to firms that are prepared to pay the wages that are specified in the relevant sectoral collective agreement. This requirement covered both contractors and subcontractors and allowed violators to be penalized accordingly. Lower Saxony granted a contract to a company to build a local prison, and this company subcontracted the work to a Polish firm that was not paying the appropriate (agreed upon) wage. The contract was terminated, and a penalty was issued. The main contractor had gone bankrupt, so Dirk Rüffert, the liquidator of its assets, took the case to court, even though the German Federal Constitutional Court had, in 2006, already considered the practice in accordance with the German Constitution. The ECJ decided that the ability to offer lower wages was an important part of a member state's ability to compete in the European internal market. Hence, by requiring foreign firms to pay locally determined wages, they were undermining another state's competitive advantage. ECJ, Case C-346/06 Rüffert (2008), ECR I-1989
Luxembourg	*Commission v. Luxembourg* (2008) The European Commission took Luxembourg to court because it didn't think that Luxembourg's labour legislation was consistent with the directive on posting of workers. Luxembourg had included all of its existing collective agreements under the rubric 'public policy provisions', as allowed by Directive 96/71, Art. 3.1.1. As a result of this, foreign service providers were expected to respect all of Luxembourg's labour law regulations, including all relevant collective agreements. (Two issues, in particular, drew the most attention: automatic pay adjustments in line with the cost of living, and the inclusion of all collective agreements.) The Commission argued this was too broad an interpretation of 'public policy provisions', and that doing so would prove an obstacle to the fundamental principle of freedom to provide services. As a result, Luxembourg was forced to change its labour law. ECJ, Case C-319/06, NZA 2008: 865

and need for, securing greater policy autonomy in recent years (see, for example, the COVID-19 response described in Chapter 7), member states are still required to abandon a series of tools, including barriers to trade, public procurement and other national regulations, that were developed to protect workers in their local labour markets.

Stabilization

While national regulatory, procurement and protection legislation could be used to help stabilize member state economies during a short-term macroeconomic retraction, the main policy tools governments have used to stabilize the macroeconomy are national monetary and fiscal policies. Here, too, we have seen a substantial reduction in the scope for autonomy.

Since at least the Second World War, democratic states have relied upon the use of both monetary and fiscal policies to steer the domestic economy in ways that are consistent with the needs and desires of its people, and so ensure that the structural power of market actors could not threaten that democratic will. The resulting welfare state depends critically on the state's ability to maintain full employment, secure significant revenues through national taxation regimes and money creation, allocate capital for social needs, provide public goods and services, and redistribute inequities. These are the sorts of things that autonomous monetary and fiscal policies can, and did, provide.

The clearest reduction in European policy autonomy is evident in the area of monetary policy. Here, many member states have been willing to liberate their central banks from political influence and have discarded their national currencies and monetary policies in order to tie themselves to the fate of a common currency. Much of the reasoning for doing this was described in Chapter 3. Of course, not all EU member states have joined the monetary union, and there is, as a consequence, some room for policy autonomy among a handful of states (see Moses, 2017a). The scope for autonomous fiscal policy has also been severely restricted – especially after the Great Recession – when the EU imposed greater surveillance and restrictions on member state fiscal policies.

In discussing how member states have sacrificed and curtailed these important policy tools, two caveats come immediately to mind. First, having the freedom to use a policy doesn't mean that it is costless. A little policy autonomy can be a dangerous thing, and there is great political responsibility tied to having control over policy. This is why we have democratic government in the first place: to ensure that policies are pursued in the interest of the people. After all, a poor policy can have enormous social and economic consequences, even those that are decided by technocrats or bound by fixed rules. I once interviewed a retired Norwegian minister of finance who told me that elected officials were scared to death of the potential downsides of monetary policy autonomy. By his account, elected officials would rather tie their hands, and leave the fate of the nation to a faceless market, than take responsibility for any gains/losses associated with political autonomy.[5] If this is true, it is cheap leadership. Democracy is about meeting the needs of the people, and elected representatives should be held accountable for the policies they administer.

The second caveat is that there are a number of constraints on autonomy that are independent of EU membership. Most developed states, EU members or not, have agreed to isolate their central banks from political influence (albeit not from the financial sector, to which they are highly receptive), because of an academic and political consensus in the 1970s that central bank independence delivered better macroeconomic results. There can be international agreements or some other public norms/trends that restrict what a country can do, or is willing to do, with regard to limiting its policy autonomy. My point is not to suggest that policy autonomy is costless, or that it is limited only by EU membership. Rather, the point is to spark a discussion about the consequences of limiting democratic authority, and pointing out who benefits/loses by jettisoning that authority. Simplistic (and often empty) threats about reduced efficiency should not suffice to scuttle a nation's policy autonomy and democratic institutions.

Monetary policy

When a country maintains its monetary policy autonomy, it wields a number of different instruments to affect the amount of money in circulation, and consequently its price.[6] For reasons of convenience, we can divide these instruments into those that deal with the external and internal value of a country's money. Some of these instruments are more effective at dealing with short-term and reoccurring events (such as the business cycle), while others are more useful to pursue long-term goals, or in response to unique shocks. Policymakers should be aware of these tools and the costs associated with losing them. None of these instruments are costless – there are risks and benefits associated with each of them. But they are instruments that can and should be used (under certain circumstances) to protect the local labour market. States that are willing to give them up, or pretend they will not be needed, must consider the real costs and alternatives (and who will pay for them)!

On the external front, policymakers can use *capital controls* to limit the amount of money flowing in and out of the country. As we shall see in Chapter 8, the unimpeded flows of capital across member states, both before and during the Great Recession, was one of the reasons that the Great Recession cut so deep in the so-called 'periphery economies/states'. Having access to capital controls is a very effective way to ensure that policymakers control the amount of money that is in circulation, and hence its price – both the internal price, the interest rate, and the external price, the exchange rate.

The second important tool is the choice of an *exchange rate regime*. In maintaining an independent currency, a state is able to adjust the value of that currency vis-à-vis other currencies in a way that can immediately affect its terms of trade. For example, Iceland devalued its currency on 8 October 2008 in response to the global financial crisis, and in one month the foreign price of Icelandic exports had dropped by something like 65%, relative to the previous year (IMF, 2008: 9). In so doing, Icelandic exports were immediately more (price) competitive on the international market, and Icelandic employment levels rebounded very quickly, despite the depths of that country's financial and debt crisis. It should be obvious, but countries that join in a common currency area lose this important instrument of policy.

Most attention to monetary policy is focused on the domestic front, where autonomous monetary authorities can determine the nature of their financial and banking regulations and the degree of independence for their central banks (not to mention, settings their steering objectives). In addition, monetary authorities can use capital controls to ensure they have full control over the amount of money in circulation and direct the money to meet specific *political* objectives. For example, during the Bretton Woods era, when capital controls were ubiquitous, states were able to allocate capital to popular political projects, ensuring cheaper loans for things that society wanted to encourage (such as education, home ownership, rural development and so on), while increasing the costs of loans on non-essentials (for example luxury purchases or second homes).

Most important of all, a country with its own currency can create its own money, and this provides significant opportunities – especially when facing severe economic crises. The revenues of a government that issues its own currency are not really constrained – governments can always print/create more money. This is not just the message of modern monetary theorists,[7] but it is explicitly recognized by central bankers around the world, including the Central Bank of England (McLeay et al, 2014), and even Alan Greenspan, former chair of the US Federal Reserve:

> Central banks can issue currency, a non-interest-bearing claim on the government, effectively without limit. They

can discount loans and other assets of banks or other private depository institutions, thereby converting potentially illiquid private assets into riskless claims on the government in the form of deposits at the central bank. That all of these claims on government are readily accepted reflects the fact that *a government cannot become insolvent with respect to obligations in its own currency. A fiat money system, like the ones we have today, can produce such claims without limit.* (Greenspan, 1997: 31, emphasis added)

From a democratic perspective, one of the most serious abdications of political responsibility must be the wilful loss of a national currency. For centuries, a national currency was seen to be an essential measure of sovereignty, and states used autonomous monetary policies as the main instrument for managing their national economies throughout the golden era of capitalism. In exchanging this autonomy for the promise of increased efficiency gains, states agreed to bind themselves to policy decisions made by some external, non-democratic body. In the EU, this body is the European Central Bank (ECB) and the euro is its shared instrument.

As Figure 6.1 shows, some EU member states have managed to keep their national currencies, as have a number of other European states, which are otherwise strongly linked to the EU common market. Every EU member state (except Denmark) is formally obligated to take up the euro, once they meet the criteria to do so, even if some states seem to be dragging their feet, for fear of the consequences.

Clearly, by adopting the euro and discarding their national currencies, policymakers have given up many of the advantages of sovereignty, including the ability to create money, limit capital flows, and devalue/depreciate their currencies. While there was some discussion about states being able to leave the eurozone at the height of the Great Recession (for example in Greece), the threat of potential consequences has freighted politicians from even considering the option. But two eurozone states, Cyprus and Greece, were able to secure *permission* to impose capital controls at the height of the crisis.[8] After all, the treaties do allow for restrictions on capital flows during exceptional circumstances.[9]

In both of these countries, massive capital flight threatened the stability of the domestic banking sector, and the governments received permission to introduce capital controls. Cyprus did so from March 2013 to April 2015, and Greece did so from June 2015 until August 2019. These two cases demonstrate the degree of flexibility that is

Figure 6.1: Three realms of European currencies

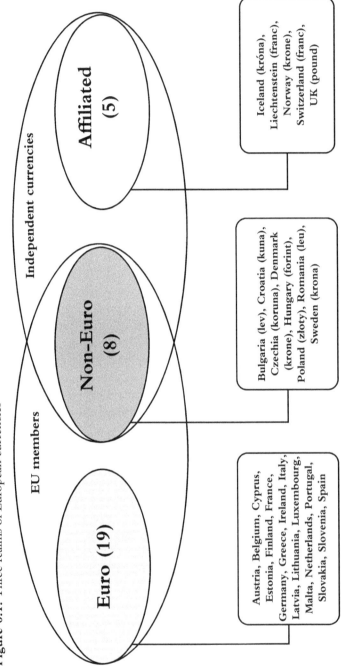

Independent currencies

EU members

Affiliated (5)

Iceland (króna), Liechtenstein (franc), Norway (krone), Switzerland (franc), UK (pound)

Non-Euro (8)

Bulgaria (lev), Croatia (kuna), Czechia (koruna), Denmark (krone), Hungary (forint), Poland (złoty), Romania (leu), Sweden (krona)

Euro (19)

Austria, Belgium, Cyprus, Estonia, Finland, France, Germany, Greece, Ireland, Italy, Latvia, Lithuania, Luxembourg, Malta, Netherlands, Portugal, Slovakia, Slovenia, Spain

Source: Author's own

possible within the EU, but it shows how much a country will be forced to suffer before it is allowed to access that flexibility. States that retained control over their monetary policy during the Great Recession, such as Iceland, were able to impose capital controls almost immediately in order to stave off massive, and potentially destructive, capital flight.

I recently wrote a book on the effective use of monetary policy in response to the Great Recession (Moses, 2017a). In that study, states that had kept their currencies, and stayed out of the euro area, were able to respond to the recession in a way that shortened the recession and lessened its impact, especially on workers. Those countries that remained committed to maintaining the eurozone paid for it with crippling international loans, extended unemployment and increased suffering and inequalities. Space precludes further discussion on the political costs of monetary union in Europe, but I hope that interested readers might turn to my 2017 book for more information.

In short, there are enormous political costs associated with ditching one's currency, and these costs have been accumulating across the EU. As we shall see in Chapter 7), there are things the EU can do to subsidize these costs, or to allocate them differently – but the costs remain and we need them to be counted.

Fiscal policy

Edmund Burke (1790) noted that 'The revenue of the state is the state.' In recognition of the incredible power of the purse, democratic constitutions around the world require legislative approval over government finances: the people's representatives are expected to have a say in how their governments' money should be raised and spent (Wehner, 2006: 767). Popular control over the budget is a fundamental component of modern representative democracy.

This principle is also (if implicitly) recognized in the TFEU, which limits the legislative authority of the EU to *coordinating* member state economic and fiscal policy (TFEU, 2012: Art. 2(3)). As we shall see, much of this coordination is secured by using a number of soft law and hybrid mechanisms – guidelines, targets, indicators, scorecards, benchmarks and so on. But the real constraint on member state fiscal policy does not come from the EU per se: as we shall see in Chapter 7, the size and scope of the EU budget is remarkably limited. Rather, the constraints on policy are more structural in form, in that a free market makes it difficult for more democratic (member state) legislatures to regulate, discipline or harness capital to meet the needs of the people.

In creating a common market for capital, the EU provides capital owners with an effective veto threat over undesirable policies (from the perspective of capital owners). By allowing free capital mobility, states are unable to pursue tax and regulatory policies that differ significantly from their main competitors.[10] The reason for this is clear: the threat of capital flight. Any country planning to fund a welfare state, absent a fiat currency, will find it difficult to tax income/wealth. Consequently, political authorities will need to transfer the tax burden over to other (less mobile) asset holders (land and labour). As we saw earlier, attempts to maintain more rigorous environmental, safety and/or labour regulations are easily 'voted' down by the threat of capital's exit (a so-called 'capital strike') or the treaty-based freedoms elaborated on in Table 6.1. In addition, those countries with highly organized income policies, for example corporatist income policies, find that the relative bargaining power of capital increases, relative to labour, as any negotiated outcome is susceptible to the threat of a capital strike (exit). On each of these fronts – money, fiscal, regulatory and incomes policies – increased capital mobility ties the hands of government.

This is clearly the case in the EU, where national tax systems have been exposed to decades of competitive pressure, resulting in member state tax systems that have been 'deeply and thoroughly Europeanised since the very moment the European Communities were established' (Menéndez, 2016: 79). This Europeanization is established as part and parcel of a legal regime, most clearly articulated in Article 119(3) of the TFEU, which requires all EU and national activities to comply with the 'guiding principles' of stable prices, sound public finances and monetary conditions, and a sustainable balance of payments. If this was not clear enough, Article 121 holds that 'Member States shall regard their economic policies as a *matter of common concern*' – aimed at the 'purposes set out in Article 3 TEU' (TFEU, 2012: Art. 119, emphasis added) – in particular, the establishment of an economic and monetary union.

In addition to the increased challenge of taxing mobile assets, the EU has placed a growing number of constraints on the fiscal powers of member states, in an effort to try and make up for the shortcomings of its suboptimum currency area. The result is a bewildering tangle of acronyms, jargon and euphemisms, as outlined in Table 6.3, with each step bringing the national budget further away from the people it is meant to serve. As Genschel and Jachtenfuchs (2016: 176) observe, in a somewhat understated manner: 'It is not easy to understand the complex system of standard EU legislation, intergovernmental Treaties,

Table 6.3: The slow erosion of fiscal sovereignty in Europe

Year	Instrument
1997	*Stability and Growth Pact* (SGP). Requires every country to maintain an annual budget balance, with a deficit not to exceed 3% of GDP and a national debt level lower than 60% of GDP. Includes both preventive and corrective elements. The Commission supervises these rules. If a country fails to meet them, the Commission can employ sanctions.
2010	*Europe 2020.* Proposed by the European Commission, this is a ten-year strategy, successor to the Lisbon Strategy (2000–10). Its aim is to further coordinate national and European policy by generating 'smart', 'sustainable' and 'inclusive' growth. Most significantly, it introduced the European Semester.
	European Semester. A six-month cycle of economic and fiscal policy coordination within the EU. During the European Semester, member states align their budgetary and economic policies with the objectives and rules agreed to at the EU level. In addition to coordinating fiscal policies, the European Semester is used to prevent excessive macroeconomic imbalances and secure structural reforms in member states.
2011	*Six Pack.* Contains five regulations and a directive (hence its name). The Six Pack is part of the European Semester and applies to all member states, and is designed to reinforce/strengthen the preventive and corrective arms of the SGP. In particular, it defines, quantitively, what constitutes a significant deviation from the medium-term budgetary objective or adjustment path, and provides a new way to operationalize debt. The Six Pack also introduced reverse qualified majority voting for most sanctions, in other words, sanctions become more likely.
	Euro Plus Pact (EPP). Initially called the 'Competitiveness Pact', the EPP is an intergovernmental agreement signed by 23 member states (all eurozone states plus Bulgaria, Denmark, Latvia, Lithuania, Poland and Romania). Hence, the EPP is voluntary and not directly integrated within the European Semester. The EPP defines a set of additional actions to foster wage cost competitiveness and employment growth, while preserving financial stability.
	Macroeconomic Imbalance Procedure (MIP). Introduced with the Six Pack, the MIP offers a surveillance mechanism designed to monitor and correct macroeconomic imbalances, such as high current account deficits, unsustainable external indebtedness and housing bubbles. The MIP includes a number of steps, such as the *Alert Mechanism Report* (prepared by the Commission), based on a *MIP Scoreboard* of indicators, to identify countries that require *in-depth reviews*. Based on these reviews, the Commission can act in a number of different ways, including triggering what is called the *excessive imbalance procedure*, leading to sanctions.

(continued)

Table 6.3: The slow erosion of fiscal sovereignty in Europe (continued)

Year	Instrument
2012	*Treaty on Stability, Coordination and Governance* (TSCG). This is an intergovernmental agreement, not written into EU law, which introduces a new stricter version of the SGP. Adopted by all EU member states, except the UK and the Czech Republic (who opted out). The main provision of this treaty binds member states to transpose the Fiscal Compact into their domestic legal orders. Out of the 25 Contracting Parties to the TSCG, 22 are formally bound by the Fiscal Compact (the 19 eurozone member states, plus Bulgaria, Denmark and Romania).
	Treaty Establishing the European Stability Mechanism. Signed by eurozone members to establish the European Stability Mechanism (ESM), this treaty establishes an international organization located in Luxembourg, to act as a permanent source of financial assistance for member states in financial difficulty, with a maximum lending capacity of €500 billion. A precondition for receiving an ESM bailout is that the member state must have ratified the European Fiscal Compact.
2013	*Two Pack.* Contains two regulations (hence its name), with a focus on coordination and the introduction of a budgetary timeline. Eurozone member states must submit draft budgets for each coming year to the Commission by 15 October. The Commission then comments and can ask for redrafting. The Two Pack also strengthens EU monitoring of national budgets by expanding the European Semester, reinforcing the *excessive deficit procedure*, and creating a surveillance mechanism for member states. In particular, any state facing 'serious financial difficulties' can be placed under enhanced supervision and is obligated to fix the problem, endure regular inspections and so on.

declarations, programmes, national action plans etc., accompanied by increasing differentiation of membership which is now summarized under the general label of "EU economic governance"'.

The erosion of sovereign fiscal power began with the Maastricht Treaty (MaT, 1992; also referred to as the Treaty on European Union, or TEU) and the Stability and Growth Pact (SGP) requirement that the Commission should monitor member state fiscal activities and initiate sanctions against excessive deficits or debt. The SGP was introduced in 1997 as part of the original Economic and Monetary Union provisions: it included restrictions on budget deficits (up to 3% of GDP) and public debt (below 60% of GDP), with deviant countries punished by a fine. As any attempt to impose sanctions required the approval of a qualified majority of member states, these sanctions were never imposed.

Although these restrictions were a clear hindrance and bother, they proved entirely insufficient. The fiscal screws needed to be tightened even more as a result of the Great Recession.[11] Not only were member states placed under stronger monitoring and punishment regimes, but a new calendar, or decision schedule, was introduced: the so-called 'European Semester'. The European Semester grants the Commission greater power to monitor and influence national budgetary processes, because states are now required to submit a draft budget to the Commission before it is even submitted to the national parliament! In addition, it extends national budgetary horizons from annual to five-year plans. This means that government budgets are now developed according to a calendar that is blind or indifferent to national electoral dates and outcomes.[12] Finally, budget decisions are now set when a qualified minority of eurozone states supports the Commission's proposals. In effect, this means that creditor states can carry the vote over debtor states' budgets (Menéndez, 2016: 114).

The Great Recession has shaken the architecture, vocabulary and accessibility of European budgeting, as laid out Table 6.3. The result is almost incomprehensible. The *Six Pack* introduced a *European Semester* to better coordinate national economic policies and budgets; it strengthened the *preventive arm* of the *Stability and Growth Pact*; tightened the *excessive deficit procedure*; and introduced a *MIP Scoreboard* and a *Macroeconomic Imbalance Procedure* to prevent and correct any macroeconomic deviations. These reforms were then followed up with a *Treaty on Stability, Coordination and Governance*, a *Fiscal Compact* and a *Two Pack* to ensure that the euro area does not suffer any further mutinies. Aaagghh!

To the extent that we operationalize democracy in terms of legislative influence over a country's purse strings, Europe's budgetary recipe is deeply undemocratic. In this way, at least, the then Commission President José Manuel Barroso was right in calling the results a 'silent revolution' (Phillips, 2011a). The budgets of European countries are straitjacketed by a series of artificial numerical values that clearly restrict the tax and spending choices of member states. Even the advocates of these types of fiscal rules recognize their undemocratic nature (Wyplosz, 2013: 504–7). In effect, member state fiscal policy is placed on a sort of autopilot, with the waypoints plotted in by the EU, and set in the direction of austerity.

Finally, as if these constraints were not enough, a handful of states – Cyprus, Greece, Ireland, Portugal and Spain – were placed under even harder restrictions, due to a collapse in their public finances, and as payment for the financial assistance they received from a handful of international, bilateral and European creditors (such as 'the troika' – the European Commission, the IMF and the ECB). Among the many conditions for this assistance was a commitment to reform programmes, laid out in a series of 'memoranda of understandings' and 'stand-by agreements' that detailed heavy oversight requirements and the implementation of serious structural and budgetary reforms, including spending cuts, privatizations, increases in taxation and significant deregulation of their labour markets. Once again, national legislatures were pushed to the sidelines.

An even greater sacrifice was required of Greece and Italy – they were forced to jettison their elected prime ministers, in exchange for technocrats who were more acceptable to their financiers. In 2011, Mario Monti, a former EU commissioner, was chosen to replace Silvio Berlusconi, the democratically elected prime minister of Italy. While Berlusconi had the ballot box, Monti was an international adviser for Goldman Sachs, the European chair of David Rockefeller's Trilateral Commission and also a leading member of the Bilderberg Group. A similar transfer of power occurred in Greece, when the Greek Prime Minister George Papandreou was so bold as to suggest that Greeks should use a referendum to decide how to respond to their onerous bailout terms. Within days, Papandreou was replaced by Lucas Papademos, former vice-president of the ECB, visiting Harvard professor and ex-senior economist at the Boston Federal Reserve.

Despite all this, some observers will continue to argue that there is sufficient scope for policy autonomy in the EU's budgetary maze. For example, *The Economist* (2020b) recently suggested that 'member states [enjoy] near-total control over central policy-levers, like the power to tax and spend, and to regulate banks'. Such observations make me realize how important initial expectations can be when studying something as political as the role and scope of the legislative budget.

I suspect that *The Economist* enjoys many fellow travellers on this point, and it is not unreasonable that economists, politicians and political theorists might see such things differently. For this reason, I should be clear and explicit: I see the scope of member state fiscal policy severely circumscribed by the following (non-exhaustive) lists of constraints, imposed by the EU. Each of these has been described in this chapter:

- The capacity of member states to increase tax revenues is constrained by the threat of mobile capital flight.
- There are real limits imposed on the size of a government's deficit and debt levels, regardless of local economic conditions. Legislatures

are not free to pursue countercyclical policies that violate these legal limits.

- Member states must submit their budgets to the EU *for approval* and follow a budget calendar (or Semester) that is insensitive to domestic needs, elections and business cycles.
- Member state budgets must be approved by the EU before they are submitted to their national legislatures.
- Member states must ask for permission to institute major policy changes, such as the introduction of capital controls.
- A qualified minority of eurozone states can veto national budget proposals.
- Elected member state officials can, under certain conditions, be replaced.

To me, the scope and intrusiveness of these measures are shocking. In the EU, national budgets (and the process for producing them) are not designed to reflect democratic needs and interests but are used to secure the sort of macroeconomic convergence required of a common currency area. These restrictions are deeply intrusive and undemocratic, and they inhibit democratically elected officials from managing their local labour markets.

Conclusion

In Chapter 5, I documented a remarkable variance in local economic conditions across the EU. There is not one common labour market in Europe, but many different labour markets. To address the unique needs of these local labour markets, elected officials need access to a wide variety of independent policy instruments. Traditionally, these instruments have included monetary, fiscal, regulatory and procurement policies (among others). These instruments, employed in different ways, have been used in the past to encourage economic development and to stabilize local/national economic conditions.

This chapter has described how these instruments have been taken away from, or watered down by, policymakers. The desire to create a level playing field, the needs of a single market, and the demands of a common currency area have required that member states jettison the sort of policy instruments they need to stabilize and grow their local labour markets. Consequently, local labour markets in Europe remain exposed to the destructive gales of the marketplace.

In other integrated markets that share a common currency, the central (or federal) state usually helps to fund and reallocate the local costs of economic adjustment. As the scope of member state policy autonomy in Europe has shrunk, we might hope that the EU would fill the resulting gap by introducing EU-wide policies, supports and transfers. Chapter 7 considers that EU response.

7

Europe to the Rescue?

The Great Recession revealed the inadequacies of Europe's economic order. Having lost many important tools of economic policymaking, as described in Chapter 6, member states were unable to protect themselves from the financial storm and were constrained in their capacity to rebuild quickly after the storm had passed. The Great Recession clearly demonstrated that Europe remains divided in terms of its levels of economic development and that its individual member states are exposed to the world's economy in significantly different ways.

In the aftermath of the Great Recession, we find a burgeoning awareness of the role that the EU could, and should, play in filling the policy vacuum. There is a growing chorus of voices calling for the EU to assist member states in overcoming their structural and cyclical challenges. As an earlier European commissioner for employment, social affairs and inclusion noted:

> It has been broadly accepted that due to the limited availability of adjustment mechanisms for national economies within the EMU, unemployment and social crises risk developing to a greater extent in a currency union than in a more flexible exchange rate regime, *unless they are anticipated and addressed by the currency union on a collective basis.* (Andor, 2013a: 2, emphasis added)

This is clearly a step in the right direction. Further progress is evident in the EU's initial response to the COVID-19 pandemic. The varied and asymmetric impact of the pandemic across member states has underscored the need to secure more local responses and resources. Still, Europe has a very long way to go. This chapter considers two of the most important things that the EU could do to help policymakers manage their local labour markets, and then evaluates the EU's progress on both fronts.

The most important thing that the EU could do to support local labour markets is to provide a strong and common regulatory floor, upon which member states could build more elaborate protections (to meet local needs). The EU has the legal authority to provide that regulation, coordinate member state policies and delegate the necessary authority and resources accordingly. Unfortunately, it has proven very difficult to secure these sorts of protections, and much of the EU's recent regulatory efforts have been aimed to facilitate market integration, rather than to protect and advance workers' interests. The first part of the chapter briefly surveys this regulatory history.

A common budget is the second tool at the disposal of EU policymakers. This budget could be structured in such a way that it redistributes income across member states and allows them to stabilize their local labour markets. The latter part of this chapter describes the size and nature of the EU budget and explains why it is too small and improperly designed to help stabilize local labour markets in Europe. The final section turns to the EU's response to the COVID-19 pandemic, as it (implicitly) recognizes the need for greater member state policy autonomy in response to economic crises.

Europe's fractured regulatory floor

The EU's legislative output in the (broad) area of social policy is remarkably modest.[1] Its output in the area of labour market policy is even smaller. Compared to the amount of legislation that has been used to create the internal market, help farmers, extend freedom, security and justice, or even protect the environment and consumers, the level of legislative activity in the realm of EU social policy is quite limited (Degryse and Pochet, 2018: 11–12).

As we might expect from the discussion in Chapter 4, it was originally assumed that social policy would (and should) remain under the control of member states. After all, the Treaty of Rome (ToR) did not include any specific legislative powers in the area of social policy, and the effort to create a European social policy was mostly limited to three areas: equal pay across genders (ToR, 1957: Art. 119); the need to harmonize member state social security systems (ToR, 1957: Art. 120, 121); and the introduction of the European Social Fund (ToR, 1957: Chapter 2) to train and resettle workers who had lost their jobs as a result of market integration.

With time, European officials gradually expanded their authority to legislate over labour markets. Many of these efforts were brought about as part of the larger push for increased economic and monetary union, as outlined in Table 7.1. The first expansion came with the (1987) Single European Act (SEA), which introduced qualified majority voting in many areas, including regulation of the working environment (albeit not in the most sensitive areas, including fiscal provisions, free mobility and 'the rights and interests of employed persons' (SEA, 1987: Art. 1A)). Then, with the 1992 Maastricht Treaty (MaT), the EU was empowered to establish minimum standards in a number of areas of labour law – *except* for the most important areas: those that concern 'pay, the right of association, the right to strike or the right to impose lock-outs' (MaT, 1992: Art. 2(6); TFEU, 2012: Art. 153(5)). Finally, the 1997 Treaty of Amsterdam (ToA) 'constitutionalized' employment policy, by including a separate chapter (Title VIa) on employment, which aimed to promote a 'skilled, trained and adaptable workforce and labour markets responsive to economic change' (ToA, 1997: Art. 109n). From these guidelines for expansion, we can see how Europe felt a need to recommodify its workers in order to create a more efficient economic and monetary union.

Formally, labour market policy in the EU rests on three levels, as sketched in Table 7.2. At the top level, we find a series of treaty articles that provide the legal foundations for a more activist social policy. The EU is also committed to a series of obligations associated with the Charter of Fundamental Rights (OJEC, 2000). Below this level of primary law lie a number of employment protections in the forms of directives and regulations. Table 7.2 offers only a sampling of these (and many of these have been subsequently amended), to give the reader an idea of their content.

The objective of these directives and regulations, and the Community's enthusiasm for them, tends to vary over time. It is common to divide EU social policy into periods of varying levels of activism. Following Kenner (2003), for example, the 1970s can be seen as a period of the 'Community's "New Deal"', while the 1980s was the era of Europe's 'Social Charter'.

In the early period, Community directives were largely aimed at protecting European workers, as seen in the sample of directives from the 1970s in Table 7.2. Examples include equal pay for men and women; comprehensive equal treatment of men and women in employment; protection of workers in the case of collective redundancies; and protecting workers in the case of transfers of undertakings and the insolvency of the employer. This was the 'New Deal' to which Kenner

Table 7.1: The push for deeper market integration

1957	Treaty of Rome (ToR)	Created the *European Economic Community*, which was resolved 'to ensure the economic and social progress of their countries by common action to eliminate the barriers which divide Europe.'
1970s	Werner and MacDougall Reports	The Werner Report (1970) provides an early blueprint for Economic and Monetary Union (EMU) in Europe, while the MacDougall Report (1977) considered the budgetary implications of that EMU.
1987	Single European Act (SEA)	First major revision of the Treaty of Rome: created the *European Community*, with the objective of establishing a single market by 1992. To do this, the decision-making process was streamlined by introducing qualified majority voting in many areas.
1992	Maastricht Treaty (MaT)	Established the *European Union* and provides most of the foundation stones for eventual monetary union in Europe. In particular, Maastricht established the European Central Bank (ECB) and introduced the convergence criteria (originally referred to as the 'Maastricht criteria'), which severely curtailed the fiscal manoeuvrability of member states.
1997	Stability and Growth Pact (SGP)	The Stability and Growth Pact is an agreement among the member states to facilitate and maintain the stability of the EMU. The pact consists of a Council Resolution (97/C 236/01) and two regulations: Council Regulation (EC) 1466/97 and Council Regulation (EC) 167/97.
1998	European Central Bank (ECB)	The European Central Bank was formally established on 1 June 1998, as spelled out in the Maastricht Treaty (1992), but it did not exercise its full powers until the euro was formally introduced in 1999.
1999	Euro introduced	The euro was established with the Maastricht Treaty (1992), and after years of preparation, a non-physical form of the currency (transfers) was introduced at midnight, 1 January 1999. In the following couple of months, there was a transition in notes and currencies, from the old (national) currencies to the euro at rates of exchange that were fixed against one another.
2012	Treaty Establishing the European Stability Mechanism	This treaty was signed by eurozone members to establish the European Stability Mechanism (ESM). The treaty created an international organization located in Luxembourg, to act as a permanent source of financial assistance for member states in financial difficulty, with a maximum lending capacity of €500 billion.

Table 7.2: Legal framework for EU labour market policies (sampling)

Instrument	Details
Primary law	Treaty of the Functioning of the European Union (TFEU, 2012): • Article 4(2)(b) mentions social policy as a shared competency; • Article 9 requires that 'the Union shall take into account requirements linked to the promotion of a high level of employment, the guarantee of adequate social protection'; • Article 19 combats all forms of discrimination (broadly); • Title IV of Part II (esp. Articles 45–48) links social policy to supporting the needs of the free movement of workers; • Title X of Part III (Articles 151–161) focuses explicitly on social policy, by promoting the role of social partners, supporting member states policies, facilitating social dialogue and so on. Charter of Fundamental Rights of the European Union (OJEC, 2000) Chapter 4 on 'solidarity' includes: o Art. 28: Rights to collective bargaining and action; o Art. 31: Fair and just working conditions; o Art. 34: Social security and social assistance; and o Art. 35: Health care.
Directives	• *75/117/EEC.* On equal pay for men and women • *75/129/EEC.* Protects workers in the case of collective redundancies • *76/207/EEC.* Equal employment treatment for women and men • *77/187/EEC.* Protects workers in the case of transfers and insolvencies • *89/391/EEC.* Framework directive for health and safety at work • *92/85/EEC.* Pregnant workers and maternity • *93/104/EC.* Working time • *94/45/EC.* European works councils • *96/34/EC.* Parental leave • *96/71/EC.* Posted workers • *97/81/EC.* Part-time workers • *98/59/EC.* Collective dismissals • *99/70/EC.* Fixed time work • *2000/43/EC.* Race equality • *2005/36/EC.* Recognizing professional qualifications • *2006/123/EC.* Services • *2014/24/EU.* Public contracts • *2018/957/EU.* Amendment to Posted Workers Directive

(continued)

Table 7.2: Legal framework for EU labour market policies (sampling)
(continued)

Instrument	Details
Regulations	• *Regulation (EC) No 883/2004* on the coordination of social security systems • *Regulation (EC) No 1408/71* and *883/2004* on social security for families moving to another member state • *Regulation (EU) No 492/2011* on free movement of workers within the EU • *Regulation (EU) No. 987/2009* on rules for coordinating social security systems • *Regulation (EU) No 1176/2011* on correcting macroeconomic imbalances (Art. 4 introduces a 'scorecard' that came to include wages policy indicators)

referred. In the 1960s and 1970s, then, we can still find 'a concerted effort by the European Commission to extend the role and scope of supranational social and welfare policy on behalf of intra-Community labor markets' (Hansen and Hager, 2010: 199).

Over time, however, the Commission came to realize that Europe's welfare state provisions were restricting the sort of interstate mobility that a common currency area would require (in that they allowed a certain degree of decommodification). In the 1980s, European labour market directives and regulations were increasingly aimed at trying to make the internal market work more effectively – by making it easier for workers to move (such as facilitating social security transfers, recognizing foreign qualifications and liberating posted workers). By the end of the decade, it was clear that the Commission viewed social policy as a useful instrument to further market integration:

> social policy must, *above all*, contribute to the setting up of a 'single labour market', by doing away with the barriers which still restrict the effective exercise of two basic freedoms: the freedom of movement of persons and the freedom of establishment. (CEC, 1988: 2–3, emphasis added)

This is not to ignore or downplay the important role that the EU's anti-discrimination regulations play for those who find work abroad, for whatever reason. As we can see from the sample of directives in Table 7.2, there has been a concerted effort, from the late 1980s onwards, to protect against different forms of discrimination in the workforce and to provide other basic protections for mobile workers.

This is the period of Europe's 'Social Charter', and it is a messy one, saturated with disagreement about what a European social policy should/might look like. This mess shouldn't distract us from the fact that the launch of the European Social Policy can be seen as a response by Jacques Delors, president of the European Commission, to protect workers in the face of increased market pressures. The general idea at the time was to create a distinct 'European social model', which could distinguish itself from a more free-market approach of the US. The problem is that this launch proved politically contentious.

The attempt to construct a new social Europe faced significant resistance, as is most clearly evident in the need for a Social Policy Protocol (see Box 7.1). As a result of the difficulty in agreeing a common policy, much of European social policy in the 1990s was two-tracked, with only 11 (of 12) member states signing the 1994 directive on European works councils; the 1996 directive on parental leave, and the 1997 directive on part-time work. As Streeck (2019: 129) recently noted, 'probably the most substantial piece of European social-policy

---

Box 7.1: Social Policy Protocol

In the run-up to Maastricht, Europe's social partners, in particular the *Union des Industries de la Communauté européenne* (UNICE), the European Centre of Employers and Enterprises, and the European Trade Union Confederation (ETUC) had agreed to a text they hoped might be inserted into the Maastricht Treaty (JASP, 1991). The subsequent Agreement on Social Policy (2 February 1992) proposed:

1. that the social partners be included and constitutionally recognized as a part of the Community legislative process;
2. a major extension of EC competences in employment and industrial relations; and
3. the use of qualified majority voting with respect to some of the new competences.

In short, the Agreement on Social Policy proposed a radical change in the Community legislative process for social policy. This change was unacceptable to the UK, which refused to sign, and the agreement was annexed to the Protocol on Social Policy to the Treaty of Maastricht – but included an 'opt-out' for the UK. This opt-out lasted until May 1997, when a newly elected UK government opted back in, and the Agreement on Social Policy was incorporated into a revised 'Social Chapter' of the EC Treaty in the 1997 Treaty of Amsterdam.

---

legislation in this period was passed outside the Social Protocol': the 1996 Directive 96/71/EC on posting of workers. This directive allows employers to skirt the Rome Convention (1980), which required workers be protected by the law of the member state in which they work. As we saw in Chapter 6, this directive became a lightning rod in the decade that follows, as the European Court of Justice (ECJ) used it to threaten national labour market arrangements (in particular Viking and Laval; see Table 6.2), and it was subsequently amended in 2018 (Directive 2018/957).[2]

Since Maastricht, EU labour market policy has taken a decidedly liberal tack, even as most of the work being done has been pushed into the legislative shadows. Unable to secure consensus on how to proceed, Europe changed its strategy from promoting legislative protections to encouraging member states to adopt non-binding policies. This change in emphasis was clearly evident in the 1994 White Paper on social policy:

> Given the solid base of European social legislation that has already been achieved, the Commission considers that *there is not a need for a wide ranging programme of new legislative proposals* in the coming period. (European Commission, 1994: 5, emphasis added)

In short, from the early 1990s, the EU believed that workers did not need more legal protections. Worse, such protections were increasingly seen as the source of Europe's economic woes and a hindrance to further integration. The problem of (un)employment was increasingly recognized as a problem of overregulation and onerous welfare protections (European Commission, 1993: 123–4). To get the labour market working again, the Commission reasoned, these member state protections needed to be slashed. In this approach, we can clearly see the logic of the mainstream labour market model (as depicted in Figure 2.1), where the market for labour is seen as analogous to other, more general markets.

The EU now works to encourage its member states to deregulate their national labour markets using a number of soft law venues and approaches, strategies and pillars (see Table 7.3), and the open method of coordination (OMC).[3] The focus of this 'soft law' approach is trained on mitigating the alleged rigidities in European employment regulations and facilitating greater contractual diversity. The new slogans in this struggle are flexibility, flexicurity, efficiency and freedom (European Commission, 2006).

Table 7.3: Soft law measures relevant to EU labour markets

Year	Measure	Description
1989	Community Charter of Fundamental Social Rights for Workers	Human rights-based charter, which includes articles on free movement of workers (for example). States can adopt this charter voluntarily: the UK originally declined, but adopted it in 1998.
1997	European Employment Strategy (EES)	Aimed to set common objectives and targets for European employment policy. The EES is linked to the requirements of EMU, in reaching mid-term objectives, indicators and convergence criteria. Actively employed the open method of coordination (OMC).
2000–10	Lisbon Strategy	Action Plan for the EU to become 'the most competitive and dynamic knowledge-based economy in the world capable of sustainable economic growth with more and better jobs and greater social cohesion'. Included a 'Strategy for jobs and growth'.
2010–20	Europe 2020	Second ten-year Action Plan to boost growth and employment. This one aims to raise the employment rate of the population aged 20–64 from the current 69% to at least 75% (one of five main goals).
2017	European Pillar of Social Rights	A new charter of social rights. Establishes 30 key principles and rights, organized under three rubrics: equal opportunities and access to labour markets; fair working conditions; and social protection and inclusion. Originally conceived for eurozone states, but applicable to all member states that want to participate.

The end result was a contradiction. On the one hand, the EU's ambition to create a regime for free movement is both unique and inspiring. The original idea was to encourage a fourth freedom, and this could be done if migrants were supported by a robust system of (national) welfare state protections. Seen from this historical trajectory, the EU is predominantly a welfare regime, and the rights of this regime travelled with workers when they migrated from one member state to another. On the other hand, it became increasingly obvious that Europe's welfare regimes were deterring the sort of labour mobility and wage flexibility that a common currency area required. Because of this tension, it became necessary to limit the expansion of these rights for fear that they deter migration (by decommodifying workers). Worse, these rights have become increasingly peripheral, as employers have discovered ways to work around them (through the system of posting workers, for example). Consequently, the EU has relied more and more on workaways as a fallback mechanism for local economic adjustment in the EU. As we shall see in Chapter 8, this trend is especially evident in response to the Great Recession.

In encouraging a more flexible and mobile workforce, the EU has facilitated a number of significant amendments to national labour laws across Europe. As a recent review of these reforms has shown, the attack on labour protections has been three-pronged: making existing labour law provisions more flexible; decentralizing collective bargaining arrangements (from national/sectoral levels to the company level); and relaxing minimum standards. In many cases, the reforms were justified as a response to the Great Recession or the need to 'modernize' national labour laws. But, in other cases, these amendments were forced upon member states by European (whether the ECB and/or the European Commission) and international organizations, such as the IMF (Clauwaert and Schömann, 2012: 5–6).

The end result is a hodgepodge of protections in Europe, constantly threatened by waves of competitive pressure. This pressure only increased in the wake of the Great Recession, when member states in Southern Europe were forced to reduce their already meagre standards of protection, cut their minimum wages and even disassemble their collective bargaining systems. Overall, legislation on social minimum standards in Europe is unsystematic and fragmentary, with important areas – such as protection against unfair dismissals – left uncovered (Weiss, 2017: 34).

While European policymakers are increasingly vocal in their recognition of the need to assist member states in stabilizing their local labour markets, developments on the ground seem to be heading in the opposite direction. Overall, the EU has largely given up on trying to legislate better working conditions for its workers. It now sees its role as the great persuader – encouraging member states to liberalize their national labour markets in an effort to create a more level playing field, with an eye on producing greater efficiencies.

The promise of a European budget

It is routinely assumed and argued that a common currency area requires the transfer of significant budget responsibility from the member states to a higher (here European) level of government. This reasoning rests on the experience of other federal states, where federal fiscal transfers to member states are able to counterbalance the mostly procyclical tendencies of member state fiscal policies, and redistribute income from rich to poor regions.[4] After the Great Recession, this argument has gained traction and there is now a greater push for stronger EU budgets and regulations. Many of these arguments point to the need for stronger European regulation of the financial and banking sectors and greater coordination of member state fiscal policies.[5]

While there is a growing recognition that Europe needs new tools to stabilize macroeconomic conditions at the member state level, there is significant resistance to doing this by means of a larger EU budget. While most analysts recognize this to be an economic necessity, almost nobody thinks that it is politically viable to transfer greater budgetary responsibility from member states to the EU, or to increase the EU budget in any significant way.

As a result, much of the most politically influential work in Europe focuses on market-based solutions to macroeconomic stabilization, such as some form of reinsurance arrangement or renewed national unemployment insurance systems (Gros, 2014; Tommaso Padoa-Schioppa Group, 2012: 30f). Others point to the need for a large rainy day fund (IMF, 2013a; Tommaso Padoa-Schioppa Group, 2012), or even a shared (union-wide) unemployment insurance scheme (IMF, 2013a).

To be honest, the resistance to expanding the EU budget is completely understandable. Member states continue to provide the bulk of citizen protections and needs; the EU is (rightly) seen to be suffering from a democratic deficit; and the effectiveness of EU programmes is frequently questioned/doubted. As it is economically infeasible to significantly increase revenues to the EU budget without decreasing them to the individual member states, increasing the overall EU budget is politically untenable.[6]

Even though it is political anathema, a larger EU budget is a necessary consequence of the choices Europe has already made on its path to market integration. In the absence of autonomous member state fiscal and monetary policies (see Chapter 6), and in a context where labour, as a factor of production, is insufficiently mobile or flexible (see Chapter 8), there are few remaining tools that can be used to stabilize local labour markets.

In fiscal federations[7] – even highly decentralized federations – the central government is responsible for three key political functions:[8] the provision of public goods (such as defence, foreign relations, justice, and infrastructure needs); income redistribution (by providing social insurance and social welfare programmes); and smoothing local macroeconomic shocks (through fiscal transfers). The last task should be familiar to readers from Chapter 3, where we briefly discussed the role of federal fiscal transfers in smoothing out regional economic differences in suboptimum currency areas.

To pay for these central functions, the size of the federal government's budget tends to be significant – it usually constitutes more than half of all government spending.[9] For example, in their recent 13-country study, Cottarelli and Guerguil (2015b: 37) found that 60% of all general government spending in fiscal federations came in the form of central government expenditures (including social security institutions). In short, central governments need access to substantial revenues to fulfil the tasks with which they are usually associated.

These revenues are nearly always secured by means of corporate and individual income taxes. In doing so, central governments bypass member state governments and tap directly into their main sources of revenues. In other words, the central government has direct access to a huge (and varied) revenue base, independent of its member states. As we shall see, this facilitates a downward flow of transfers, as the money is aggregated, in bulk, at the central level and subsequently distributed downward to the member states. This arrangement provides the central government with significant economic muscle.

There are many advantages to organizing the budget in this way: the central authorities are able to coordinate fiscal, monetary and structural powers (say, countercyclically); they can leverage the financial capacity of the (larger) central government; they can organize the budget in a way that insures against idiosyncratic member state economic shocks; and they can internalize any interregional spillovers. In short, the design of federal revenue/expenditure programmes allows the central state to better manage cross-regional redistribution, as well as stabilize local labour markets. These are exactly the functions that member states in the EU have jettisoned, in exchange for greater market integration and monetary union.

For our purposes, the promise of increased fiscal transfers are three in number.[10] First, these transfers facilitate redistribution, by permanently transferring funds from richer to poorer regions – bringing about the sort of wealth convergence that the EU says it wants (and needs).[11] Second, fiscal transfers help member states to stabilize the local economy. They do so by acting as a form of insurance, allowing member states to protect against both unique regional (or member state) shocks (read risk sharing), as well as common shocks – those affecting all members states (read stabilization). Finally, during periods of extraordinary crisis (such as the Great Recession or the COVID-19 pandemic), the central government can use fiscal transfers to bail out member states under financial stress. They can do this more efficiently due to lower borrowing costs and their capacity to issue credit (or 'print' money).

We know about the important role that central (federal) budgets must play in common currency areas through a plethora of studies on the US. We considered some of these studies in Chapter 3, and the role they delegate to federal fiscal transfers in smoothing out regional economic differences in a shared currency area. As a general rule, local and state government budgets in the US tend to be procyclical, in part due to state rules that require annual balanced budgets. These budgets are also relatively modest: state and local budgets make up just 40% of total government spending in the US (Henning and Kessler, 2012: 14). Luckily, American workers don't have to rely on their state governments alone (as these have few means for stabilizing their local labour markets) – the great stabilizer, in the US, is the federal government.

The mechanism is simple – a federal budget allows for risk sharing across member states – in terms of both revenues and expenditures. When it comes to revenues, the federal government receives much of its money in the form of income taxes, from individuals and firms, scattered across 50 states. As incomes go up in one state (the result of a local economic boom), the federal government receives greater tax revenues from individuals and firms in that state. As incomes go down in another state, individuals and firms in that state will send less tax money to the federal government. As a result, revenues to the federal government are directly linked to local economic activity.

On the expenditure side, the pattern is reversed. Many federally funded programmes are closely (but inversely) linked to local economic conditions, for example unemployment or Medicaid (a programme that pays the medical costs of people with limited income and resources). A state suffering an economic recession will have more people needing unemployment benefits, and the federal government will send it more money to help pay for that increase (at the same time, the federal government will send less unemployment money to those states that are enjoying stronger economic conditions). Other federally funded programmes are fixed, and not linked to the local business cycle (for example infrastructure projects). Most of the money that states receive from the US federal government goes to meet federally funded mandates, including grants-in-aid, Medicaid and education, but the federal government can also pour in massive amounts of money during periods of extraordinary crisis, such as we saw during the Great Recession and the first round of the COVID-19 outbreak.

In 2012, C. Randall Henning and Martin Kessler mapped the scope of US federal support to US states during the Great Recession. In Table 7.4, I've converted these figures into a (% GDP) format that can facilitate a subsequent comparison with the eurozone. Here, we can see that the US federal government's overall level of expenditures, during the Great Recession, was in the neighbourhood of 25% of GDP.

Although the US federal government is not known for its extravagance, the scope of US federal government activities is still larger than that of the EU (just think of defence spending), so it may be unreasonable to expect the EU to manage a budget that corresponds to a quarter of its GDP (but see MacDougall et al, 1977: 13). If we scale down our ambitions, we can see that the amount of money that goes directly to 'federal transfers' is more limited, just 6–7% of total US GDP. Granted, these figures capture an extraordinary period, at the height of the Great Recession, so they are probably larger than usual. But almost everyone agrees that the size of these transfers was insufficient for restarting the US economy at the time. More to the point, we might expect the need for federal transfers in the US to be smaller than in Europe – given that the American labour force is more mobile and its wages more flexible than its European counterpart (for reasons that are rather obvious).

Other large economies that share a common currency have learned of the necessity and utility of a significant central (or federal) budget. When designed properly, this type of central budget can play a significant role in helping member state economies adjust to asymmetric shocks. In this way, the central budget is used to compensate member states for the loss of policy autonomy required of an integrated market that shares a common currency.

As we shall see in the following section, the EU has not been able to leverage this knowledge and its (central) budget remains too small (and improperly designed) to protect member states from the frequent economic storms to which they are exposed.

The European budget in practice

The budget of the EU is quite different from most government budgets, especially the budgets of federal states, in terms of both its size and the way it is funded. These unique characteristics place significant

Table 7.4: US federal support to states, 2009–11 (billions USD)

	2009			2010			2011		
	Federal transfers	Of which, from stimulus package	Share of GDP	Federal transfers	Of which, from stimulus package	Share of GDP	Federal transfers	Of which, from stimulus package	Share of GDP
Federal transfers									
Grants–in–aid	482.4	70.3		531.5	100.8		504.3	43.5	
Medicaid	264.4	41.3		281.5	45.9		265.3	2.7	
Education	59.8	21.3		71.8	30.9		67.9	24.3	
Other	158.3	7.6		178.3	23.7		171.1	16.5	
Total transfers	964.9		6.7 %	1,063.1		7.1 %	1,008.6		6.5 %
Total federal gov. expenditures	3,777.5		26.1 %	4,005.8		26.7 %	4,026.8		25.9 %
GDP	14,448.9			14,992.1			15,542.6		

Notes: Federal transfers from Henning and Kessler (2012: 15, Table 2); Federal expenditures and GDP from OECD 2020a and OECD 2020b, respectively). GDP figures based on output approach. The 2011 federal transfers are for Q1–Q3, annualized.

Sources: Adapted from Henning and Kessler (2012: 15, Table 2); OECD (2020a, 2020b)

constraints on what the EU can do to help stabilize labour markets across its many member states.

The first European budget was adopted by the European Council in 1958. For the first few years of the European Economic Community (EEC), the budget was remarkably modest: it covered only administrative expenditures. But as the political ambitions of the EEC grew, so too did its budget. In the initial years, most of the budget was dedicated to starting up the European Social Fund (ESF) and the Common Agricultural Policy (CAP). Over time, as the Community began to grow, the budget grew accordingly. All the while, however, it remained remarkably small, as a share of member state economies, as shown in Figure 7.1. At the height of European central government spending, in the mid-1990s, expenditures never exceeded 1.2% of the aggregate gross national income (GNI) of member states.

The EU budget is subject to a remarkable array of principles, procedures and regulations. These include two limiting factors that are especially relevant to our study. The first is buried in the 384 pages of the current version of the EU's Financial Regulation (European Commission, 2018b). In particular, Article 17 includes a 'principle of equilibrium,' requiring that the EU's revenues and expenditures always be in balance. Indeed, a balanced budget is said to be 'the guiding principle' behind the EU revenue system (European Council, 2020a), and it prevents the EU from issuing credit and/or debt to finance itself.[12] The other important limiting factor comes from Article 3 of a 2014 European Council Decision (2014/335/EU), which sets an

Figure 7.1: EU expenditures, % of GNI, 1958–2020

Source: Adapted from European Commission (2008: 51–6, 2019a: 64–5)

explicit ceiling on annual expenditures: they shall not exceed 1.23% of the sum of all the member states' GNIs (European Council, 2014). In short, the EU budget is hobbled: its expenditures are not allowed to exceed 1.23% of its GNI, and its revenues must be set equal to its expenditures. This is *remarkably* small, especially when compared to the US federal budget, as outlined in Table 7.4.

Union revenues

When the scope of the Community budget remained limited, funding it was not particularly complicated. At the start, the EEC budget could rely on agricultural and customs duties, along with a sugar levy, and any discrepancy between revenues was filled by member state contributions. Today, the EU relies heavily on member state contributions, in the form of direct payments and a share of their value added tax (VAT). The European Commission (2019a: 38) divides the main sources of current (2018) revenue into four categories, as described in Table 7.5.

The bottom two sources of revenue (Traditional own resources and Other) are the only sources of revenue that are integrally allocated to the EU central budget. The top two sources arrive at the EU via the member states. The first source (National contributions) is by far the largest, but it was originally introduced as a means to balance revenues and expenditures. The structure of these budget revenues

Table 7.5: EU revenue sources (2018)

Source	Share of 2018 revenues	Description
National contributions	66%	A specific contribution by each member state, based on its GNI.
VAT	11%	Member state contribution based on a standard percentage of the harmonized VAT base in each EU country.
Other	13%	Revenues generated from a variety of sources, including taxes on EU staff salaries, fines, bank interest and contributions from third countries.
Traditional own resources	10%	These are mostly in the form of customs duties on imports from outside the EU.

Source: Adapted from European Commission (2019a: 38)

means that the EU suffers from what the federal fiscal literature calls a 'substantial reverse vertical fiscal imbalance'. Whereas most of the money in traditional federations flows downward (from the central government to the member states), in the EU it mostly flows upward! In 2018, 79% of EU transfers flowed upward (via VAT and the national contributions) into the EU central budget. Indeed, it appears that the EU is the only contemporary case of a central budget stably funded primarily by upward transfers (Escolano et al, 2015: 34). As we saw earlier, this resource pattern is a serious problem if the EU hopes to use its central budget to stabilize local labour markets.

There has been some recognition of the need to develop new sources of revenues, even if the Commission is reluctant to reveal as much in its public dealings.[13] In particular, the EU first introduced the possibility of a common corporate income tax in 2011, which could partially contribute to the European budget. While it met significant initial resistance, the proposal was relaunched in 2016 (European Commission, 2016). In the same year (2011), the Commission also proposed a financial transaction tax (European Commission, 2011a: 3), with the intent of 'creating a new revenue stream with the objective to gradually displace national contributions to the EU budget'.

There are two significant shortcomings with EU budget revenues: they are too small and too dependent upon member states to be able to help those member states address pressing needs in their national labour markets. To compensate member states for their loss of policy autonomy, the EU needs to be able to secure a direct source of financing – for example through individual or company income taxes – from across the EU, and to increase those revenues precipitously. While there is a growing realization of the need to broaden the revenue base and bypass member states, these changes are politically contested, and unlikely to happen in the near future. These limits on the revenue side are serious enough, but the limitations continue on the expenditure side as well.

Union expenditures

As we already know, the size of the EU's expenditures are currently limited by a 2014 Council Resolution (2014/335/EU) to just over 1% of member state GNI (European Council, 2014). This is remarkably small compared to other central government budgets. But the content of those expenditures is also rather unique, in that the EU does not fund social protection, primary education or national defence. Rather, the EU budget is primarily an investment tool used to boost growth and competitiveness in the broader EU economy.

The EU works with two forms of budget: one long term, the other annual. The long-term budget – the so-called 'Multiannual Financial Framework' (MFF) – provides a strategic investment overview, while each annual budget is then set within the MFF expenditures' ceilings. In 2018, the annual budget totalled €173.1 billion in commitment appropriations and €156.7 billion in payment appropriations. About half of the funds (€87.4 billion in commitments) were earmarked to stimulate growth, employment and competitiveness – through facilities such as the European Fund for Strategic Investments, the Connecting Europe Facility and the European Structural and Investment Funds (European Commission, 2019a: 5). This annual budget was embedded in a larger MFF, for the 2014–20 period, in which the EU allocated up to €1,087 billion in commitments and €1,026 billion in payments (European Commission, 2019a: 13), divided under six headings, as shown in Figure 7.2.

The official breakdown of EU expenditures does not really lend itself to our purposes. While it is impressive that nearly 40% of the current long-term budget's expenditures are aimed at delivering sustainable growth, this does not help us think about how the EU might bring

Figure 7.2: Main EU expenditure categories, 2014–20

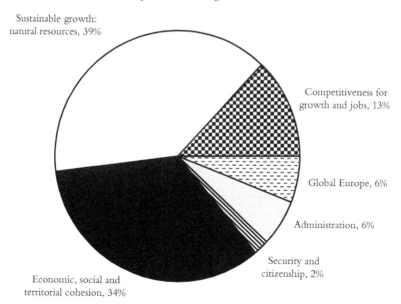

Sustainable growth: natural resources, 39%

Competitiveness for growth and jobs, 13%

Global Europe, 6%

Administration, 6%

Security and citizenship, 2%

Economic, social and territorial cohesion, 34%

Source: Adapted from European Commission (2019a: 13)

its member states closer together (call it convergence, cohesion or redistribution) or help its member states smooth out local economic maladies (macroeconomic stabilization).

Cohesion Policy

Europe's Cohesion Policy receives a great deal of attention but has been marred with controversy.[14] While recognition of the need for a regional policy can be traced back to the original Treaty of Rome, and a number of the instruments we associate with Cohesion Policy are dated to that time, European Cohesion Policy was fuelled by three related factors: the inability of markets to shrink the economic gap that separated Europe's poorest and richest member states; Europe's expansion to include poorer member states; and the difficulties that new member states had (and have) in meeting the demands of an increasingly integrated market.

The first two factors are perhaps the most obvious: the growth of Europe's Cohesion Policy goes hand in hand with the growth of an increasingly diverse membership in the European Community (as outlined in Table 7.6), and the deepening of market integration (as outlined before, in Table 7.1). As we shall see, the biggest injections of money, and the largest regulatory reforms, came in 1988 and during the 2013–17 budgetary period – immediately following expanded membership drives.

The need to ensure a 'harmonious development by reducing the differences existing between the various regions and the backwardness of the less favoured regions' was a motivating factor behind the Treaty of Rome (ToR, 1957: Preamble). To satisfy this need, the ToR laid the groundwork for three financing instruments: the ESF (introduced in chapter 2 of the Treaty); the European Investment Bank (EIB, the subject of Title IV); and the European Agricultural Guidance and Guarantee Fund (justified in Title 2, esp. Art. 40 and 41, but not created until 1962). See Table 7.7 for an overview of the EU's diverse cohesion tools.

Other important funding instruments for European Cohesion Policy are a direct result of expanding membership. For example, the European Regional Development Fund (ERDF) was a product of the first wave of membership in the 1970s, in recognition that economic integration had not managed to deliver the 'balanced expansion' as promised by the Treaty of Rome (CEC, 1973: 2).[15] When the EU was expanded to include Greece, Spain and Portugal, the (1987) Single European Act (SEA) encouraged the Community to use its Structural Funds

Table 7.6: Waves of expanding EU membership

Date of entry	Country
1952	Belgium
	France
	West Germany
	Italy
	Luxembourg
	Netherlands
1973	Denmark
	Ireland
	United Kingdom
1981	Greece
1986	Portugal
	Spain
1995	Austria
	Finland
	Sweden
2004	Cyprus
	Czech Republic
	Estonia
	Hungary
	Latvia
	Lithuania
	Malta
	Poland
	Slovakia
	Slovenia
2007	Bulgaria
	Romania
2013	Croatia

and the EIB to help achieve 'Economic and Social Cohesion' (SEA, 1987: Title V, Art. 130b). In 1987, as part of the Delors-I package deal (CEC, 1987), the Structural Funds received a major cash injection (doubling their budget over the 1989–93 period) and underwent a series of regulatory reforms (Dudek, 2014: 5).

Finally, the last big push for Cohesion Policy came with the most recent waves of expansion into Eastern and Central Europe – states with significantly lower levels of per capita income. First of all, the Cohesion Policy underwent a set of substantial regulatory changes in 2013, setting it off in a new policy direction – one that more closely aligned the objectives of the European Structural and Investment Funds to the

Table 7.7: European cohesion tools

Start	Tool	Description
1957	European Social Fund (ESF)	Included in the Treaty of Rome, this is the oldest of the Structural Funds. The Community's main instrument for supporting employment. Covers all regions (but uses a complex formula), with a focus on improving employment and education opportunities across the EU, but does so, among other things, by 'supporting labour mobility'.
1962	European Agricultural Guidance and Guarantee Fund (EAGGF)	Originally set up to finance the CAP. Contained two sections: a 'guarantee' section financed measures intended to regularize agricultural markets and the refunds for exports to third countries; and a 'guidance' section financed rural development measures covered by activities under Objective 1 and the EU rural development initiative. Replaced in 2007 by the European Agricultural Guarantee Fund and the EAFRD.
1975	European Regional Development Fund (ERDF)	Investment fund for strengthening economic and social cohesion in the EU by correcting imbalances between its regions. Funds are allocated by theme and level of development.
1988	Structural Funds	Contains two funds: ERDF and ESF. Introduced as part of Europe's 'Cohesion Policy' with the entry of Greece, Spain and Portugal into the Community.
1988	Cohesion Policy	Umbrella term that covers ERDF, CF and ESF. Designed originally to help Greece, Spain and Portugal integrate. Key principles include: focusing on the poorest and most backward regions; multiannual programming; strategic orientation of investments; and involvement of regional and local partners.
1993	Cohesion Fund (CF)	Introduced with the Maastricht Treaty. Along with Structural Funds, this is a major tool of EU regional policy. Aimed at members states whose GNI per inhabitant is less than 90% of the EU average. The objective of the CF is to reduce economic and social disparities and to promote sustainable development. The focus is on environmental and transportation/ infrastructure projects.
2002	The European Union Solidarity Fund (EUSF)	Provides assistance in case of natural disasters.

Table 7.7: European cohesion tools (continued)

Start	Tool	Description
2005	European Agricultural Fund for Rural Development (EAFRD)	Funding instrument for the CAP. In particular, the EAFRD is used to finance the Rural Development Programme.
2014	European Maritime and Fisheries Fund (EMFF)	Funds the EU's maritime and fisheries policies, for example to help fishermen and coastal communities transition to more sustainable activities. Replaced the European Fisheries Fund (from 2007), which had previously replaced the Financial Instrument for Fishing Guidance.
	European Structural and Investment Funds (ESIF)	Umbrella term that covers five funds: ERDF, CF, ESF, EAFRD and EMFF.

overall priorities of the EU. More significantly, a great deal of money was distributed to the new member states in the 2007–13 long-term budgetary period. Indeed, the ten new member states received more than half (€175.5 billion) of the total €336.5 billion that was earmarked for Cohesion Policy in the 2007–13 period (Gorzelak, 2017: 33).

The year 2015 represents the apex of cohesion spending. Since the creation of the ERDF in 1975, the budget for cohesion has increased steadily, from a mere 5% to around 36% of the EU budget during the 2007–13 period (Manzella and Mendez, 2009: 21). While these higher spending levels continued into 2015 and 2016, to overlap with the next budgetary period (2014–20), cohesion spending was deprioritized.

A commitment of 36% of the EU budget is not to be sneezed at: it shows that the EU is serious about the need for greater redistribution across its diverse member states. But this number needs to be placed in a context that recognizes the small overall size of the EU budget. Figure 7.3 does just that, showing the scope of EU Cohesion Policy, as it varies over time, and as a share of EU GDP. This figure draws on the three main components of EU Cohesion Policy (see Table 7.7): the Cohesion Fund, the ERDF and the ESF (which is coupled with the Youth Employment Initiative). Here, we can see that the highpoint of Cohesion Policy occurred in the wake of the EU's eastward expansion, but topped out in 2015 – at under *half of one per cent* (0.47%) of EU GDP.

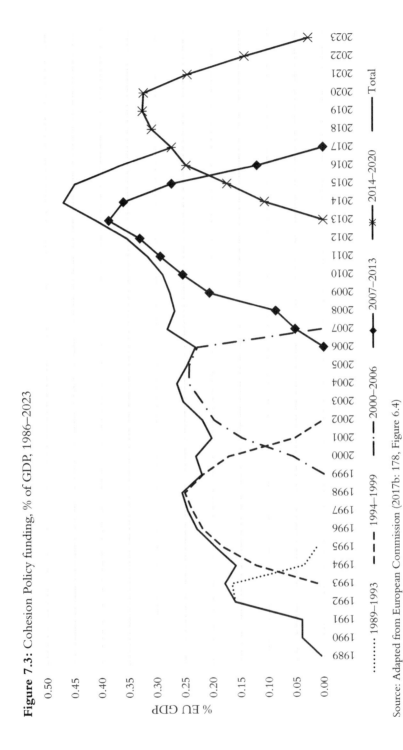

Figure 7.3: Cohesion Policy funding, % of GDP, 1986–2023

Source: Adapted from European Commission (2017b: 178, Figure 6.4)

Macroeconomic stabilization

As we saw in Chapter 4, European policymakers have long been aware of the need to balance the desire for further economic integration with the need to maintain sufficient political autonomy. In the early decades, this balance was secured by limiting the extent of integration, so that further constraints on member state autonomy would not be necessary. Over time, the common market has been extended to a broader selection of member states (both rich and poor), and has deepened in form to incorporate a greater economic and monetary union. As a result, the process of integration has undermined member states' capacity to manage their local labour markets.

In the 1970s, Europe was hit by a number of economic shocks – among them, two oil crises, the collapse of the Bretton Woods regime, and rampant inflation – and these shocks sparked an interest in the need for deeper forms of market integration, including economic and monetary union. It is in this context that European officials were first introduced to the necessity of growing the EU budget.

The Werner Report (1970) provided the first blueprint of an eventual economic and monetary union in Europe. Contemporary readers of the report will be surprised by its cautious and modest approach to the subject matter and its explicit recognition of the need to direct resources from the member states up to the European level. The report speaks of the desire to create an area where 'goods and services, people and capital will circulate freely and *without competitive distortions, without thereby giving rise to structural or regional disequilibrium*' (Werner et al, 1970: 9, emphasis added). To arrive at this desirable outcome, the report recognized that:

> Economic and monetary union means that the principal decisions of economic policy will be taken at Community level and therefore that the necessary powers will be transferred from the national plane to the Community plane. (Werner et al, 1970: 26)

The nuts and bolts of this transfer of power were considered in detail by the MacDougall Report (1977). This report considered the budgetary implications of greater economic and monetary union, in light of the experiences of other federal systems. Here, too, we find a clear warning that the size of the common European ('federal') budget needs to be expanded significantly to facilitate the sort of macroeconomic stabilization that a common monetary union requires. The MacDougall

Report concluded that a future 'Federation in Europe' should expect to adopt a public budget of *around 20–25% of aggregate GDP* (MacDougall et al, 1977: 13). As we have already seen, this figure is very close to what we find in the US today (see Table 7.4).

Recognizing that such a large European budget was not politically feasible, the report proposed a smaller, short-term 'federal' budget, in the order of 5–7% of GDP (MacDougall et al, 1977: 14). This is roughly the same size as US federal transfers to the states, as shown in Table 7.4. In addition, the MacDougall Report recommended (among other things) a community unemployment fund to cushion temporary setbacks; a budget equalization scheme for weak member states (of up to 65% of the average fiscal capacity); a system of cyclical grants to local and regional governments ('that would depend upon regional economic conditions'), and a 'conjunctural convergence facility' to counteract cyclical crises (MacDougall et al, 1977: 16). These are the sorts of supports a central government needs to provide its member states when the currency union undermines the policy autonomy of local authorities.

It was also made clear that the absence of a sufficient Community budget made monetary union impracticable:

> If only because the Community budget is so relatively very small there is no such mechanism in operation on any significant scale as between member countries, and this is an important reason why in present circumstances monetary union is impracticable. (MacDougall et al, 1977: 12)

Hence, from the very start of Europe's plan to create a common monetary union, there was an explicit recognition of the need to shift budgetary authority (and resources) upward in the system, from member states to the European level. But there was also an acute awareness that this would be politically contentious. In the end, this awareness has not had any effect, as the size of the EU's overall budget (as a share of member state GDP) is capped, and the source of EU revenues flow upward through the member states.

It should not be surprising to learn that there have been numerous studies on the effect of fiscal transfers, and how they might have helped the EU deal with its many economic crises.[16] The results from a recent study by Allard et al (2015: 235–6) are not uncommon or atypical. They found that the lack of sufficient fiscal transfers makes it much more difficult for eurozone member states to smooth out local economic shocks. For example, when GDP in the eurozone drops by

1%, household consumption in member states drops by as much as 0.6% (in other words, about 40% of the decline is still dampened by an ineffective fiscal union). But in other federal states, such as Germany, the US and Canada, the nature of fiscal transfers can dampen a much larger share (80%!) of the hit: under these systems, household consumption in the different regions/states only drops by 0.2%. Worse yet, the authors find that the capacity of eurozone member states to respond to local shocks has declined over time (with the creation of the euro): 58% of the local shocks remained unsmoothed in the 1979–99 period; increasing to 66% in the 1999–2010 period (Allard et al, 2015: 237).

After the Great Recession, there has been increased awareness that the design of the common monetary union is insufficiently 'genuine' (see, for example, Cottarelli, 2016). In December 2012, the European Commission (EC) and the president of the Council, in close collaboration with the presidents of the EC, the Eurogroup (eurozone finance ministers) and the ECB, both issued proposals for a roadmap towards greater fiscal integration (European Commission, 2012c; European Council, 2012a). This was followed up with a call from eurozone leaders, in June 2012, 'to develop a specific and time-bound roadmap toward a genuine Economic and Monetary Union', including greater fiscal integration (European Council, 2012b: 3). In the wake of one severe economic crisis, and before it was even aware of the coronavirus to come, the European Commission and eurozone leaders had rediscovered MacDougall.

At the time of writing, I find room for more optimism. COVID-19 has shaken the way that Europe approaches its fiscal account, and there is growing public recognition of the social costs tied to Europe's fiscal tightening in response to the Great Recession. Europe's first response to the COVID-19 crisis was aimed to prioritize the needs of its citizen. This is a hopeful sign.

The COVID-19 response

The coronavirus projected a new and different type of threat to the EU, with manifold effects and lessons. On the one hand, the pandemic has revealed many of the hidden costs to employers who rely heavily on workaways. Migrant labour is now more difficult and costly to secure, due to quarantine restrictions, testing regimes and a dwindling supply of foreign workers. Worse, Europe may be witnessing a rise in xenophobia, as host populations fear the virus can be spread by migrant workers. Consequently, it would seem that the immediate threat of workaway has been reduced with the spread of COVID-19.

On the other hand, the varied nature of the COVID-19 threat (how its economic impact varies across the EU) clearly demonstrates the importance of providing member states with the tools they need to support their local economies. Indeed, it is a relief to see EU authorities finally triggering the emergency 'escape clauses' that exist for just such occasions (even as one might wonder why this crisis qualifies as a trigger, when previous crises did not). Unfortunately, EU authorities have made it abundantly clear that these responses are meant to be temporary.

Although it is too early to evaluate the effects of the EU response, and many of the changes are explicitly temporary in nature, it can be useful to map the EU's initial response, in light of the challenges that motivate this book. The response, thus far, has come in three waves: a first response; the erection of safety nets; and a full-blown recovery plan.

Initial response

As early as April 2020, an initial EU response began to take form around three main components: relaxing EU rules and regulations; redirecting EU funds; and increased financing.[17] In this response, we can find an (implicit) recognition on the part of EU officials that its rules have limited member state capacity, and that member states require greater policy autonomy to respond to such crises.

From the perspective of this book, the most important development was the immediate suspension of some of the EU's binding rules and regulations. In particular, the European Commission (2020b) suspended the Stability and Growth Pact (SGP) and granted member states the fiscal breathing space they desperately needed. By recognizing that member states would be producing larger budget deficits than the SGP formally permits, the Commission needed to loosen the SGP's fiscal straitjacket. This decision followed the Commission's adoption of a Temporary Framework for State Aid (European Commission, 2020h), which promised to relax state aid rules, so that member states could provide financial support for companies and citizens who are struggling due to the COVID-19 economic fallout. As I have been arguing throughout the book, this is the sort of policy flexibility that member states require in response to unexpected shocks.

The second response was to redirect and free up EU funds for the battle against the virus. In total, the EU added €3.1 billion in COVID-related expenses to its 2020 budget. Among the most notable changes were efforts to: redirect €37 billion from the EU budget to support healthcare systems, small and medium-sized enterprises (SMEs) and labour markets via the Coronavirus Response Investment Initiative (European Commission, 2020i); to free up all unallocated funds in the 2014–20 structural funds 'national envelopes', so they can be repurposed to help with the crisis (up to €28 billion); and to extend the scope of the European Solidarity Fund to include public health crises – unlocking another €800 million for the hardest hit countries (see European Council, 2020c).

The third response came from the ECB (2020), in the form of its Pandemic Emergency Purchase Programme (PEPP). Compared to its response to the Great Recession, the ECB was mercifully quick this time around. The PEPP complements the asset purchasing programme that the ECB established in 2014 and allows for so-called 'quantitative easing'. In effect, the ECB buys bonds from banks and financial institutions, which frees up their funds, allowing them to lend more money to households. The original tranche of the PEPP was announced on 8 March (€750 billion), while an additional tranche of €600 billion was added on 4 June 2020. Hence, the PEPP now totals €1,350 billion, and is designed to last until the end of June 2021.

Safety nets

Alongside these three initial responses, the Eurogroup proposed a €540 billion emergency support package on 9 April 2020 (European Council, 2020d). This package included three safety nets: one for member states, one for businesses, and one for workers, as depicted in Figure 7.4.

The biggest of these nets was designed to catch eurozone states: a Pandemic Crisis Support (PCS) programme, totalling €240 billion in loans (European Parliament, 2020a). The PCS is based on the European Stability Mechanism's Enhanced Conditions Credit Line, which allows euro member states to access a line of credit up to 2% of their GDP, but with a total cap of €240 billion. The PCS extends this line of credit to include spending associated with member state responses to the COVID-19 pandemic (European Council, 2020e).

The second largest safety net was erected to catch European companies: a Pan-European Guarantee Fund (EGF). This fund was established by the EIB, and endorsed by the European Council on 23 April 2020. The programme invited all 27 EU member states to contribute to the planned €25 billion EGF – each member state was to contribute a share of the €25 billion, equal to their share of EIB capital.[18] This fund is mobilized to secure €200 billion of funding, 65% of which will go to SMEs in Europe (EIB, 2020c).

Figure 7.4: Three COVID-19 safety nets, totalling €540 billion

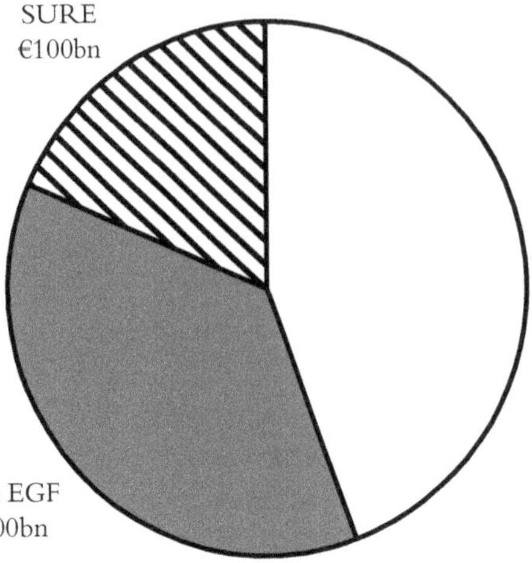

Source: Adapted from European Council (2020c)

The third safety net is the most relevant for European workers. As we can see in Figure 7.4, it is also the smallest of the three safety nets. This net falls under the title of SURE: Support to mitigate Unemployment Risks in an Emergency, and is characterized by three unique components: it is accessible to all member states (not just eurozone states); it comes without any conditions attached; and it is designed to include the 'self-employed'. SURE is a €100 billion instrument, based on guarantees provided by member states and the EU budget. In short, SURE provides access to loans on relatively favourable terms to countries affected by the pandemic so that they can finance temporary unemployment support schemes to keep people at work.

The Commission itself describes the SURE as a second line of defence, 'supporting short-time work schemes and similar measures, to help Member States protect jobs and thus employees and self-employed against the risk of unemployment and loss of income' (European Commission, 2020j: 2). In effect, member states are allowed to access loans when their public expenditures increase as a result of rising unemployment.[19] By the end of October, €87.7 billion (of €100 billion) had been distributed to 17 member states – the largest recipient state was Italy, as shown in Table 7.8. Most importantly, it is important to underscore that SURE is *not* designed to be a permanent tool, a stabilization tool, or even an insurance mechanism: it is an explicitly temporary response.

Table 7.8: SURE allocations (2020)

Member state	€ million
Italy	27,400
Spain	21,300
Poland	11,200
Belgium	7,800
Portugal	5,900
Romania	4,100
Greece	2,700
Czech Republic	2,000
Slovenia	1,100
Croatia	1,000
Slovakia	631
Lithuania	602
Bulgaria	511
Hungary	504
Cyprus	479
Malta	244
Latvia	193
Total	**€ 87,664**

Note: Allocations as of September and October, 2020.

Source: Adapted from European Council (2020e)

The recovery plan

It did not take long before the EU again realized that more money would be needed. In the middle of July 2020, after a historic five-day meeting of the European Council in Brussels, a €1.8 trillion recovery plan was launched (European Council, 2020f). The agreement contained two component parts, the largest of which was a €1,100 billion commitment to the overall (long-term) budget. The second, more controversial, element was to create a recovery fund, worth €750 billion.

Despite urgent need, the details and fate of this recovery plan have still not been settled at the time of writing (14 December 2020). The plan has been delayed by discussions as to whether or not 'rule of law' conditions should be imposed on member states. In November 2020, member states and Parliament managed to strike a deal (European

Commission, 2020k), which has passed through the Council (10–11 December) and will likely pass through Parliament by the end of the year. For this reason, it is somewhat premature to discuss the 'recovery plan' response. For us, the relevance of this plan concerns the debate that surrounds it: about the perceived limits to government budgeting, financing and regulations.

The first component – increasing the budget – is fairly straightforward. As we have already seen, the Multiannual Financial Framework (MFF) is the standard long-term (seven-year) budget for the EU. To prepare for the anticipated response, the EU has produced a new MFF, totalling €1.1 trillion. This is roughly the same size of the budget being proposed before the pandemic hit,[20] and the money spent will be stretched out over seven years.[21]

The second component of the July meeting was more interesting (and more controversial). This was the introduction of an extraordinary €750 billion recovery fund, the so-called 'Next Generation EU' (NGEU) fund. The reason for controversy is that the NGEU represents the first time that the EU has been willing to run a common deficit in response to an economic shock. EU member states have promised to lift the resource ceiling so that the European Commission will be authorized to borrow funds from capital markets, on behalf of the EU (up to €750 billion, in 2018 prices). It is important to underscore that this is seen as a temporary ('one-off') measure: it will not be repeated. Most significantly, member state parliaments still need to agree to lift the EU's so-called 'own resources ceiling', allowing it to borrow the hundreds of billions of euros it needs to raise for the recovery fund.

The hope is to raise commonly issued debt over six years, with bonds issued at maturities extending to 2058. When complete, the NGEU will raise funds that constitute about 4.7% of EU annual GDP (but spread out over several years).[22] The funds raised will be distributed in two main forms: €390 billion will be distributed as grants; the rest (€350 billion) will come in the form of loans – and the money issued will cover seven main programmes, as outlined in Table 7.9.

It is both remarkable and hopeful that the EU is finally discussing ways to increase its central budget in response to a serious crisis, and is willing to relax its rules to facilitate the required borrowing. Just as significantly, member states have been given more freedom to respond, as needed, to the economic shocks being produced by the pandemic. But this hope promises to be temporary, and the EU will continue to keep a strong hand on the tiller – monitoring and approving the way member states will be allowed to employ these funds.

Table 7.9: NGEU's seven main programmes

Programme	€ billion
Recovery and Resilience Facility	672.5
ReactEU	47.5
Just Transition Fund	10.0
Rural Development	7.5
InvestEU	5.6
Horizon Europe	5.0
RescEU	1.9
Total	**750**

Source: Adapted from European Council (2020g)

Europe's COVID-19 response has provided some grounds for optimism. The EU has suspended some of its most stringent fiscal rules, provided the necessary scope for larger fiscal recovery packages, and allowed new loans to member states, funded by common debt. It is far too early to see whether this hope will be sustained, as the EU has promised to return to its former, more austere, path. What is clear is that these reforms provide Europe with some needed breathing space, and a welcome opportunity to rethink its approach to Community building.

Conclusion

We know that Europe's common currency area is creating severe hardships in local labour markets, and that national policy authorities lack the tools to address them adequately. We also know that European policymakers could fill that policy void by developing a common EU budget that could provide risk sharing and stabilization support (not to mention redistribution). The costs of not doing this are clearly evident, when we consider the effects of fiscal transfers in other federal systems.

Over the years, the European Community/Union has secured the legal authority to develop widespread worker protections, but it has not had the political will (or requisite consensus) to bring these about. The likelihood of reaching consensus seems to have diminished with each outward expansion of member states. As a consequence, social policy has been, and remains, firmly in the hands of member states, but the tools that these states have at their disposal have been dwindling in both number and effectiveness (as described in Chapter 6). Worse, the EU now coaxes member states into a regulatory race to the bottom, with hopes of creating a more flexible workforce – one that can respond quickly to each market downturn.

Even if there is little hope to be found on Europe's regulatory horizon, there is now broad awareness of the need to expand Europe's central budget and let it play a larger role in both redistribution and macroeconomic smoothing. This could provide some relief to local labour markets, but there remains significant political resistance on both fronts.

The simple fact is that the EU budget needs to grow: it must expand its expenditures on centrally provided public services (not only unemployment insurance benefits, but also, for example, infrastructure supports). In this way, the EU budget could facilitate increased risk sharing, allowing local markets better protection. This risk sharing should occur on both the revenue side (as countries hit by negative shocks would automatically contribute less) and on the spending side – as countries hit by negative shocks could still benefit from centrally provided public services (such as infrastructure projects), and use the outlays in a countercyclical fashion.

I believe there is widespread recognition of this fact. The difficulty in achieving a larger and more effective EU budget lies in the political terrain. Member states have different views of the role to be played by political authority and markets, and many Europeans are loath to extend greater budgetary authority and responsibility to EU officials. Although I believe it is important to respect these (varying) national interests and preferences, this is not the place to engage these potential challenges – I can only acknowledge the important role they play in limiting the EU's course of action. My focus is restricted to showing how Europe's chosen path to market integration has limited the scope for policy autonomy, and this path requires a large toll in human costs.

Put simply, the EU budget is too small to do what needs to be done, and it is too dependent on member state financing to employ fiscal transfers effectively. Member state monetary policy has been eviscerated, member state fiscal policy has been reduced to a number of scorecards, and the results are procyclical and ineffective member state budgets. In other aggregated (federal) political entities, the central government's budget plays an essential role in helping its member states overcome these limitations to their autonomy. The EU does not, and cannot, do this.

As a consequence, the EU is unable to fill the void created by the hollowing out of its member state economic policies. When labour markets can no longer be managed at the member state level, and the EU budget is unable to fill the gap (by providing additional support), the only adjustment mechanism left to deal with local economic downturns is the hope and promise of increased factor mobility. This is the subject of Chapter 8.

8

Money and People on the Move

Given the degree of local labour market variation, as seen in Chapter 5, and the absence of other available adjustment tools (whether at the national or the EU level, as seen in Chapters 6 and 7), member states have remarkably little capacity to influence their local labour markets. As a result, much of the burden of economic adjustment has been pushed down to lower levels of the economy. In particular, European policymakers hope that an integrated market can clear itself, without local political interference, and that mobile workers and capital can fill the void created by the absence of other instruments for economic management.

European labour markets are still exposed to any number of different economic shocks and crises. Over the past decade, local labour markets have needed to respond to a global financial crisis (2008–10), a dramatic fall in the price of oil (2014), a refugee crisis (2015) and the COVID-19 pandemic (2020–21). In the face of such crises, how can a member state buoy its labour market when its monetary policy is set in Frankfurt, its regulatory and fiscal policies are largely set in Brussels, and there is little fiscal capacity at the EU level? What can a poor state do?

Let's imagine that the poor state is Greece, and that it is hit harder by a shock than any other member state. (This is not purely a hypothetical example.) Because Greece is a part of the eurozone, it cannot devalue its currency or impose capital controls (unless granted permission by EU officials). Its fiscal hands have been tied (both by the troika, but also by more general EU restrictions, as described in Chapter 6), and the Greek economy is no longer able to compete with its European brethren.

Under these circumstances, the path to Greece's recovery will be strewn with the unemployed. In order for Greece to become competitive again (vis-à-vis other eurozone members), its prices/wages need to fall precipitously. Because wages are notoriously sticky, Greece will need to suffer significant unemployment before Greek wages will begin to move downwards. When the Greek unemployment level rises high enough, and lasts long enough, two concurrent developments will slowly deliver Greece's subsequent recovery: falling wages and increased workaways. As wages fall (along with the hope of finding a job in the local labour market), unemployed Greeks will be forced to look elsewhere in Europe for work. Those who remain in Greece will need to reduce their wage demands if they hope to stay employed. In effect, Greece has become a nation of Amelies, as described in Chapter 2.

Before the COVID-19 pandemic, this was Europe's solution to every economic crisis. A market-based response relies heavily on workaways: both to reduce the excess labour created by the crisis/ recession, but also to discipline the wage claims of the workers who remain. For those who hope to stay near family and friends, the threat of workaway will force them to concede to further wage reductions. For those who might be more willing to emigrate (the young), or are more desperate (the poor), workaway offers the best possible alternative, but it is a very costly one for them and their families. Either way, for this economic adjustment to take place, Europe must devalue the needs of Greek workers, and force them to behave like any other commodity on the market – they need to chase down the best prices, regardless of where they live. If Greek labour is not sufficiently mobile, or if Greek wages are not sufficiently flexible, then the crisis will be prolonged.

Europe's second adjustment mechanism relies on the investment acumen of European capitalists. Once unemployment takes hold, and Greek workers begin to leave, we can expect wages to fall (and fall significantly). These falling wages should make the Greek labour market more attractive to outside investors, who will be enticed to move production to Greece and take advantage of the resulting wage savings. From this view of the market, falling wages attract a substantial inflow of private capital and this investment capital is key to a region's subsequent economic recovery.

In this example, we can clearly see the important roles that factor mobility – both labour and capital – play in the design of Europe's integrated market. This chapter examines the scope of European labour and capital mobility in general, and in response to the Great Recession of 2008 – what Paul Krugman (2012: 444) referred to as 'the mother of all asymmetric shocks'. The pattern of mobility we uncover is somewhat different than expected, given the market-based example sketched before. On the one hand, it is clear that workers are being forced to find work in foreign labour markets, but the level of mobility is entirely insufficient to facilitate the necessary adjustments (prolonging them, unnecessarily). On the other hand, capital mobility in Europe has worked to exacerbate more than facilitate any necessary adjustments. In looking at how European labour and capital flows responded to the Great Recession, we can see how ineffective factor flows have been in taking up the policy slack we have uncovered in the preceding chapters.

Labour mobility

We can begin by looking at general patterns in Europe. This is not as easy as it sounds, as the type of labour mobility in Europe is as varied as its regional/national conditions. It is also important to recognize that there can be many reasons for the migration trends we observe – they are not all motivated by labour market conditions. Still, there are good reasons to suspect that employment motives are important, given the fact that most of the migrants tend to be in prime working age, and their level of labour market integration is comparable to the host populations. We can also avoid counting other types of migrants (for example students and pensioners) by focusing on the working-age population (20–64) in the migration statistics.

My ambition is to measure the degree to which migrants are taking advantage of a common European market, to see whether the level and type of migration is changing over time, and to find out whether workaway has become a more common/likely means for member states to adjust to local economic challenges. This is what we might expect, given the erosion of other (state-level) tools for economic adjustment. In examining these trends, we might interpret the migration flows as a sort of signalling device for dysfunctional states in Europe (Moses, 2017b), as workers are fleeing the failed policies of their home states and, in effect, voting with their feet.

The European Commission focuses on three main forms of labour mobility: cross-border mobility; posted workers; and long-term mobility (see Table 8.1). To get an idea of their relative size and importance, we can begin by noting that there were nearly 305 million people who were of working age in the EU28 (in 2018), 220 million of which were actually employed (European Commission, 2020d: 18).

Cross-border movers

The smallest group of migrant workers are those in the cross-border category: it is estimated that about 1.5 million European workers live in one country, yet work in another (in 2018).[1]

Table 8.1: European workers adrift, 2018

	Number	% of total
Total working-age population	304.6 million	
Total employed	220.1 million	72%
Cross-border workers	1.5 million	0.5%
Estimated posted workers	1.9 million	0.6%
Long-term EU28 (Eurostat)	12.9 million	4.2%

Source: Adapted from European Commission (2020d: 18–19)

In thinking about cross-border workers, the first image that might come to mind are those Europeans who live along border regions, for example a worker who lives in Malmö (southern Sweden), but who travels across the Öresund Bridge to work in Copenhagen (Denmark), or a worker who lives in the Netherlands but works in Germany (or vice versa). This would be the kind of 'commuting zone' migration we saw in Chapter 5, and we might expect it to be the least onerous for workers. After all, such workers could commute across a national border, earn a pay cheque and return home for dinner.

Should this be the case, it is unfortunate that cross-border mobility is the smallest class of migrants in Europe, constituting just 0.5% of the total number of employed Europeans. But when we look closer at the nature of these cross-border movers, we find it to be much broader than daily commuters. Figure 8.1 ranks cross-border out-migrants as a share of their home employment population (age 20–64) in 2018. This allows us to see which states are exporting the most workers (relative to their home employment population). It then breaks up this cross-border group of workers by the states in which they found jobs. In this way, we can see where the largest share of these foreign jobs was located, in each case.

In Figure 8.1 we can clearly see how Slovaks are most reliant on foreign employment (while still living at home). The equivalent of almost 5% of the employed population in Slovakia worked in another country, but lived at home in 2018. The largest share of these jobs was in neighbouring states, such as Austria and Czechia. Still, Germany (which is not a neighbouring country) employed more than three times the number of Czech workers than neighbouring Hungary (26,000 vs 8,000). Likewise, there were 12,500 Romanian workers living at home, yet working in the UK. It is doubtful these workers were commuting back and forth daily. Figure 8.1 provides an interesting mix of more

Figure 8.1: Cross-border workers in the EU, 2018

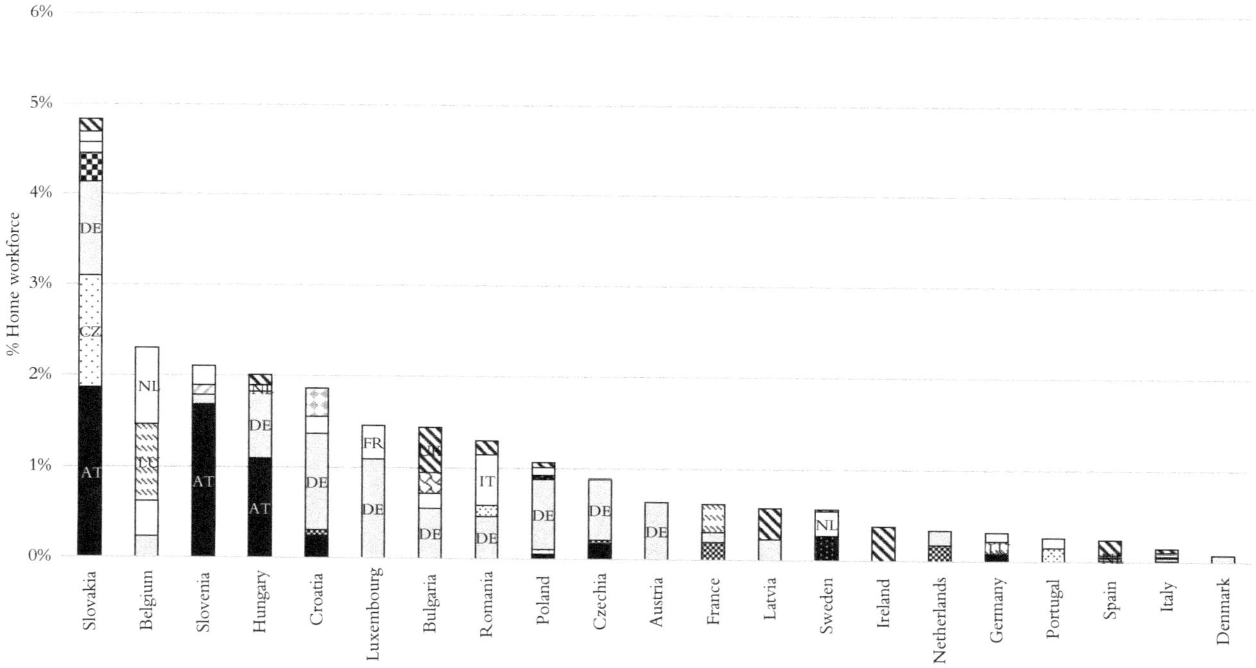

Notes: Cross-border data come from EU LFS 2018 data on EU citizens who reside in one EU country and work in another. Home employment is employment (age 20–64), figures from Eurostat (lfsi_emp_a).

Source: Adapted from European Commission (2020d: 143–4, Table 27) and Eurostat (lfsi_emp_a).

and less affluent states (Belgium and Luxembourg are nestled between Slovakia and Bulgaria) sending their workers abroad, while Germany was by far the biggest magnet state: about 32% of all Europe's cross-border workers went to Germany in 2018.

Posted workers

The next largest group of European migrant workers, but only marginally so, are so-called 'posted workers'. As we saw in Table 8.1, these workers are estimated to total 1.9 million in 2018, less than 1% of Europe's total working population. Posted workers are workers who employers use to bypass existing regulations and standards at the actual place of employment. In particular, a posted worker is one who is 'regularly employed'[2] in one member state but sent to another member state by the same employer to work there for a limited period of time. These workers follow regulations from their point of origin, as described in Box 8.1. We saw some of the political fallout from posted

---

Box 8.1: Point-of-origin regulations

Most goods and services are regulated at the point of consumption. European officials have decided to regulate its posted workers at the point of origin.

If you think about it, this is a rather astonishing way of regulating a market. I am not aware of another market where the price of the good/service, or the regulations that pertain to it, are set at the point of origin, not the point of consumption. After all, if a Belgian consumer buys a car made in India, they expect that car to meet the regulatory requirements at the point of use (for example Belgian safety regulations) and be bought at Belgian prices – not Indian regulations and prices (which are presumably lower). For most of us, this is common sense, as we cannot be expected to familiarize ourselves with the nature of regulations at each and every point of origin.

The same expectations apply to the purchase of financial goods: even though a foreign (say, Chinese) bank may be conducting business in Germany, German consumers of financial products expect that German financial regulations (rather than Chinese) apply to their purchases.

But workers posted from Romania and sent to Sweden will abide by Romanian regulations and pay levels – not Swedish.

---

workers in the handful of European Court of Justice cases described in Chapter 6.

As posted workers constitute less than 1% of the total working-age population in the EU, it may seem odd that they receive so much critical attention. There are perhaps two reasons for this. First, these workers pose the biggest threat to undermining the higher pay and regulatory standards in Northern Europe, as they compete directly with workers in those markets, but do so backed by their home (not the local) standards. Second, the number of posted workers is growing *much faster* than other types of migrant workers. While the total growth of long-term EU movers (inflows) between 2012 and 2017 was just 19%, the increase in posted workers over the same time was 84% (see De Wispelaere and Pacolet, 2018: 21, Table 4)![3]

We can use these posting permits (so-called 'Portable Document A1', or 'PD-A1') to get an idea of which countries tend to send more posted workers, but it is important to remember that we are comparing the number of permits, not the number of workers.[4] Figure 8.2 illustrates the net issuance of permits in 2018, as a share of home employment (ages 20–64). In other words, this figure lists the number of PDs-A1 issued (Article 12 type) minus the number received. Hence, a positive balance depicts net senders of posted workers (13 states), while the bottom 15 states (negative balance) were net recipients of posted workers. With the exception of Luxembourg, we find the same group of states haemorrhaging their workforce as we did in Figure 8.1.

It is perhaps easiest to think of these movements in bilateral terms, but then we need to return to nominal (not % share) figures (where large states will dominate). In 2018, most postings were from Poland to Germany (120,540 PDs-A1). Indeed over 50% of Poland's total PDs-A1 went to Germany alone. Other significant flows (more than 40,000) were from Germany to Austria, Germany to France, Germany to the Netherlands, and from Slovenia to Germany (De Wispelaere et al, 2019: 23).

Long-term movers

The largest group of migrant workers, by far, are Europe's long-term migrants. There are different ways of measuring the size of the overall migrant stock, and the measures can vary slightly. For example, when we use the EU Labour Force Survey (EU LFS) estimate there are 11.7 million in this group, but the Eurostat estimate (used in Table 8.1) is 12.9 million. When a person of working age

Figure 8.2: Net postings, % employed, 2018

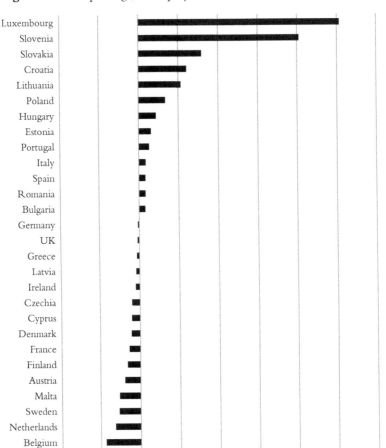

Notes: Net balance between the number of PDs-A1 issued and received according to Article 12 of the Basic Regulation. (Net balance = issued – received.) The original data source is 'Administrative data PD A1 Questionnaire 2019'. Home employment is employment (age 20–64), figures from Eurostat (lfsi_emp_a).

Source: Adapted from Eurostat (lfsi_emp-a) and De Wispelaere et al (2019: 25, Figure 4)

(20–64 years) moves to another country (other than their citizenship) and stays for at least a year, then that person is counted among the long-term movers. This is by far the largest group of mobile workers in Europe, and it has been growing slowly, but steadily over the years (albeit not as quickly as the number of posted workers). Figure 8.3 shows the total number of Europeans (EU28, 20- to 64-year-olds) who either were employed in, or commuting to, a foreign country.

Figure 8.3: Number of Europeans working abroad, 2002–2018

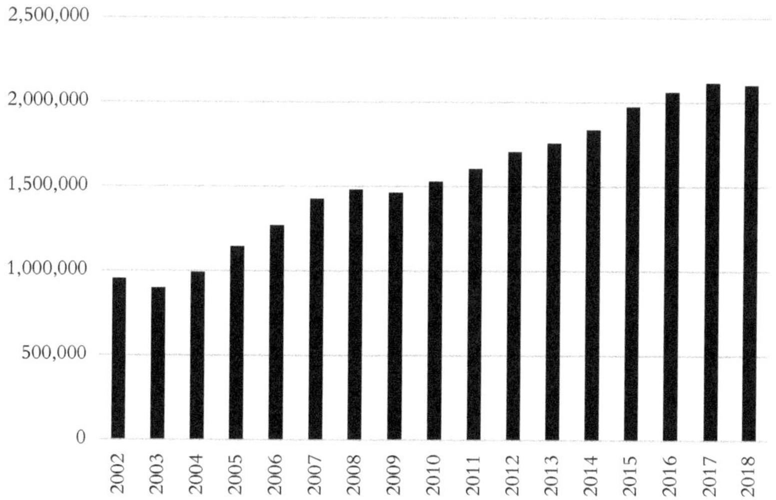

Note: Employment and commuting in a foreign country; EU28; 20- to 64-year-olds.

Source: Adapted from Eurostat (lfst-r-lfe2ecomm)

Although there was a slight decline in 2008–09 (counter to expectations), long-term migrants have been growing steadily ever since, except in 2018, when we again see a minor downturn.

I should point out that when we look closer at the overall growth in Europe's migration figures, we find some surprising trends. For example, when we measure foreign workers as the share of the working-age population living in a European country, but holding citizenship in a different country, it is possible to distinguish between EU28 migrants and non-EU28 migrants (Eurostat, migr_pop1ctz). Using this indicator, we find the same gentle increase in the number of European migrant workers, but see that the increase is mostly driven by *the non-EU28 share* (both EFTA and third-country workers).[5] In 2019, for example, over 56% of the migrant population was from non-EU 28 countries. In short, most of the migrant workers in the EU28 member states were from non-EU28 states!

To get an idea of where these migrants are going, we can look at the net flows of the long-term migrant workers in 2017,[6] as a share of the domestic workforce (employed, age 20–64, in home country). Figure 8.4 shows six countries (on the left-hand side) with net negative mobility, which means that more people have left the country than entered it in 2017. These countries – Lithuania (LT), Croatia (HR), Latvia (LV), Romania (RO), Bulgaria (BG) and Poland (PL) – are

Figure 8.4: Net migration, share of employment, 2018

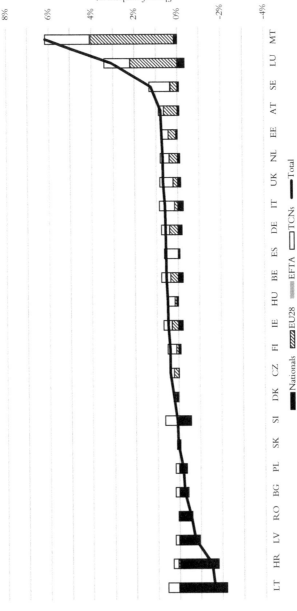

Notes: Net mobility flows by country of residence, by broad groups of citizenship, share of home employment. Citizenship groups include nationals, citizens of the EU28 member states, European Free Trade Area (EFTA) and so-called 'third-country nationals' (TCNs) – those who are neither EU28 or EFTA citizens. Note, data were missing on Greece, France, Cyprus and Portugal. Employment data is total employment, 20- to 64-year-olds, Eurostat (lfsi_emp_a). Underlying data is from Eurostat (migr_emi1ctz) and (migr_imm1ctz).

Source: Adapted from European Commission (2020d: 125, Table A13) and Eurostat (lfsi_emp-a).

unable to sustain their national labour markets, as more people are leaving them than entering. Lithuania, for example, has a negative net mobility level that is equivalent to 1.7% of its home labour market. At the other end of the figure, countries such as Luxembourg (LU) and Malta (MT) rely heavily on foreigners to get the job done.

Figure 8.4 also tells us what kinds of citizens were coming and going. Here, we can see that it is mostly nationals leaving the countries on the left-hand side of the figure, even as a significant number of immigrants from third-country nations are entering (for example in Lithuania, Croatia and Latvia). This makes me wonder what kinds of jobs are found in these countries – jobs that attract workers from outside the EU, but which are apparently unsuitable for domestic workers. Slovenia (SI) also has a significant outflow of nationals, even if its net migration balance is slightly positive, because it takes in so many 'third-country' migrant workers.[7] As these figures are framed in terms of the size of the domestic labour force, they hide some of the larger flows. For example, Romania (RO) experienced the largest exodus of domestic workers in 2017 (49,380), even if this was not a particularly large share of the country's working population. Indeed, of the stocks of long-term mobile workers, over half of them (or 6.1 million people in 2018) come from just four states: Romania, Poland, Italy and Portugal (European Commission, 2020d: 21).

Likewise, Germany (DE) doesn't stand out in this figure, but it was the largest recipient of migrant workers, with 306,450 people coming to Germany in 2017, while 75,428 nationals left Germany for employment elsewhere. Finally, Malta (MT) looks like a great magnet for foreign workers (mostly from the EU28), but because it is such a small country, it masks the fact that there were, in fact, only 8,240 workers coming to Malta from the EU28.

Finally, we might wonder what kinds of workers are taking advantage of this large European marketplace; in other words, which professions are the most mobile? To answer this question, we can access the European Commission's (2020e) 'EU Single Market: Regulated Professionals Database' for professionals moving abroad. Here, it is possible to download aggregate figures for the types of workers who have applied to (permanently) transfer their professional credentials or certificates to another European country, so-called 'establishment' movers (European Commission, 2020f).

This database collects records for (certified) professionals who applied for official recognition when moving to a different country within Europe (EU member states, plus Switzerland, Iceland, Liechtenstein and Norway). For example, if you are a registered doctor in Spain and you want to move to France, you have to reregister with the French authorities. Of course, not every profession has a recognition regime, but you would be surprised at how many professions are listed in this database: since 1997, people from 404 different occupations have asked to transfer their credentials!

When we look at the entire period covered in the database, from 1997 to 2019, we find that a total of 827,513 asked that their professional qualifications be recognized in another European state. Among these, the 50 most mobile professions are listed in Figure 8.5. Almost 19% of the total registered migrants over this period were 'doctors of medicine' (n =154,863), followed by nurses (n = 151,178) and secondary school teachers (n = 111,106).

Figure 8.5: Fifty most mobile professions in Europe, 1997–2019

Source: Adapted from European Commission (2020e)

The most mobile professions in this list tend to include high-skilled professionals (architects, lawyers and secondary school teachers), but especially those working in the health sector: doctors, nurses, dentists and so on. Among the top 100, my favourite movers were in the category of 'shotfirers', 546 of whom moved during this period (ranked 88th). A shotfirer is someone employed to detonate an explosive.

Figure 8.5 reveals the promise of free migration in Europe. Because these figures are aggregated over a longer period of time and conceal the pattern of migration (for example home/host states), it is impossible to say much about their motivations for moving. But the dominance of higher skilled professionals suggests that it is unlikely these migrants are being forced to workaway because of dysfunctional labour markets at home. Over a longer arc of European history (1997–2019), then, we can see many professionals have been able to enjoy the freedom of mobility, and the EU's anti-discrimination legislation provides these workers with important protections (see Chapter 7).

This sort of freedom of mobility is less evident in the other indicators surveyed in this section. In these figures, where we can examine the pattern of flows and the types of migrants, workaways appear to be more prominent. Generally, we can see that the number of migrant workers is slowly increasing over time and most of this increase is associated with non-EU28 migrants. Long-term migrants clearly constitute the largest group, although the number of posted workers is increasing very rapidly. The direction of these migrant flows, across all three types of migrant groups, seem to indicate that market motives are propelling the migrants: of the EU member states, it is the poorer states in Eastern Europe that are unable to sustain a viable labour market at home for their workers, and it is the wealthier and more developed member states that are attracting these workers. When we look to the types of migrants who are moving, over recent decades, a more nuanced picture develops – but this picture is confined to those professions that require some sort of certification or official recognition.

Post-crisis mobility

In this section we turn to see how labour markets responded to the Great Recession, and whether workers are sufficiently commodified to move in response to the failures of local labour markets (increased local unemployment).

There have been a number of sophisticated empirical studies on the effects of the crisis on European labour mobility.[8] Some of these examine the effects using national-level data, while others focus on the regional (subnational) levels.[9] While there are minor differences in approaches, there is a broad and clear consensus that labour mobility has increased slightly in response to the Great Recession, and that workers in Europe (especially low-skilled workers and those from new member states in Eastern Europe) are increasingly responsive to labour shortages (see, for example, Kahanec and Guzi, 2017; Kahanec et al, 2016).

It is not necessary to dive into the details of these empirical studies. A quick comparison of the migration flows before and during the crisis confirm the more general impressions: migration flows are closely related to economic developments and/or desperation. Consider for example, Figure 8.6, which summarizes the nature of member state migration changes before (top panel) and during (bottom panel) the Great Recession. These figures show the change in the working-age population abroad, either in an EU28 state, or not.

Before the crisis (Figure 8.6, top panel), the more developed economies in Northern Europe (BE, LU, SE, UK, DK, FI) were clearly able to attract immigrant workers, and these countries continued to host attractive labour markets during the Great Recession. Labour markets in Ireland and Spain fared less well: they were extremely attractive destinations before the crisis but shrivelled up in the Great Recession (bottom panel) – indeed, both countries began to lose workers during this period. At the same time, we can see that a number of poor states (Croatia, Estonia, Latvia) were exporting their workers, even in the pre-crisis period.

When the crisis hit, there is a clear and obvious pattern to the data: almost all the countries on the right-hand side of the bottom panel (Hungary, Greece, Bulgaria, Romania, Poland, Spain, Slovakia, Croatia, Lithuania, Estonia and Latvia) top the list of the EU's poorest countries, in terms of GDP/capita, as shown in Figure 5.1. The one outlier on the right-hand side of the bottom panel is the Netherlands, which experienced an inexplicable decline in its foreign labour force during the Great Recession.

The kinds of workers who are moving during the Great Recession are also different. In contrast to the general tendency for service professionals to top the lists of mobile workers over the past couple of decades (as seen in Figure 8.5), the nature of the mobile labour force has changed in response to the Great Recession. Figure 8.7 takes data that the European Commission (2020f) collects on *temporary* mobility for the regulated professions in its Regulated Professions Database. This is a different database than the 'establishment' database used in Figure 8.5 (which lists permanent transfers). Figure 8.7 lists the number of declarations received (and, where applicable, decisions taken) for

Figure 8.6: Pre/post mobility patterns

Panel A: 2005–2008

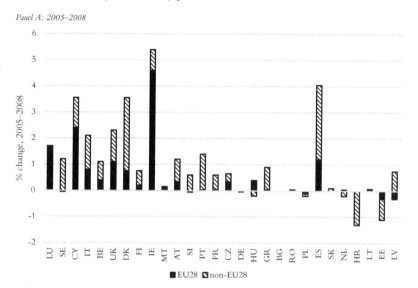

Panel B: 2008–2013

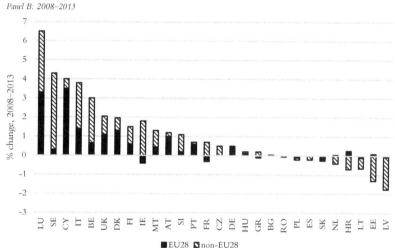

Notes: Change in the share of the working-age population born abroad, pre-crisis (top panel) and during the crisis (bottom panel). These figures are then divided between those born in the EU28 and those who were not. The figures for Bulgaria, Germany and Ireland are for 2006 instead of 2005. For Germany, the value is for all foreigners and no further breakdown was available. Countries are ranked according to changes from 2008 to 2013. The underlying data source is a special extraction from the EU LFS.

Source: Adapted from Arpaia et al (2016: 6)

Figure 8.7: Twenty-five most mobile professions, temporary, 2008–09

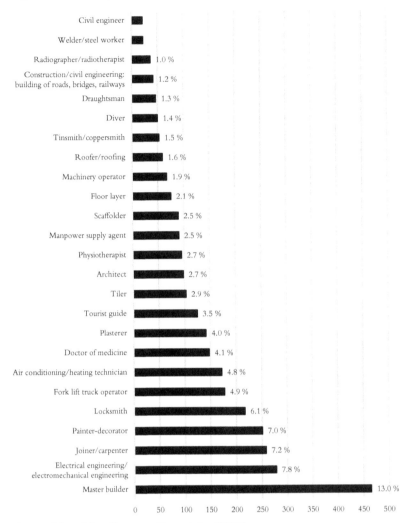

Source: Adapted from European Commission (2020f)

temporary provision of services within EU member states, European Economic Area countries and Switzerland.

In other words, Figure 8.7 counts only temporary movers, for both 2008 and 2009, and ranks them in terms of their frequency. The most mobile professions are listed at the bottom of the figure: with 'master builder' being the most common type of worker to move temporarily during the crisis. Compared to the general tendency for professionals to move permanently (in Figure 8.5), the dominant movers in Figure 8.7 were from the building trades: carpenters, locksmiths, plasterers, tilers, scaffolders and so on.

This seems to suggest that local authorities in many European states lacked the capacity to maintain or manage their local labour markets in the face of the Great Recession; they were forced to send their workers out into Europe, in a desperate search for employment elsewhere. In choosing this means to 'fix' local labour markets, the EU imposes a huge human cost on its population, and this burden is heavier in some trades and countries than in others. To be clear (if somewhat blunt): the left-hand side of Figure 8.4 provides a list of countries that cannot provide for their workers – Lithuania, Croatia, Latvia, Romania, Bulgaria, Poland and Slovakia. During the Great Recession, these countries were joined by a few more (Greece and Spain).

Whereas professionals were more likely to take advantage of Europe's common labour market when times are good, they seem to be well-enough positioned to ride out the Great Recession in their home markets. It would appear that other workers, especially in the building trades, are more likely to face the threat of workaway when an economic crisis hits. This is the story told in Figure 8.7 (see also European Commission, 2020d: 68).[10]

In conclusion, there was not any sort of radical jump in European migration levels in response to the Great Recession. This was already evident in Figure 8.3. But it seems clear that the number of workaways is increasing over time, and especially in response to economic crises. From the perspective of European decisionmakers, it would seem this is a proud accomplishment:

> The movement of workers from one EU country to another has become an increasingly important adjustment mechanism for the European economy, particularly since the introduction of the euro ... workers have become more likely to move to another EU country in response to economic shocks affecting only some countries. Movements in response to shocks have increased significantly since the introduction of the euro ... [and] real wages also became more responsive to asymmetric shocks during the same period. (European Commission, 2015: 19)

While I can agree about the trend towards increased mobility/ workaway, I cannot agree that this is a sign of progress. Instead, I see a disciplining and recommodification of European labour. During periods of economic crisis, increased labour mobility looks to me like the desperate choice of workers who have been abandoned by their national policymakers.

Capital markets

In stark contrast to the pains associated with long-distance labour mobility, it is relatively easy and costless for money to move quickly around Europe. Indeed, this was one of the primary motives for creating a common currency area – to make it easier and cheaper to move money from one member state to another, without incurring any exchange rate risk – prices are now directly comparable in a common currency, making it easier to find bargain purchases and investments on the other side of the EU.

Such is the promise of a unified capital market in Europe. The costs are also evident, if often downplayed. First and foremost, financial markets are notoriously unstable, and it is risky to expose European polities to this volatility. National policymakers have long recognized that risk and they once tried to contain it by controlling cross-border capital flows and regulating national capital markets. But contemporary policymakers have downplayed the risks and exaggerate the promised efficiency gains from greater mobility.

Increased capital mobility is also a problem to the extent that it limits political autonomy. As described in Chapter 6, increased capital mobility undermines member states' capacity to maintain autonomous regulatory, fiscal and monetary policies. This is not news, of course: these are the very reasons that international capital mobility was limited for most of the postwar period, as part of the Bretton Woods arrangement.

As with the first part of this chapter, we can begin with a general survey of capital flows in Europe and its component elements. We will then turn to the role that capital flows played in the Great Recession.

Markets for money

When looking at the nature of capital markets in Europe, it is important to recognize its many varied components. Just like the demand for plumbers might differ from the demand for school teachers, different types of capital respond to varying market conditions. To understand these different markets, we can think of how they affect a member state economy. To do this, we look at a country's current account balance, which can be defined in terms of a simple accounting identity (in which we neglect the balance of the capital account as well as errors and omissions):

$$current\ account\ balance\ +\ private\ capital\ inflows\ +\ official\ capital\ inflows\ =\ 0$$

At this level of aggregation, we can see how capital flows (both private and official) can be used to correct for a country's current account imbalance. But this level of aggregation obscures the subtle variations that exist within both private and official types of capital movements.

Consider first, the official (or public) flows. In Europe, the most important sources of public capital flows are associated with the intra-Eurosystem liabilities programme (TARGET2) as well as loans and transfers from the European Financial Stability Facility (EFSF); the European Financial Stabilization Mechanism (EFSM); the European Stability Mechanism (ESM); international support programmes (say, from the IMF); and the Securities Markets Programme (where the ECB purchases government securities from residents).[11] As the TARGET2 programme is perhaps the least well known of these, but most relevant for our purposes, it is described briefly in Box 8.2.

We don't usually pay much attention to these official capital flows, because the market is supposed to clear itself. The public focus tends towards private capital flows. To facilitate these private capital flows, policymakers lowered barriers to cross-border capital mobility and encouraged a common market for financial services, which became more competitive (and concentrated) over time.[12] Once liberated from national regulations and control, and believing its risks were minimal, capital flowed out from the wealthier countries in search of investments promising higher yields in Europe's less developed markets (now sharing the same currency).

As with the official capital flows, there are different types of private capital flows as well. Europe's liberalization process attracted a great deal of foreign (non-EU) capital into the EU, but it also enticed a great deal of mobility within Europe. In this way, developments parallel those in the labour markets – where immigrants from outside the EU make up a significant share of the labour mobility in and out of member states. Much of this capital was moving to avoid paying their fair share of tax – for example moving to Ireland to take advantage of that country's low level of income tax. The scope of this movement is so large that we are beginning to correct for the role that 'phantom' capital plays in national statistics on foreign direct investment (FDI).[13]

Box 8.2: The TARGET2 system

The TARGET2 system (Trans-European Automated Real-time Gross settlement Express Transfer) plays a very important role in addressing European current account imbalances. TARGET2 is the eurozone's interbank payment system: it processes the majority of cross-border transactions between eurozone countries. It works by automatically extending payments credits to central banks in countries where payments deficits are causing an outflow of commercial bank reserves.* For example, when money is moved from a Spanish bank to a German bank (for example a deposit is moved), the transaction is settled between the Spanish (*Banco de España*) and German (*Bundesbank*) central banks – the Spanish bank incurs a liability to the German bank. It is important to note that these claims can be generated from all kinds of different transactions – they might have a real economic counterpart (for example the result of an import that requires cross-border payment), or they might be the result of a purely financial transaction (for example an interbank cross-country loan). Whenever a transaction occurs, an opposite flow is recorded as a TARGET2 flow, so that at any time the balance of payments accounts will add up to zero, with the resulting TARGET2 net flow being recorded as a central bank inflow or outflow vis-à-vis the rest of the Eurosystem.

*For example, net outflows from private commercial banks in Spain are matched by credits to the Spanish central bank, with the credits extended collectively by the other central banks in the eurozone.

When capital in Europe is not avoiding taxes, it is frequently invested in more speculative property and equity market ventures. A significant share of private capital in Europe, whatever its origins, does not seem particularly interested in securing long-term returns on real investments. A unified capital market in Europe brought cheap credit to consumers in Europe's less developed regions – credit mostly used to finance increased consumption and inflate housing/equity market bubbles. With access to cheaper capital, and now absent the risk of a devaluation, the periphery economies (Greece, Italy, Ireland, Portugal and Spain) came to borrow heavily from Europe's core economies (in particular Germany, but also Finland, the Netherlands and Luxembourg).[14] This is yet another example of a common policy (emanating from the ECB) that may be suitable for some countries, but which was clearly inappropriate for others – because Europe's different regional economies have varying needs.

It is also clear that much of this foreign capital movement is not related to productive enterprises. For example, Hobza and Zeugner (2014) find that these financial flows do not map onto trade flow patterns, but rather depict a debt relationship between core and periphery countries in the eurozone – and this relationship was not based on trade linkages:

> Financial flows within the euro area and particularly towards the periphery countries were dominated by debt instruments. For example, debt flows accounted for over ¾ of the total gross financial flows in the euro area in 2004–6. In Spain, the share of cross-border loans and portfolio debt exceeded 95%. A significant part of this was short-term inter-bank lending and investments of banks and other financial institutions into sovereign debt of the periphery countries. (Hobza and Zeugner, 2014: 299)

Finally, Europe's shared capital market has made it possible to set new records in the level of destabilizing capital flight. The amount of money fleeing the eurozone periphery during the Great Recession (when measured as a share of GDP), proved to be

> far larger than the flight that precipitated changes in currency regimes during the most notable balance of payments crises of the past twenty years. This includes the 1992–93 ERM crisis affecting Italy, Spain, and the United Kingdom; the 1994–95 Mexican crisis; the 1997–98 Asian crisis affecting Indonesia, Korea, the Philippines, and Malaysia; the 1998 Russian crisis; and the 2000–02 Argentine crisis. (Higgins and Klitgaard, 2014: 4)

Lane's (2013) study for the European Commission, although slightly dated, still provides a good overview of the behaviour of capital flows (both gross and net) for eurozone member countries. Here, one can see how Europe has experienced extraordinary boom–bust cycles in both gross and net capital flows, since at least 2003. His work also shows an enormous reversal in net capital flows during the Great Recession and he recognizes how costly these flows have been for the macroeconomic and financial outcomes for the high-deficit countries. Lane's figures (1 and 2, pp 28–9) on aggregate flows to the eurozone show an enormous inflow of capital, slowly, over time, and then its dramatic collapse in 2009. In this regard, the European experience was not different from other economies on the world stage. What has changed is that Europe no longer has the regulatory bulkheads that used to limit destabilizing financial flows across national boundaries.

The Great Recession

As with the impact of the Great Recession on European labour mobility, there is also a larger literature that examines the response of capital markets in Europe.[15] Here, too, it is possible to depict a consensus on the nature of the flows and the challenges they posed to Europe's integrated markets.

The main story is one of pre- and post-crisis imbalances in private capital markets. As we saw earlier, access to cheap (and apparently risk-free) capital fuelled a consumption boom and corresponding asset bubble, which left the private sector heavily indebted. When the crisis hit, it brought a 'sudden stop' to these flows (Merler and Pisani-Ferry, 2012), massive capital flight, a protracted contraction in domestic demand, and a significant deterioration in the periphery's public finances. In short, when it was most desperately needed, private capital hightailed out of the periphery, leaving the local labour markets high and dry of needed investments.

The capital flight was of two types: first, it was the money of more footloose capitalists from core countries and beyond, who feared for their money and repatriated it as soon as possible. These speculators lost interest in investing in the stressed eurozone countries: they planned to weather the financial storm at home, in safer investment havens. But the flight also included 'investors' from within the periphery, who 'disproportionately shifted capital into debt securities of non-stressed euro area countries' (Beck et al, 2015: 1).

By 2012, the scale of capital flight from the periphery was astounding. Foreign investors from both inside and outside the eurozone liquidated a total of €525 billion (!) worth of assets from the periphery economies, €224 billion of which were from Spain alone (Higgins and Klitgaard, 2014: 4). Most of this money had been invested in portfolio assets, a broad category that includes sovereign bonds and notes and private security instruments other than derivatives. But foreign investors also liquidated sizable investments in bank loans and other periphery economy assets. At the same time, as noted previously, investors located in the periphery added to the net capital outflow by buying foreign assets. If we combine both foreign and domestic capital flight from the periphery, the net value of private funds exiting the periphery was estimated to be something like €676 billion (Higgins and Klitgaard, 2014: 4)!

In short, rather than helping with the need for regional adjustment, private capital exacerbated the problem by fleeing from the scene of the crisis. Rather than taking advantage of the recessed economies in the region and the growing unemployment (and falling wages), private capital returned to safe havens. Worse, the private capital market was completely unable to deal with this shock on its own. The huge gaping hole that was created by massive private capital flight was filled with public lending, and it was this public money that kept these regions afloat.

To see how this works, we can look briefly at the case of Greece, and then at the periphery as a group. Figure 8.8 employs data from the European Commission (2015) to distinguish between Greece's total and private capital flows during the period in question. The dashed line that moves steadily upwards is the total net inflows into Greece – the money that is keeping the Greek economy (barely) afloat. Until 2010, Greece was able to rely on private capital inflows, and it seemed sufficient to meet that country's financial needs. But when the crisis hit, all that private money fled – as seen in the rapid drop of the solid line in Figure 8.8 – like rats from a sinking ship. The only thing keeping the Greek economy afloat was the public money (mostly in the form of TARGET2 flows and programme assistance). The difference between the total net and private net flows in Figure 8.8 is made up by these kinds of public support.

A similar picture can be drawn for the eurozone periphery, in general. Figure 8.9 draws on the work of Steinar et al (2019) to combine the balance of payment figures for Greece, Ireland, Italy, Portugal and Spain, and then separates them into their component parts (current account, private capital flows, official/public capital flows [16] and central bank reserves). In this figure, we see that the periphery countries were experiencing a growing current account deficit until about 2012, but since that time it has largely flattened out. Before 2011, this deficit was mostly covered by private capital inflows – but with the 'sudden stop' that came with the crisis, this private money fled. Since that time, the current account deficits are being covered by 'official' capital.

In short, the periphery countries could not rely on private capital markets to deal with the crisis. When nearly €700 billion in capital fled from the periphery, these countries needed to turn to official financing sources – financing the necessary adjustment came mostly from TARGET2 (in Spain and Italy), sometimes combined with the support from EU institutions and the IMF (in Greece and Portugal).

European financial markets were both unwilling and unable to finance the investments necessary to help periphery countries

Figure 8.8: Greek cumulative capital flows, 2002–14

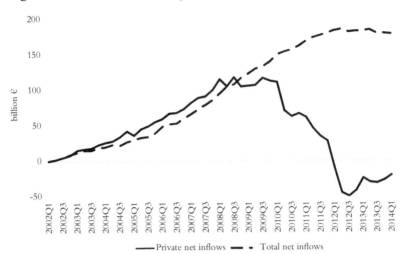

Notes: Cumulated flows. An upward-sloping line represents net inflows. Private net flows are computed by subtracting the other investment balance of general government (essentially programme assistance) and central bank (essentially TARGET2 flows) from the total net inflows.

Source: Adapted from European Commission (2015: 10, Graph 1.2); Eurostat (BPM5)

climb out of the recession. During the crisis, investments declined significantly and (in 2018) they had not yet rebounded from their pre-crisis trend, despite the fact that the ECB had employed a very expansionist monetary policy throughout this time (Ademmer and Jannsen, 2018: 3787; see also European Commission, 2015). Official EU sources do not employ a convenient time series indicator for real business investment in the euro area, but Ademmer and Jannsen (2018: 3789) have constructed a useful proxy indicator, which I have reproduced in Figure 8.10; here we can clearly see how business investment in the eurozone declined rapidly by about 15% during the Great Recession. As you can see in Figure 8.10, the level of business investment in 2016 had still not recovered – it remained below the 2008 level.

The reason for this weak investment behaviour is complex and related to relatively weak economic activity, such as insufficient aggregate demand, high real interest rates, and credits issues related to deleveraging (see European Commission, 2015; Barkbu et al, 2015). The reasons for the insufficient investment are not as important as the recognition that private capital flows are unable to play the role that Europe's common market requires them to play.

Figure 8.9: Balance of payments, euro periphery

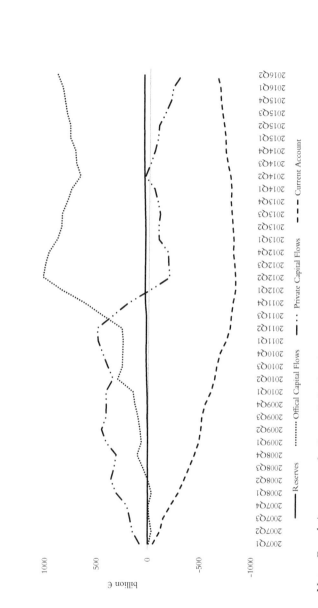

Notes: Cumulative accounts for Greece, Ireland, Italy, Portugal and Spain. Official capital flows refer to the sum of all bilateral and multilateral lending, including loans from the EFSF, the EFSM, the ESM, the IMF and the intra-Eurosystem liabilities (TARGET2).

Source: Adapted from Steiner et al (2019: 95), IMF BOP Statistics

Figure 8.10: Business investment in euro area, 2001–16

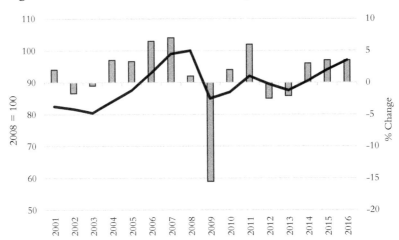

Notes: Annual data, index 2008 = 100. The line presents annual changes in an index, where 2008 = 100 (left hand axis). The histogram columns capture the year-on-year growth rate, marked on the right-hand axis, as percent change.

Source: Adapted from Ademmer and Jannsen (2018: 3789)

Conclusion

To secure greater room for a more efficient market in Europe, members states levelled their regulatory authority and their capacity to manage local labour markets. An integrated market in Europe was to provide the stimuli and incentives necessary to secure local economic adjustments. The need for local policy scope was often downplayed by assuming that regional differences to economic shocks would slowly disappear over time, and by hoping that markets would self-correct. If adjustments were required, policymakers believed they could be secured by European-wide factor markets, in which capital and labour would flow freely to fill any economic void. In short, increased factor mobility – for both capital and labour – plays a central role in Europe's integrated market.

This chapter has demonstrated how this trust in a market-based solution is entirely misplaced. This is especially true with regard to capital markets: private capital did not behave as anticipated – it did not race to impoverished areas and invest in productive enterprises to raise periphery economies from the ashes. As Furceri and Zdzienicka note:

> market-based insurance tends to be suboptimal in currency unions as private agents do not internalize the

macroeconomic stabilization effects of the portfolio choices. In addition, the recent financial crisis has shown that shocks hitting a member country's economy are quickly transmitted through the international financial system, and that credit markets tend to freeze up during downturns and, in some cases, contribute to amplify these shocks. The recent experience with recessions has also shown that domestic fiscal policy cannot fully offset output shocks. (Furceri and Zdzienicka, 2015: 684)

Credit flows have become more procyclical since the creation of the EMU, rather than less (Allard et al, 2015: 237). In fact, private capital flows exacerbated the crisis – they contributed to an unhealthy economic imbalance before the crisis, and mobile capital pulled the economic rug out from under these countries when the crisis hit. When the private markets imploded, it was up to state and official capital sources to step in with massive public funding and support.

This left European workers terribly exposed. They could not get adequate help in the form of national fiscal, monetary or regulatory policies (see Chapter 6). There was no support to be found in the form of European transfers, at least not at the scope that was required (see Chapter 7). Capital was only concerned with finding a safe haven and fled the crisis-hit areas almost immediately (see the preceding discussion). All this meant that most of the burden of adjustment landed on those that remained: European workers, who were forced to workaway and accept lower wages.

But the Great Recession also revealed that labour mobility, in itself, is entirely insufficient for meeting the needs of local economic adjustment. The size and scope of workaways is increasing, especially in response to the Great Recession, but it remained relatively limited. More to the point: the scope of workaway in Europe will never be sufficient, given the nature of labour, as human life. Europe's local labour markets are being asked to make enormous sacrifices, for an economy that simply doesn't work as designed.

A recent report by the European Commission (2019b) surveyed the challenges of 'Imbalances and Adjustments' within the eurozone and concluded with some good and some bad news. The bad news was that the various regions of Europe were not pulling in the same direction and were unable to respond effectively to the common shock of creating the EMU itself! For the European Commission, it was good news that 'the adjustment mechanisms worked as predicted, with competitiveness reacting in such a way as to absorb asymmetric shocks' (European Commission, 2019b: 43). What the Commission means by this is that countries that were negatively affected by the Great Recession were able to slowly crawl out of it by reducing their labour costs and 'shedding' their labour:

> A process of unit labour costs being significantly reduced was observed in the countries most affected by the crisis, notably Ireland, Cyprus, Greece, Spain and Portugal. This partly reflected increases in labour productivity due to labour shedding but also reflected in some countries a downward adjustment in wages. (European Commission, 2019b: 53)

This is exactly what is wrong with Europe's effort at creating a common labour market. For the market to function as designed, workers need to suffer. Clearly, a process of reduced 'unit labour costs' and 'labour shedding' can only be embraced by somebody who does not work (or does not rely on others who work) in Ireland, Cyprus, Greece, Spain and Portugal, not to mention Hungary, Bulgaria, Romania, Poland, Slovakia, Croatia, Lithuania, Estonia and Latvia. For Europe's integrated market to work, these workers had to be 'shed' from their jobs and homes, in order to force down their wages, in the hope that this eventually (over a relatively long period of time, for an unemployed worker) *might* attract the investment needed to create new jobs (but now at lower wage levels).

European policymakers have been able to shift the burden of adjustment onto the backs of workers because the relative power of labour, as a class, has been falling for decades. Labour's decline is due, in large part, to the sort of market integration reforms I have been describing in the preceding chapters. This decline in the relative power of labour is the subject of Chapter 9.

PART IV

Results

9

The Power of Labour

This chapter considers the effect of market integration on organized labour in Europe. To the extent that workaway and competitive wage pressure have become a more important means for securing local labour market adjustments, they are bound to affect the relative power of labour. This chapter considers the impact of these changes on the power and influence of workers as a class, and how organized labour in Europe has responded to these changes.

As mentioned in Chapter 2, it is common to measure labour power along two dimensions: in terms of both structural and associational power. Most of this book has aimed to describe how changes in European markets have undermined the structural power of labour. In the preceding chapters, we have seen how many instruments have been removed from the policymakers' toolbox, leaving national authorities with less capacity to manage their local labour markets. Member states have jettisoned their monetary and regulatory policies, and their fiscal policies have been severely constrained by the needs of a monetary union (Chapter 6). The resulting policy void has not been filled by a suitable common budget or social policy at the European level (Chapter 7). Finally, European factor flows (Chapter 8) have proven entirely inadequate for the job: capital flows tend to make things worse, not better, and the scope of labour flows across Europe is entirely insufficient (and for good reasons). The result of these changes can be seen in a significant decrease in the structural power of labour, as evident in high levels of unemployment, low wages, increased workaway, dwindling social service protections and other indicators.

These changes have also necessitated increased competition among European labour markets. While the motivation behind these reforms may not have been to undermine the power of labour, this has clearly been the effect. In the same way that unorganized labour bids against unionized labour to secure scarce job offers, workers in Europe are now locked in a competitive wage struggle, where each local labour market has an incentive to underbid the others in a race to the bottom. European policymakers explicitly advocate wage flexibility as the key to economic (competitive) survival and this tends to increase the vulnerability (and commodification) of European workers. As Clauwaert and Schömann (2012: 17) have suggested, the EU seems to see quality employment (and pay) as being incompatible with competitiveness.

This chapter shows how the integration of European markets, as described in the preceding chapters, has been accompanied by a significant decline in the associational power of labour. It does so in three parts. First, we examine evidence of a very broad decline in labour power around the world – to underscore that the challenge to labour is not limited to the EU. Second, we focus in on recent developments in Europe, to show clear signs of a decline in associational power among European workers. This second section examines the growing precariousness of the European labour force, its shrinking wage share, a decline in the density and coverage of organized labour, and its reduced willingness or capacity to strike in support of its demands. In the third and final section, we consider how organized labour in Europe has responded to the challenges of increased market integration and the threat it poses to their power. Here, we turn our attention to the promise that works councils, coordinated wage bargaining and minimum wage legislation offer to European workers.

The slow decline of labour

For the past 40 years, the power of labour has been in retreat across most developed economies in the world. While there is little agreement over the exact causes of this decline, it is clearly evident in the two most common (and central) measures of labour power: the voting share and the income share of labour have been falling for decades.

On the political front, the vote share of social democratic parties in Europe has been in decline since at least the 1970s, and continues to be dismal. Figure 9.1, from Benedetto et al (2019), shows the aggregate vote share of social democratic parties in 31 European countries since the end of the Second World War. Not even the suffering generated by the Great Recession was able to spark increased voter interest in Europe's sundry labour parties. While there is little consensus as to why these parties are shedding voters, a number of recent studies paint

Figure 9.1: Social democratic party vote, share of electorate, 31 countries

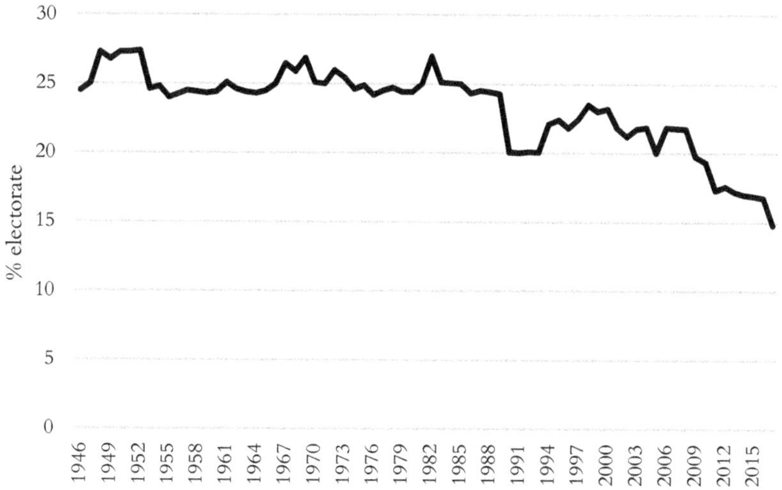

Notes: The total share of the electorate (%) is the total votes for social democratic parties in a year in 31 countries, divided by the total number of eligible voters in an election. The 31 countries in the study are all in Europe: Albania, Austria, Belgium, Bulgaria, Croatia, Cyprus, Czechoslovakia/Czech Republic, Denmark, Estonia, Finland, France, Germany, Greece, Hungary, Ireland, Italy, Latvia, Lithuania, Luxembourg, Macedonia, Netherlands, Norway, Poland, Portugal, Romania, Slovakia, Slovenia, Spain, Sweden, Switzerland and the UK.

Source: Adopted from Benedetto et al (2019: 4, Figure 1). Underlying data based on Nohlen and Stoever (2010)

a dire picture of labour parties in 'crisis', 'retreat', on the 'back foot' or even 'dead'.[1]

On the economic front, evidence of labour's demise is most clearly seen in the downward trend of labour's share of income in national economies. As with the political trend, there is much disagreement about the reasons behind labour's shrinking share of the economic pie, but the overall change is dramatic and serious, as seen in Figure 9.2. In the most developed economies, the labour share has been shrinking since the 1970s. We do not have comparable data for emerging markets and the developing economies, but the existing data clearly show that workers in these countries are securing an even smaller (and still falling) share of national income.

Labour's share of income is the premier indicator of labour power, as it shows the share of national income that is paid out in wages (and benefits). A stable labour share of GDP was once considered to be a 'stylized fact' of growth (Kaldor, 1961). But that was a long time ago,

Figure 9.2: Labour share of income, globally, %

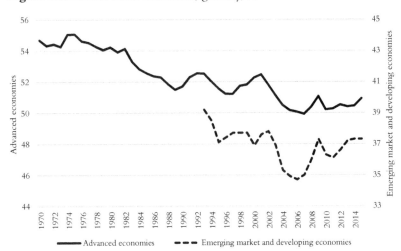

Notes: For advanced economies the figure shows averages, weighted by nominal GDP in current US dollars. For emerging market and developing economies, the figure shows year fixed-effects weighted least-squares-regressions (using nominal GDP weights) that also include country fixed effects. Year fixed effects are normalized to reflect the level of the labour share in 2000. See the original source for more details.

Sources: Adopted from IMF (2017: 122, Figure 3.1). Underlying data is from the CEIC database; Karabarbounis and Neiman (2014); national authorities; OECD; and IMF staff calculations

under a very different balance of power between labour and capital. A falling labour share implies that workers' product wages are growing slower than the average level of labour productivity. In other words, workers are less able to secure the gains made from added productivity. More often than not, capital absconds with these gains. This is one of the reasons why a shrinking labour share is often accompanied by increased income inequality.

Economists disagree about the reasons for this decline and different analysts tend to focus on different explanatory variables. In all likelihood, there are several reasons why labour shares are falling, but the most common explanations include technological change (such as robotization), increased trade and financial integration, as well as changing labour market policies, institutions and regulations.[2]

The decline in European labour power

There is no good reason to think that the technological challenge to labour should be different in Europe than in other developed nations/

regions. For this reason, we can assume that some part of Europe's declining labour share should be attributed to technological changes. But the other main explanations for declining labour shares *are not* coincidental to the strategy for European market integration. As we have seen in the preceding chapters, increased trade and financial integration are two driving forces behind the common market. These forms of integration were sold to the public with the promise that a rising economic tide would lift all boats, but a declining share of labour income casts doubt on that promise.[3]

More to the point, regulatory changes and labour reforms are fuelling the falling labour share and increasing the precariousness of work (Standing, 2011). This was clearly the result (if not the intent) of the European Directives for Services and for Posted Workers. As we saw in Chapter 7, member states are encouraged to 'modernize' their labour markets by allowing for greater contractual diversity through increased flexibility (that is, introducing more flexible forms of employment, while reducing employment protections against dismissals).[4]

When we look at the details of these reforms, we find that this modernization effort was aimed to reduce so-called 'labour segmentation', where widespread labour market deregulation is encouraged in hopes of promoting employment on the margins (among so-called 'outsiders'). In encouraging 'employment friendly' reforms, the European Commission (2012d: 103–4) has proposed a number of changes, including: decreased statutory and contractual minimum wages; decreased bargaining coverage; decreased (automatic) extensions of collective agreements; decentralized bargaining systems; decreased generosity of unemployment benefits; and reduced wage-setting power for trade unions. These changes clearly undermine labour's relative power.

Consequently, economic growth in Europe produces mostly non-standardized types of employment. While this type of employment is better than none, it tends to be low paid and difficult to organize – such that it does not (yet) lend itself to strengthening the relative power of labour, as a class. Before the Great Recession – and during a period of economic expansion – Europe experienced a substantial rise in the use of temporary contracts, part-time employment and the number of self-employed. After the Great Recession, as seen in Figure 9.3, the growth in part-time and self-employed jobs was increasing even faster than the total number of jobs in Europe. Today, part-time work accounts for almost 20% of all jobs in the EU (24% in the EU15), up from 16% in 1996, and the involuntary share of that part-time work had risen from 22.4% in 2007 to 29.1% in 2015 (Eurofound, 2018: 1).

Figure 9.3: Net job growth by forms of employment, EU28

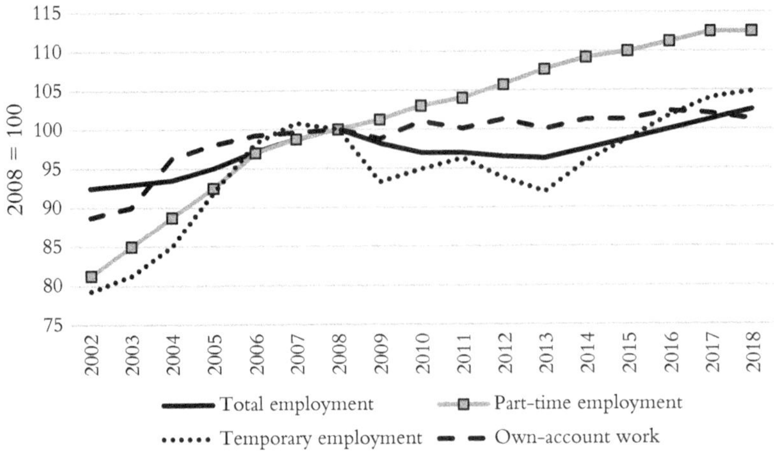

Note: Comparison of 2nd quarters; change in thousands; index 2008 = 100.

Source: Adapted from ETUI (2019: 26, Figure 2.2); underlying data is Eurostat (lfsq_epgaed, lfsq_etgaed, lfsq_esgaed)

The scope of this temporary work (both voluntary and involuntary) varies substantially across the EU. In the 17 older member states (EU17), roughly 30% of those employed find themselves in some form of non-standard employment arrangement.[5] In these states, the share of workers able to hold down a full-time job has been falling for the past two decades: in 1996, over 77% of workers in the EU15 were able to enjoy a full-time position (36 hours or more per week); while 20 years later, in 2015, that share had fallen to 66.7% (Eurofound, 2017: 16). In the newer member states (EU11), the figures are much lower: only 15% of their workforce, on average, is stuck in non-standard forms of employment.

These new types of employment – gig economy, employee sharing, causal/temporary work and so on – tend to skirt around social protection requirements. Not only are these types of workers difficult to organize, they undermine the relative bargaining power of organized labour, fuelling the trend in falling wage shares. It is not surprising, then, that research 'points to [the] increased precariousness of casual work contracts, less favourable working conditions, and lower wages compared to regular and permanent employment' (Eurofound, 2018: 38).

The European Trade Union Institute (ETUI) mapped the scope of recent labour market reforms in Europe. This mapping offered a damning conclusion, it:

demonstrates the major negative impact of labour law reforms on workers' rights and fundamental social rights under cover of the economic and financial crisis. National reforms tend to deregulate already flexibilised labour law regulations and thus in most cases represent a step backwards in terms of workers' protection. A recurrent feature of these labour law reforms and flexibilisation is the explosive growth of inequalities and insecurity in most of the countries concerned (Mazuyer et al 2012: 5). Setting this alongside measures affecting social security, such as pension reforms or public sector reforms, reduction of job seekers benefits, salary cuts and so on, calls into question the European concept of 'quality employment' and the international concept of 'decent work', which national labour law reforms in Europe no longer seem to meet. The meaning of the European social model is also undermined. (Clauwert and Schömann, 2012: 16)

Labour share

For all these reasons, it is not surprising to see that labour's share of income in the EU15 has been falling since the mid-1970s, as shown in Figure 9.4. This figure employs the European Commission's AMECO indicator for wage share (using current prices). What *is* surprising is that the aggregate wage share of EU national incomes is falling faster and steeper than in the US – until 2006, where there was an increase in the wage share around the Great Recession, and a flattening ever since. It should be noted that the spike in the labour share around the Great Recession is not the result of wage increases for workers, but a statistical artefact of a falling GDP after the subprime and financial crises.

When we disaggregate the EU figures into new and old member states, as is done in Figure 9.5, we can clearly see how workers in the EU17 (older) member states have managed (mostly) to hold on to their shares of national income in the 2000s (after the earlier long decline, as shown in Figure 9.4). Workers in the EU11 (newer) member states have not been so fortunate: their income share has been falling significantly during this period (until 2015).

As with many of the other indicators in this study, there are substantial differences across member states, but the general picture is clearly one of a fall in European labour share of income over time, especially in the EU11. This decline occurred at the very time that the EU was

Figure 9.4: Wage share, current prices, US and EU, 1960–2021

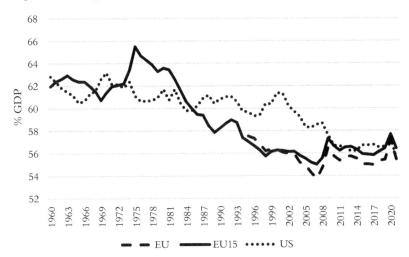

Note: Adjusted wage share: total economy, as percentage of GDP at current prices (compensation per employee as percentage of GDP at market prices per person employed).

Source: Adapted from AMECO (2020)

Figure 9.5: Weighted average wage share, EU17 and EU11, 2000–17

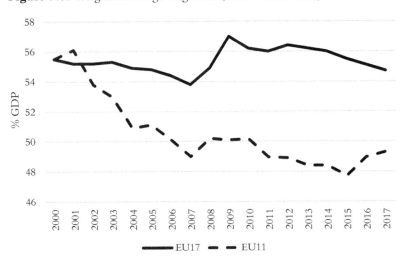

Notes: Weighted by GDP. Underlying data from Müller et al (2019a: Table A1.B) and European Commission, AMECO Database, GDP at current prices.

Source: Adapted from Waddington et al (2019: 14, Figure 1.2)

pursuing its ambitious reforms for market integration, as described in the preceding chapters.

As increased trade and financial market integration is a common explanation for the demise of labour power elsewhere, it is not unreasonable to suggest that the EU's approach to market integration is responsible for much of labour's relative decline. At the very least, we can be certain that Europe's approach to market integration has not managed to increase labour's relative share of income.

A similar relationship can be traced to the decline in the associational power of European labour, as seen in three related statistics: a decline in union density; collective bargaining coverage; and the use of strikes – the subjects of the next three subsections. These indicators are emphasized in traditional analyses of trade unionism (Webb and Webb, 1894; Perlman, 1928), as they can be used to mobilize workers, improve the terms and conditions of their employment, and reduce overall inequality.[6]

Union density

Since the 1990s, overall union membership in Europe has been falling. In 2015, there were 37 million registered trade union members in Europe, down from 52 million in 1990 – a decrease of almost 30% (ETUI, 2019: 59)! Most of this decline occurred in the 1990s, and the highest casualties are to be found in Central and Eastern Europe.

The most useful indicator of union strength is not the number of union members, however, but the density of that membership – that is, the proportion of union members divided by the total number of wage/salary earners in the economy. Not surprisingly, union density is also on the decline across the EU, although the amount of decline varies significantly across member states. It is for this reason that Figure 9.6 divides the EU up into old (EU17 in top panel) and new (EU11 in bottom panel) member states. Here, we can clearly see significant changes over time, from the 1980s to the 2010s. In studying these figures, it is important to focus on the temporal trend in each country (from 1980 to 2010), and not be distracted by their horizontal presentation, which ranks countries by their level of union density in the 2010s.

In Figure 9.6, we can see that a handful of countries are doing better than others. The decline in union density seems to be smallest in those countries that use a 'Ghent' system of unemployment benefits: Belgium, Denmark, Finland and Sweden. (See Box 9.1 for a short description of the Ghent system.) But, in other countries, the large decline in union

Figure 9.6: Union density, EU17 and EU11, by decade average

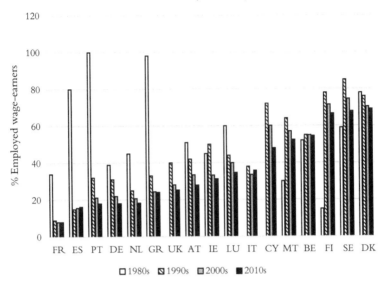

Union density, EU17, by decade

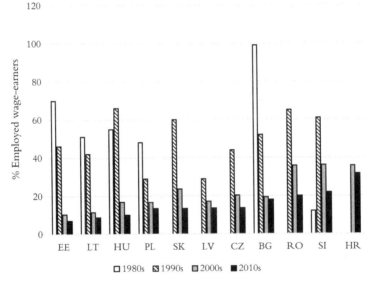

Union density, EU11, by decade

Notes: Decade averages. As the data end in 2016, the 2010s decade average is truncated, 2010–16. Union density is calculated by expressing net union membership as a proportion of wage earners in employment. In both panels, countries are listed by their level of union density in the 2010s. See original source for more information about the nature and sources of data.

Source: Adapted from Müller et al (2019a: 677, Table A1.H). Underlying data from OECD and Visser (2016)

Box 9.1: The Ghent system

The Ghent system refers to a system of benefits, originating in Ghent, Belgium, where trade unions (rather than governments) are responsible for paying welfare benefits, especially unemployment benefits. In the Ghent system, the government transfers the administration of these benefits systems to labour unions. These funds are then closely regulated and kept separate from other union finances. The system is voluntary, and workers are directed to the local occupation or industry union office in order to register for the system and pay a small fee (most of the financing is through government tax revenue).

The Ghent system is still used in Denmark, Iceland, Finland (but see Böckerman and Uusitalo, 2006) and Sweden. (The system in Belgium is actually not a full Ghent system.) Welfare benefits provided by the Ghent system tend to have better coverage and take-up rates than systems that are mandatory and government run. This approach to organizing welfare benefits also makes union membership more attractive, so that union membership rates tend to be substantially higher in Ghent systems, relative to other countries (see, among others, Scruggs, 2002; Böckerman and Uusitalo, 2006).

---

density has been eye-popping, and the pattern is revealing: Greece, Portugal and Spain have experienced huge drops since the 1980s, but so too have Bulgaria, Estonia and Lithuania. Much of this decline is probably associated with fundamental and obvious political changes occurring in each of these countries, and the changed role that labour unions played in very different political contexts.

But the sort of decline that we see across the board since the 1990s is evidence of a shared experience of reduced labour union power in the EU. These declines are particularly steep in the new member states, as seen in the bottom panel of Figure 9.6. As Boeri et al conclude in their exhaustive – if now somewhat dated – review of union membership in Europe:

> this downward trend in unionization is related to the rise in unemployment during these years and to structural changes in labour market participation and employment, bringing in groups with a lower propensity to unionize (service workers, workers finding employment in small firms) and groups that go into non-standard employment (for example,

part-timers and workers on temporary contracts). (Boeri et al, 2001: 45)

Bargaining coverage

By joining together and confronting employers as a group, workers can leverage their influence over wages, working conditions and even employment levels. Coordinated, multi-employer bargaining systems based on broad-based collective bargaining partners deliver higher employment, lower unemployment, reduced wage inequality and higher wages for the workers covered (OECD, 2018: 74ff). Remarkably, and in contrast to the OECD, the European Commission (2018c: 101) believes that collective bargaining coverage and union density have little impact on long-term wage growth.

In the early postwar period, from the 1950s to the 1980s, labour markets in Western Europe relied upon collective bargaining arrangements with high levels of coverage and based mostly (but not exclusively) on multi-employer industrial bargaining (Crouch, 1993). As a result, a large share of private sector wages in these countries was removed from direct market competition (yet another form of decommodification). In Eastern Europe, for obvious reasons, the situation was quite different: collective bargaining was mostly absent in Eastern Europe before the 1990s. But one of the perceived benefits from these countries joining the EU was the hope of eventually establishing collective bargaining arrangements (Müller et al, 2019: 625).

This was not to be. The demands of market integration discouraged union membership, and workers in Eastern Europe had an incentive to compete on the basis of cheaper wages, rather than by way of collective bargaining. In the 1990s, union density was falling across most of the EU11 (see Figure 9.6). One reason for this might be that the EU prioritized the need for flexibility in the face of changing market conditions. Indeed, in response to the Great Recession, the EU participated in several financing programmes (such as in Latvia and Romania) and memorandums of understanding (Greece, Ireland, Portugal) that applied enormous pressure on member states to reform their labour law and social protections. The extent of these pressures is evident in the fact that two national trade unions (in Spain and Greece) filed a complaint with the ILO that the EU's collective bargaining reforms ran counter to the principles of trade union freedom and/ or free collective bargaining (Clauwaert and Schömann, 2012: 16).

While the nature and scope of changes to European collective bargaining vary significantly, there has been a clear decentralization of bargaining arrangements – both with respect to how wages are secured and regulatory capacity. Wages in both Eastern and Western Europe are now exposed to more competition, sometimes fiercely so. Indeed, since the 1980s, one can see a clear tendency towards increased decentralization of bargaining arrangements, from multi-employer to single-employer (Visser, 2016) – even if multi-employer bargaining systems are still predominant in the EU28 (Müller et al, 2019: 629). Another related trend is the devolution of regulatory capacity to the company level, providing employers with more flexibility (and workers with less power).

Figure 9.7 provides an overview of the changing scope of collective bargaining arrangements in Europe. As with Figure 9.6, the data are presented in two panels, to underscore the different experiences separating old and new member states. Among the EU17, we find higher levels of coverage, but also more stable levels of coverage. Indeed, coverage in the Netherlands, Finland and France has been *on the rise* over the decades. Other countries, such as Portugal, Italy, Denmark, Belgium and Austria are holding steady. In the EU11, by contrast, we find reduced bargaining coverage in every single state – even though most of the new member states started from much lower levels.

As there are so many differences in the starting points and nature of changes in collective bargaining arrangements across EU member states, it is difficult to summarize the extent of these changes and the effects they have had on labour's associational power. Perhaps the best synopsis is provided by a group of editors at the conclusion of their recent 670-page survey of *Collective Bargaining in Europe*:

> A quick glance at the titles of the various country chapters of this publication illustrates the dire straits of collective bargaining in Europe. Stability and resilience are the most positive developments referred to in the titles of, for example, the chapters on Belgium, Croatia and Italy. The titles of most of the other chapters contain some kind of reference to erosion, decentralisation or fragmentation. If there is one feature shared by almost all countries covered in this publication it is that over the past 20 years the regulatory capacity of collective bargaining has decreased, albeit to varying degrees; and that in most cases policymakers at European and national level have played an active role in advancing this development. (Müller et al, 2019: 657–8)

Figure 9.7: Bargaining coverage, EU17 and EU11, by decade average

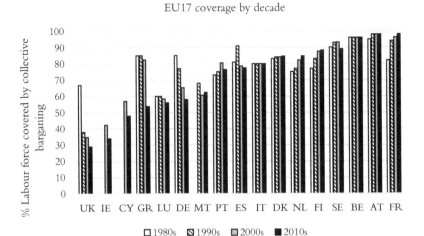

EU17 coverage by decade

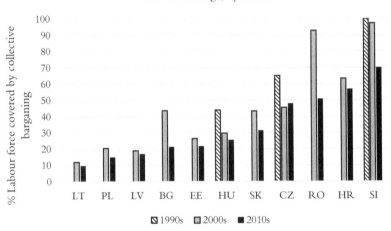

EU 11 coverage, by decade

Notes: Decade averages. There is no EU11 data for the 1980s. As the data end in 2016, the 2010s average is truncated, 2010–16. Bargaining coverage expresses the number of employees whose terms and conditions are set by collective bargaining as a proportion of the labour force (adjcov). In both panels, countries are listed by the strength of their bargaining coverage in the 2010s. See original source for more information about the nature and sources of data.

Source: Adapted from Müller et al (2019a: 670, Table A1.A). Underlying data from Visser (2016) and OECD

Disruption

In addition to collective bargaining, the other main tool that labour can use to exert power over employers it to disrupt the production process, using strikes or more general protest actions. Unfortunately, cross-national data on industrial disputes are very patchy, even in the EU. For example, Greece has not collected statistics since 1988, and Bulgaria, Croatia, Czechia, Latvia and Lithuania don't publish their strike statistics. Worse, the legal rights to strike differ across EU member states and the relevant EU law is ambiguous.[7]

The ETUI has worked hard to paint a picture of the degree to which strikes are still used as an instrument of influence. Figure 9.8 shows the weighted average of the days not worked due to industrial action, per 1,000 employees, in most European countries, especially Western Europe. The number of states included in the analysis varies from 19 (1990, 2016) to 25 (1992–2006), so the total number of strikes is surely higher. But, for our purposes, we are mostly concerned with the trend, which is clearly downwards (and the downwards trend would be even more severe, if we had data stretching back to the 1970s and 1980s). The two recent peaks (2002 and 2010) apparently capture responses to the 'dot.com' bubble of 2002 and the French 'national days of action' in 2010 (ETUI, 2019: 60).

While the trend in economic strikes is clearly declining, there has been a recent uptick in general strikes against governments, beginning in about 1980, and especially after the Great Recession. We might also expect to find an increase in rioting, in response to a growing string of crises (Clover, 2016). Before the Great Recession, trade unions were increasingly threatening a number of general strikes across Western Europe, apparently (at least in part) in response to unions being excluded from the reform process (Hamann et al, 2012: 1031–2, 1048). More recent data from the ETUI (2020) show an explosion of general strike activity in 2010 and 2012, before slowly returning to the long-term norm. Most of this recent strike activity occurred in Greece, Italy and France. Evidence of the same pattern can be found in analyses of media accounts (Schmalz and Weinmann, 2016: 559–60).

In this section we have seen how three of the most common indicators of labour's associational power – union density, bargaining coverage, and the use of strikes – all show a marked decline across Europe. Although this decline varies across states, it occurred simultaneously with a strong push for market integration in Europe. As with Europe's declining labour share of income, Europe's path to market integration

Figure 9.8: Days lost to industrial action in Europe, 1990–2018

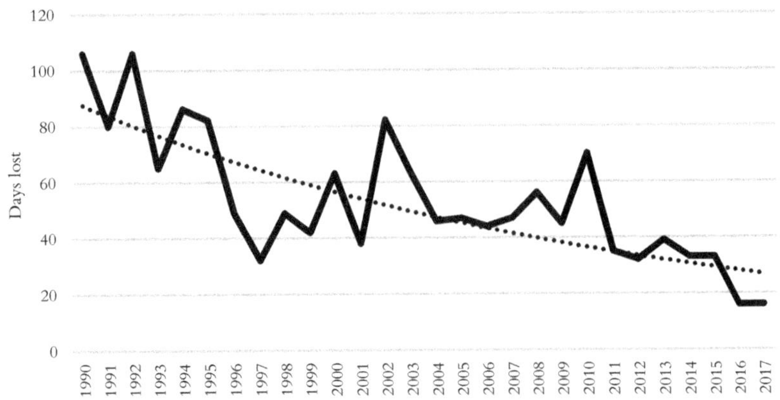

Notes: Underlying data from ETUI (see, for example, Müller et al, 2019a), based on data from national statistical offices. See original source for data on the number of states producing data each year. For details about the availability and reliability of data, see Dribbusch and Vandaele (2016).

Source: Adapted from ETUI (2019: 60, Figure 3.15)

has not managed to increase the associational strength of labour. The opposite effect seems more likely.

What is to be done?

This chapter concludes by looking at the response of European organized labour to these developments. In particular, this section will survey the prospects of three important and potential reforms that organized labour has offered in response to increased market integration: works councils, collective bargaining, and minimum wages. Before discussing these three responses, it may be useful to describe the power of labour as an interest group, relative to the organized interests of employers in Europe.

Unequal partners

From the very start, the European project has aimed to facilitate economic integration, and for that reason it quickly attracted the interests of both employer and employee organizations – even if employers were much quicker in organizing their initial response. After all, the European Economic Community was created at a time when European labour markets were increasingly structured by organized representatives in different forms of collective bargaining arrangements.

At the time, and in a handful of national markets across postwar Europe, labour movements proved themselves to be relatively strong, compared to their employer counterparts. In these states, labour could use its strength to secure more favourable working conditions and pay. In most states, however, the balance of power leaned more heavily in the direction of employers – even as workers still benefited from growing associational and structural power. At the European level, however, the contest has always been remarkably lopsided – in favour of employers. This is in part because of divisions within the labour movement itself, but also because of the structural power of capital in the European market.

Consider, first, the main interest organizations representing labour and capital. Today, employer interests are represented by BusinessEurope (the Confederation of European Businesses), whose institutional legacy can be traced back to 1949. At that time, the national industrial federations from the six member states of the European Coal and Steel Community (ECSC) formed the *Conseil des Fédérations Industrielles d'Europe* and the *Union des Industries des pays de la Communauté européenne* to monitor developments in the ECSC. When the Treaty of Rome was signed in 1958, the organizations evolved into the *Union des Industries de la Communauté européenne* (UNICE), which has been active in European politics ever since. In 2007, UNICE changed its name to BusinessEurope. Today, BusinessEurope includes 40 member federations from 35 countries in Europe (both inside and outside the EU) and is run by a 50-person staff (BusinessEurope, 2019).

By contrast, the European Trade Union Confederation (ETUC), the major trade union organization in Europe, is a spring chicken: it arrived on the scene about a quarter century later. The ETUC came into existence in 1973, as a collection of existing umbrella organizations (Barnouin, 1986). The delay was due in part to the challenge of overcoming a series of religious (Catholic/Protestant), regional (EFTA/ EEC) and political (communist/socialist) cleavages that divided the European labour movement. Today, the ETUC comprises 90 national trade union confederations in 38 countries, plus ten European Trade Union Federations (ETUFs), and is run by a 31-person staff (ETUC, 2020). Those ten ETUFs represent workers from different industrial sectors (such as manufacturing, journalism, public services and so on) and are responsible for the European social dialogue at the sectoral level.

Although the ETUC was late to the scene, it can be seen as a more robust organization – relative to BusinessEurope (Hyman, 2005: 17). Still, its influence will always be limited by the structural power of capital. In the EU, just as in the member states, governments depend upon the investment decisions of individual employers. Consequently, capital is able to exert enormous pressure on political developments without having to mobilize collectively (see Offe and Wiesenthal, 1985: 191–3; Przeworski and Wallerstein, 1988). This imbalance in power is evident in the enormous lobbying industry hovering around Brussels, and the significant influence exerted by the European Round Table of Industrialists and other business organizations (see Balanyá et al, 2003; CEO, n.d.). But it also evident in the fact that the European Commission tends to consult BusinessEurope on a wide variety of matters (as the main representative of 'industry'), but it mostly refers to the ETUC on issues restricted to social policy.

It is also important to realize that the ETUC lacks the authority to call workers out on strike. Indeed, the majority of ETUC members are not unions (or workers, directly), but national federations of trade unions and industrial committees who do not, themselves, have the authority to call a strike. In short, the ETUC is unable to exercise anything near the sort of power that national trade union federations can, as it lacks control over the two central instruments of worker mobilization: collective wage bargaining and strikes.

Despite this imbalance, the ETUC has been one of the most enthusiastic supporters for more extensive forms of European integration. Hyman (2005: 19) even suggests that the ETUC is home of the Commission's most reliable interlocutors. This sort of supporting role can also be seen in the fact that the ETUC approved every major proposition for further market integration before 2010 – that is, the Single European Act, the Maastricht Treaty, the European Constitution and the Lisbon Treaty.[8]

By 2010, however, the ETUC began to change its tune. As the EU's response to the Great Recession was largely restricted to a coordinated contraction of aggregate demand, and when the Commission's new European economic governance proposals began to imply that member state economic imbalances were caused by overgenerous social policies or wage increases in the eurozone's periphery, the ETUC voiced its opposition (Phillips, 2011b; Erne, 2015: 352).

The current challenge facing organized labour (in general) and the ETUC (in particular) is to increase worker voice and power at a time when larger political and structural changes have undermined their traditional sources of power and influence. Three policy proposals are often offered as opportunities for extending worker voice and influence in Europe's common marketplace: works councils; new collective bargaining arrangements and minimum wage legislation. The first aims to improve worker voice in the economic life of Europe; whereas the latter two proposals provide different means to shield local wages from direct market competition.

Works councils

While economic strikes, union density and bargaining coverage in Europe have been declining for decades, there seems to be at least one bright light on labour's horizon: the rise in institutionalized forms of workplace labour representation.

This light was lit a quarter century ago with the Works Councils Directive of 1994 (Directive 94/45/EC) and was subsequently 'recast' in 2009 (2009/38/EC).[9] The Works Council Directive requires large firms (over 1,000 employees in the EU) that are located in more than one member state (in particular, 150 workers in at least two member states) to recognize and consult a multinational delegation representing their workforce: a 'European Works Council' (EWC). In EWCs, workers are granted legal rights to access information and to be consulted about decisions that affect them. As such, EWCs allow workers' representatives, from different countries, to meet regularly and exchange information and sometimes even coordinate their activities.

In 2018, more than two decades after the directive was introduced, there were 1,150 EWCs actively operating in Europe, mostly in the metals, chemicals and service sectors (ETUI, 2016). It is estimated that these councils represent roughly 17 million workers, through their 20,000 delegates (ETUI, 2019: 86; Jagodziński, 2016). These councils come from an estimated total of 47,000 potential 'multinational enterprise groups', employing over 43 million employees (ETUI, 2019: 86) – so just under 40% of Europe's eligible workers have joined EWCs.

There are significant differences separating the functions and responsibilities of EWCs and the works councils that are set up on the basis of national labour law in a number of EU countries (Glassner and Pochet, 2011: 10). For this reason, the changing role and influence of EWCs is both complicated and contested (Hann et al, 2017: 210), and their effectiveness varies significantly across national jurisdictions. Not surprisingly, countries with strong unions and high levels of union density are better positioned to take advantage of the opportunities offered by EWCs. In some countries (such as Germany, Italy and the Nordic states), works councils are entitled to negotiate works agreements at the company level (in other words, they wield the power of 'co-determination'), but in most other countries, the scope for EWCs is much more limited.

While EWCs are sometimes touted as an experiment in workplace democracy (for example, Jagodziński, 2016), they offer a rather feeble voice for workers. This is primarily because the councils are only granted access to information and consultation – they do not empower workers to have a formal voice in the decision-making process of the firms where they work. (The political equivalent would be a law that allows citizens to be informed and consulted on important decisions that affect their lives, but not be allowed to actually vote.) But even in their limited form, EWCs don't function as intended and are hampered by a number of legal and practical hurdles (European Commission, 2018d). As a result, the ETUI (2019: 86) concluded: 'it is obvious that the implementation and enforcement of workers' fundamental rights to information and consultation at the appropriate level is not currently being achieved'.

Collective wage bargaining

More than anything else, organized labour in Europe needs to stop workers from underbidding one another – to inhibit Latvian workers from underbidding Spanish workers and vice versa. At the national level, after the Second World War, this sort of protection was accomplished by organizing workers and coordinating their wage claims. By introducing collective bargaining arrangements, organized labour can take wages out of direct competition and provide employers with a higher level of predictability and social peace.[10] Indeed, in small open economies, corporatist wage policy agreements were (and are) used to secure a more just distribution of wages in such a way that wage gains in the sheltered sector will not undermine the competitiveness of wages in the exposed (tradable) sectors (see Aukrust, 1977; Katzenstein, 1985).

The advantages of collective wage-bargaining arrangements are not limited to shielding wages from competition. They can also be used to secure greater voice for workers in the production process, in a way that can easily dovetail with the spread of EWCs. Sometimes, workers will agree to exchange wage increases for increased influence. Collective wage bargaining can also be used to secure a larger share of the economic pie, by ensuring that the rewards from productivity gains are returned to workers. It is because of these three benefits from collective wage bargaining (solidaristic wages, voice and redistribution) that Europe's postwar economic growth brought increased wage solidarity and decreased inequality (Meidner, 1993; Schulten, 2002).

In Europe's common currency area, there is constant pressure for downward wage competition across member states. In this context, lowering wage costs is often heralded as one of the most effective means of maintaining (or securing) competitiveness within the European market. For these reasons, it is especially important for European workers to organize and coordinate their wage claims. Indeed, some form of supranational (pan-European) corporatism may be the only means by which Europe can break out of the competitive wage battle that the common market and monetary union encourages (Glassner and Pochet, 2011; Grote and Schmitter, 1999).

The problem, of course, is that neither employers nor policymakers in Europe are particularly interested in securing solidaristic wage policies, economic redistribution and increased worker voice.[11] To the extent that there is any discussion of the need for more coordinated wage bargaining, it is the sole result of labour movement pressure (Glassner and Pochet, 2011: 12; Léonard et al, 2007) – and the labour movement itself can be divided over the utility of greater collective bargaining.[12]

The need to coordinate wage demands across the breadth of an integrated market is not news to trade unionists. As early as the 1950s, we can trace an ambition among some trade union actors in the EEC to construct a new type of supranational collective bargaining apparatus (Dukes, 2014: 155). This interest was again piqued in the 1970s, as the economic crises of that time sparked interest in transnational trade union cooperation, especially in the exposed (tradeables) sector. It was at this time that unions from the metal sector first began to establish informal cross-border institutions for the exchange of information and policy coordination.

In 1975, the ETUC successfully lobbied the Council of Ministers to create a tripartite conference of capital, labour, government and European Commission representatives (Barnouin, 1986). The formal objective of this conference was to discuss how Europe might achieve full employment by 1980, and the scope of discussions included a general reduction of working time (a 35-hour working week), and five weeks of paid vacation. These talks continued for three years, across four tripartite conferences, in which a whole range of neocorporatist solutions were discussed. But when Europe's employers refused to make the results binding, the ETUC left the talks (Erne, 2008: 83).

As the destructive effects of a common monetary policy became more evident, organized labour in Europe began a second push for greater coordination. Academics, analysts and trade union economists alike began to recognize the need for a wage determination system that was organized at the same level of aggregation as the monetary system, 'to keep workers from being played off against each other, undermining wage and labour standards' (Martin and Ross, 1999: 312).[13]

Around the turn of the millennium, the ETUC, the European Metalworkers' Federation and most other ETUFs noted the need to coordinate national wage policies in order to prevent harmful economic imbalances caused by increased wage competition (Erne, 2008: 86–90). In 1999, in preparation for the coming euro, an ETUC Congress adopted a resolution that highlighted the need to coordinate wage-bargaining policies and established the ETUC Collective Bargaining Coordinating Committee (Cochet, 2002; cited in Erne 2008: 89). On the ground, the metalworkers' unions were at the forefront of developments, as the products of their labour are most exposed to competition in global markets.[14] Other ETUFs have followed suit, adopting formal guidelines for wage setting (based mostly on inflation targets and productivity gains). Despite these initial efforts, however, a European-wide and fully integrated system of industrial relations has yet to emerge – and seems very unlikely in the foreseeable future.[15]

Minimum wages

The last front for progressive worker action might be the battle for a minimum wage in Europe. Securing a hard floor for wages provides labour with more power, because workers no longer need to accept sub-floor wage proposals and working conditions.

As it is now, only 21 of the EU27 member states have statutory minimum wage laws. In other words, six countries do not – but these countries enjoy traditions of autonomous collective bargaining and strong unions, so unions are able to use their labour market power to set the wage floor. Of the 21 countries that do have minimum wage laws, most are set below what is customarily accepted as the poverty threshold, or the equivalent of a 'living wage'.[16] Indeed, only four countries (France, Portugal, Romania and Slovenia) set their minimum wages near or above the poverty threshold (Schulten and Müller, 2019: 273). In addition, the difference between member states is staggering: the highest minimum wages are found in Luxembourg (roughly €12/hour) and the lowest are in Bulgaria (€2/hour) – a difference of €10/hour (Schulten and Lübker, 2019).

These differences have sparked renewed discussion about a minimum wage policy in Europe. For example, when Ursula von der Leyen, the newly elected president of the European Commission, presented her 'Agenda for Europe' in 2019, she included a new European initiative on minimum wages (Schulten and Müller, 2019: 268).

But there are at least three reasons why we shouldn't hold our breath for a European minimum wage. First, the very scope of the differences separating Europe's existing (member-state based) minimum wages makes it difficult to agree to a common European floor. Second, there is much resistance to a minimum wage law in Europe – and not only from employers. Nordic labour unions (and their governments), for example, are strongly opposed to a European minimum wage, as they fear it will undermine their existing wage-setting models (Alsos et al, 2019). Given the strength of organized labour in these countries, workers are able to secure better terms by negotiating in local labour markets than they are through (national) political channels and elections. Finally, there is a formidable legal challenge: wage determination and collective bargaining are explicitly excluded from EU competence under Article 153(5) of the TFEU.

This section was meant to survey the most promising responses that European labour could use to protect its collective interest and to deflect some of the more threatening consequences from market integration in Europe. Unfortunately, developments on each of these fronts – works councils, collective bargaining and minimum wages – provide little room for optimism. In each area, the rhetoric seems to be thicker than the commitment, and the challenges of creating such broad political alliances, across the EU, appear both complex and daunting.

Conclusion

While most of this book has aimed to reveal the demise of structural power for European workers, this chapter has documented the decline in labour's associational power. When put together, we can see a remarkable decline in European labour power, across the board, in terms of: the labour share of national income; union density; the coverage of collective bargaining arrangements; and even the capacity to use strikes to secure more favourable outcomes.

Like its political forms of organization – labour and social democratic parties – the economic organization of labour power is clearly on the back foot. Its most hopeful strategies – increasing worker voice through EWCs, extending collective wage-bargaining arrangements, and establishing a common minimum wage – are all fraught with difficulties and face mountains of resistance. As a consequence, it is difficult to find much room for optimism that a stronger labour movement can rise to improve worker conditions in Europe.

On one measure after the other we have seen a decline in labour's associational power. There have been significant shifts from centralized to decentralized systems of employment relations; a series of labour market reforms designed to undermined labour's relative position; a rapid growth of 'non-standard' employment contracts; the replacement of collective forms of bargaining with more individualized arrangements; and a diminishing role for the traditional social partners in industrial relations, as coverage by union and employee associations declines.

In the end, there seem to be at least two major challenges that can limit the rise of labour power across Europe. The one is legal, the other more political. On the legal front, the scope for active assistance at the EU level remains unclear. This is because Article 153, para. 5 of the TFEU places clear limits on what the Community can do:

> The provisions of this Article *shall not apply* to pay, the right of association, the right to strike or the right to impose lock-outs. (TFEU, Art. 153, para. 5, emphasis added)

This constraint is frequently held up as a means to check the feasibility of any proposal to strengthen worker wage claims in Europe and it will be difficult to change.

On the political front, organized labour confronts a powerful adversary. As in the case with collective wage bargaining, the opposition from employer groups – and the powerful influence these groups hold over European policymakers – provides a second reason for pessimism. In Europe, the organized interests of employers are substantially more powerful than those of workers, and policymakers often end up siding with the employers.

Given the structural and organizational power of employers in Europe, labour has little chance of securing better terms at the European level. But it would be a mistake to focus blame solely on European employers: Europe's divided labour movement is partly to blame for its current sorry state. Like Europe's many varied labour markets, it has proven remarkably difficult to coax European labour movements together to speak with an effective and unified voice.

10

Reducing Workaway

Labour markets are the most sensitive and protected markets we have, as the very health and wellbeing of our citizenry depend upon them. All of us, regardless of our background, education and/or skill level, rely on the labour market to some extent – and some of us are much more dependent upon it than others. For good reasons, there are significant constraints placed on what people are allowed to sell/buy on the formal market for labour, and some of these constraints have been with us for centuries. This is one important reason why the world's labour markets – beyond Europe – remain protected behind imposing border walls and fences, while the barriers to other markets (capital, services and goods) have been slowly rescinded.

In this global context, Europe's willingness and ability to reduce barriers to human mobility is both astonishing and commendable. Because my criticisms of the EU are sometimes misunderstood, let me be absolutely clear on this point: I have long advocated for a world with fewer limits on human mobility (see Moses, 2006), and I see free mobility within Europe as the Community's greatest achievement. But there is more to creating a common labour market than simply reducing barriers to entry. (Just as there is more to securing freedom than the lifting of restrictions.) As described in Chapter 2, local labour markets are highly regulated, and for good reasons. These regulations provide a legal and institutional context, within which individual wage bargains are secured. Europe's integration of these highly regulated markets threatens this dense network of protections in ways that are both complex and costly (for workers).

It is rather remarkable, then, that there has been so little written about the integration of labour markets. Unlike our effort to create a common currency union in Europe, there has been no attempt to commission work that can describe how (or why) we should integrate local labour markets, or even what an optimum labour area might look like. I am not aware of any attempt to collect, systematize and/or compare the experiences of large states when they integrated their local/regional labour markets. One can only speculate as to why Europe has chosen to push forward, blindly, in its effort to create a common labour market.

With this book, I have aimed to fill this void. In so doing, I have approached the study of labour markets in a very different manner from others who are interested in the same topic. I do this because I think the damage being done to labour is deep and structural, and the result is a threat to representative democracy. By looking critically at Europe's decades-long effort at market integration, this study has shown how these efforts have *not* resulted in an increase in the relative power of labour in Europe – either structurally or associationally. On the contrary, Europe's pursuit of market integration is likely responsible for much of labour's relative decline in power. I seriously doubt that this was the original intent of the market reformers, but it is likely the result.

It is time to re-evaluate our relationship to markets and how we choose to integrate them across political territories. This is especially true with respect to labour market integration. The efficiency gains from market integration have been relatively small, but the human costs – in the form of unemployment, poverty and workaway – have been enormous, and unevenly distributed. While the scope of workaway is still relatively limited in Europe, even a single case of market-forced migration is one too many. What is more problematic is the reigning belief that we can build a market that assumes workaway is reasonable, because it is somehow seen as efficient.

This concluding chapter has three parts. First, I want to retrace the steps of my argument to remind readers of the lessons learned. In light of these lessons, I then propose two possible paths forward. The first path offers a strategy to strengthen local political autonomy in Europe. In pursuing this strategy, the EU can weaken the bonds of integration to return more political autonomy and authority to member states (and their capacity to manage local labour markets). This strategy enhances democracy and can help provide the sort of legitimacy that the EU so desperately needs. In this strategy, market integration is managed and strategic – it is encouraged only when it can be done in a way that is clearly beneficial to local authorities and the voters who put them in office. This strategy is derived from the optimum labour area (OLA) approach introduced in Chapter 3 and is closest to the original intent of the EU's founding members, as described in Chapter 4.

A second path offers a different strategy that emphasizes the need to strengthen community: it accepts the current levels of market integration but ensures that the costs and gains are more equally distributed across the community of member states. This strategy is akin to the suboptimum labour area described in Chapter 3, where we recognize and address the substantial human costs of market integration. In pursuing this strategy, Europe should expand its common facilities and institutions, so that local authorities have access to the sort of resources they need to manage their local labour markets during periods of crisis and to deter workaway.

Looking back

Local markets are propelled by the rise and fall of creative destruction; international markets produce one wave of crisis after the other. Labour markets are especially susceptible to these types of shocks, and European labour markets continue to be local, unique and vulnerable. This is a serious problem for the European community, in that every community needs stable access to well-paid jobs; but no community should plan to build its economy on the backs of workaways. There are good reasons why workers prefer to work nearby, and policymakers need to manage/stabilize their local labour markets, so that workers can retain fruitful employment near their homes, friends and families.

When member states lose their local and discretionary tools (Chapter 6); when the EU is unable to replace these tools at the supranational level (Chapter 7); and when factor mobility is entirely inadequate to fill the resulting void (Chapter 8); then the burden of economic adjustment falls disproportionately on workers – in the form of rising unemployment, downward wage pressure and a growing need for workaways. This is unjust.

Unfortunately, this is also the current state of European affairs. European policymakers have created a market that presumes – worse, requires – the greatest inefficiencies of all: increased unemployment and workaway. For Europe's local labour markets to clear, workers have to suffer. In so doing, Europe has also devalued political voice, in that our elected governments have become more responsive to the needs of the market than they are of their own citizens. In Europe, when push comes to shove, the weight of lenders is much greater than the weight of voters (witness the examples of Italy and Greece, as described at the end of Chapter 6).

Perhaps the best example of this hollowing out of democracy can be seen in the 2011 Irish elections, where the Labour Party (in opposition) turned the election into a referendum on Ireland's troika bailout package. The issue facing Irish voters was whether to follow the ECB's advice (emanating from Frankfurt), or to stake out their own democratic route to recovery. In the words of Labour's campaign slogan: 'It's Frankfurt's way or Labour's way.' The resulting election was a landslide, from which Fine Gael and the Labour Party formed the largest majority in Irish electoral history. The Irish people's voice was clear and strong: they wanted to change economic course. It mattered little. Despite overwhelming democratic support for an alternative (less austere) recovery path, little changed: Ireland's fate was to be determined by the needs of the eurozone, not those of its voters. Clearly, elections don't count for much in today's Europe.[1]

In the preceding chapters we have seen how the integration of European markets has made local labour markets more vulnerable. From this work, I have derived six specific lessons that should be heeded as Europe moves forward:

1. Labour markets are different from other markets and should be treated as such. We should stop introducing reforms that try to make labour look more like any other commodity and start creating a market that is more in tune with labour's unique needs and promise.
2. We need to be more critical of attempts to integrate markets and evaluate any proposed reform in terms of *both* justice and efficiency. This is especially important with respect to labour market reforms. Policymakers need to balance the proposed economic gains from a reform against the costs it will impose on democratic voice and legitimacy. Policymakers also need to consider redistribution mechanisms for each market reform, to ensure that the gains are spread more evenly across the community.
3. The integration of European markets has not delivered the convergence, efficiency gains or self-corrections that were promised. Labour markets, in particular, continue to perform asymmetrically and require constant rebalancing and assistance. We need to recognize this lack of convergence and provide the local, elected officials with the tools they need to manage and stabilize their local economies.
4. We need to return more sovereign authority to local and national policymakers, so they can stabilize local economies, where the

jobs are. When policymakers are left without policy tools, many Europeans will be forced to workaway.

5. Not all types of market integration are equal, necessary or beneficial. We need a more nuanced discussion about how to integrate European economies, but our focus should be on trying to balance democratic accountability with any promised efficiency gains.

6. If migration is to become a fourth freedom, we have to lower barriers to mobility *and* stabilize local labour markets. In this way, workers can migrate on their own terms, not out of need or necessity. This provides a more positive form of freedom, where capabilities and (the absence of) constraints are more equally balanced.

In these lessons, we can clearly see how Europe has lost its way. Its member states have agreed to sacrifice their democratic and sovereign authority in exchange for the promise of a more perfect market. To make matters worse, the meagre gains from greater market integration have been distributed unequally: the groups making the largest sacrifices receive the smallest rewards.

Because we have chosen to integrate our markets in this way, we can also unchoose it. Europeans need to regain sovereign control and use it to build a better market in Europe – one more sensitive to our own needs. In so doing, Europe should revisit our earlier discussions about how to integrate markets and remind our policymakers of the need to protect democratic institutions and local labour markets from the plethora of private risk taking and market instabilities that constantly threaten.

In light of these lessons, how might we create a better market, for the benefit of all Europeans? In responding to this question, I fear coming across as someone who romanticizes the historical account. This is because I use previous experience as evidence that alternatives are both possible and practical. To the extent that I see the past providing us with lessons for how we can better protect the weak, distribute the gains from economic growth, and secure greater voice and influence for European voters, then I am perhaps guilty of this form of romanticism. But I also recognize that it is too easy to idealize the past and I see no reason why we should follow these (historical) experiences blindly.

As in the past, there remain two basic strategies for integrating European labour markets: we can strengthen the autonomy and capacity of local markets to adjust to the integration of other markets; or we can strengthen the broader community in Europe, so that it can provide local labour markets with the support they need during periods of economic downturn.

Strengthening autonomy

Because we cannot expect local markets to clear themselves (at least not in the short run), and because the social and human costs of workaway are larger than the promised gains from integration, elected officials need access to more policy tools for managing and stabilizing their local economies. In deciding what sorts of reforms to adopt, policymakers will need to balance the needs of justice and efficiency.

I realize that many of the reforms I am proposing will seem politically untenable. But this is exactly the nature of the threat to democracy that concerns me. Communities need to decide for themselves what is feasible, and how much democratic authority they are willing to sacrifice in exchange for (often hollow) promises of increased economic gain. To kick-start a discussion that could facilitate more democratic decision making, Europe might consider six general reforms to boost our capacity to manage local labour markets. These reforms are aimed at returning just outcomes to local markets, and some of the changes will require a reallocation of resources.[2]

First, member states might exit the common currency area and reintroduce their national currencies. I see this reform as the most significant, but also the most unlikely, given the apparent costs involved. The fastest, fairest and most efficient way for correcting local current account deficits is by way of a depreciation/devaluation of the national currency (supported by incomes policies that deter subsequent inflation). In addition, the many benefits of sovereign money creation should not be lost on policymakers.[3] This is the clear lesson of Europe's divergent responses to the Great Recession (Moses, 2017a). Even though there is broad recognition of the costs of Europe's suboptimum currency union, it will prove very difficult, risky and costly for states to break out of it.

There are basically two approaches to thinking about this radical option. On the one hand, and as Clause Offe (2016: 55, emphasis in original) notes: '*The Euro, in short, is a mistake the undoing of which would be an even greater mistake.*'[4] On the other hand, doing nothing may very well bring the whole system tumbling down. This possibility has been suggested by László Andor, the then (2010–14) European commissioner responsible for employment, social affairs and inclusion:

> The only remaining adjustment mechanisms are loss of population through emigration, and internal devaluation, with all its adverse effects on aggregate demand, human capital and social cohesion. If these existing ways to

restore competitiveness prove more painful than currency devaluation, we cannot assume that the commitment to the single currency can last forever. (Andor, 2013b: 3)

Limiting interstate capital mobility is the second important reform that member states can undertake. Local communities need to have more say in how social investments are made, and controlling capital is the most effective way of doing so. Creating more public and community-based banking services will also prove helpful. Clearly, this will be difficult, given Europe's current political order, but controlling capital is absolutely necessary if Europe is to reassert democratic control over its economy. Limiting the threat of capital flight is necessary for several of the reforms noted later, including the possibility of increased taxation, regulations, local procurement plans, and to level the playing field between labour and capital within national contexts. In the end, foreign investors who wish to invest in a new community must be willing to accept the rules imposed by that community.

A third reform is to provide member states with greater fiscal autonomy and flexibility so that local and national governments can again prioritize constituent interests over contractual obligations for the sake of a common currency. States should be held responsible for their own fiscal decisions, and policymakers should be held accountable to their electorates. This means that states should have the freedom to run budget deficits and accumulate debt during times of economic crises (and pay the requisite economic price to lenders), and sovereign legislatures should be free to decide the size, scope, timing and nature of their national budgets.

Fourth, states need to be allowed to regulate their home economy in ways that reflect democratic norms and ambitions. Democratically elected officials should be free to set their own regulations and make them as onerous (or as attractive) as they wish: outside producers, contractors and investors should be expected to meet their requirements if they want to compete in those local markets. There is no need for point-of-origin regulations in any integrated market.

Fifth, local government officials need the freedom to prioritize local producers and set local guidelines for their procurement needs. Communities should be able to decide for themselves how they want to spend their money. If these procurement programmes are abused, then voters should enjoy the authority to address and correct such abuses.

Finally, member state governments need to work closely with labour organizations to strengthen their relative bargaining position and to raise the local floor for wages and working conditions. They might do this by creating diverse incentives for trade union membership (for example by adopting the Ghent system); by encouraging and facilitating collective bargaining arrangements, and by introducing legislation that will strengthen worker voice on investment and management decisions.

All of these reforms can be introduced without limiting labour mobility, or reintroducing restrictions on cross-border labour flows. In this way, the reforms could truly enhance freedom. Our objectives should be to secure the gains from market integration by focusing that integration in areas that have the smallest impact on democratic accountability and economic inequality. It is entirely possible to embrace free trade in goods and free migration, while limiting capital mobility and maintaining strong welfare regimes and workplace regulations that reflect the needs of varying (and different) political communities.

For those who are sceptical of the economic feasibility of such reforms, I direct your attention to the world's oldest and most successful exercise in labour market integration: the Nordic Common Labour Market (NCLM).[5] Established in May 1954, the NCLM granted Nordic citizens the right to settle in any other Nordic country (Denmark, Sweden, Norway and Finland – Iceland joined in 1982), even if they did not have work. In the following year (1955), these same countries signed the Nordic Social Security Convention. This convention required that Nordic states treat immigrants from other Nordic countries as they would their own with respect to social security entitlements (and to cover the costs of such equal treatment if necessary). This arrangement provided Nordic immigrants free access to extended services in health and insurance, but also the right to unemployment benefits. In short, the NCLM is more than a common labour area: it is a common citizenship area, where migrants cannot be discriminated against on the basis of their nationality, and they enjoy full citizenship (and worker) rights across the common labour market. These rights are not granted for a limited period of time.

This integrated labour market was secured *before* the establishment, in 1960, of a free trade agreement (EFTA), and continues to exist among countries that (mostly) maintain monetary policy autonomy and do not share a common monetary union. Although Finland joined the eurozone, Sweden and Denmark (both EU member states) have retained their own currencies, and Norway is not a member of either the EU or its eurozone. Indeed, during the Bretton Woods era, international capital mobility was limited across NCLM member states. This context provided Nordic states with the breathing space they needed to pursue popular and effective domestic policies. Over the decades, Nordic authorities have been able to maintain high levels of employment, by wielding a full spectrum of policy tools: they have devalued; developed regional investment funds; introduced language and licensing restrictions; employed tariff and non-tariff barriers to trade; and so on – each in an effort to protect local markets and encourage local producers. In effect, the Nordic countries integrated their markets by prioritizing the rights of their citizens over the needs of traders and financiers/investors.

Just as importantly, this shared labour market did not undermine labour power in the Nordic region. The Nordic countries are known for their strong labour movements (and social democratic political parties), active manpower policies, corporatist and flexicurity traditions. The terms of the Nordic Common Labour Market allow local officials to manage local economic conditions and labour unions to maintain (perhaps even increase) their relative positions of power. This economic growth and stability has occurred without the need for workaways:

> Despite tariff and non-tariff barriers to trade and a limited capital mobility, extensive personal freedom of movement in the Nordic Common Labour Market did not result in any mass migration. On the contrary: since the establishment of the Nordic labour market, migration levels relative to migration to and from countries outside the Nordic countries have fallen in both absolute and relative terms. (Fischer and Straubhaar, 1996: 200)

The Nordic region is made up of countries that share similar economic characteristics: they are wealthy, their wealth is equally distributed, and they share a tradition of strong labour movements (and social democratic parties in government). This may make the lessons generated by the NCLM difficult to transfer to the larger and more diversified common market in Europe. But the NCLM clearly demonstrates that there are different ways to integrate labour markets, and that it is possible to secure a more just and efficient form of integration (than we see in Europe today).

While we cannot be sure whether the NCLM is responsible for labour's strong showing across the Nordic region, or whether the factors that generate a strong labour movement also explain the nature of the NCLM, there can be little doubt that labour market integration in Northern Europe is concomitant with a strong labour presence. The same can be said of the Nordic region's broader economic achievements: the NCLM has clearly not hindered the Nordic region's ability to grow and remain competitive in the international economy.

The NCLM is perhaps the closest example we have of an OLA, as outlined in Chapter 3. Its track record clearly demonstrates that it is neither utopian, inefficient nor unrealistic to create an OLA. For this reason, it proves a useful example as to how Europe can better integrate its sundry labour markets.

Strengthening community

A second strategy for integrating Europe's labour markets recognizes the efficiency gains that can be secured by greater integration, but redistributes those gains in a more just manner, and in ways that build democratic support and legitimacy for this integration.

The underlying logic for such an approach can be found in the way economists often justify and sustain support for trade, more generally: such as by expanding the European Globalization Adjustment Fund and redirecting it inwards. As a similar challenge faces all types of market integration, Europe might develop an integration adjustment assistance programme that provides support for those people and regions that are negatively impacted from integration. This was, after all, the original intent of the European Social Fund, as described in Chapter 4. But any such programme would have to be substantial if it is to be effective. If properly designed and funded, underdeveloped areas or regions/member states that experience a local economic downturn could receive more support from the larger community, in payment for the sacrifices they have made in the name of increased efficiency gains.

In short, this second strategy accepts the common currency area and the other forms of market integration, but uses OLA theory to help devise a support system that can redistribute the uneven costs associated with market integration. The most important part of this response is a need to expand the EU budget – both in terms of its size and the way in which the EU collects and spends its resources, as described in Chapter 7. It should be clear that the nature of European market integration requires a much more active and interventionist policy at both the micro and meso levels of the economy, and this policy could be directed from Brussels (Scharpf, 2016: 43). But this type of intervention is not costless.

There are many ways this money can be spent, and there is much discussion about the costs and benefits of each. Andor (2013a, 2013b), for example, has focused on the need for greater EU-level capacity to support recovery from cyclical downturns in each member state, along with an EU-wide unemployment benefit scheme. Alternatively, Phillip van Parisj (2013) has proposed the creation of a euro dividend.

Claus Offe (2016: 124–7) offers a number of policy proposals aimed at creating a stronger commitment to a social Europe. Among his proposals are the need for a more progressive system of taxation; the Europeanization of unemployment benefits and poverty relief; and the introduction of a lid/ceiling for permissible Gini coefficients. We do not lack ideas, only the requisite money and political will.

Given the scope of capital mobility within Europe, EU-wide tax harmonization is especially important, as competing tax regimes allow investors to 'regime shop' and encourage interstate capital flight. As we saw in Chapter 7, it is also important for the EU to secure access to its own source of tax revenues (such as personal and corporate income taxes), and increase them significantly, to facilitate a greater downward flow of transfers. Once Europe builds up its capacity to tax capital, and gets rid of the incentives for capital to strike (flee), member state budgets can be funded by higher taxes on income and wealth – rather than relying on austerity measures and internal devaluations.[6]

In addition to introducing significant changes to the EU's central budget, Europe should provide better and stronger regulations and legislation to secure binding employment and social standards (see Andor, 2013a, 2013b). In effect, EU regulations need to establish protective/regulatory floors, and then raise these floors over time. Given the diminished structural and associational power of labour, as described in Chapter 9, this will be anything but easy.

Just as the first strategy for labour market integration can be informed by the NCLM, this second strategy can build on the experiences of other large continental economies sharing a common currency, such as China, India or the US. Given the amount of research on the case, the US Common Labour Market (USCLM) is perhaps the most relevant model. From the perspective of labour, this should cause some concern – as the US approach is hardly worker-friendly: workaway was (and probably still is) the dominant means by which local economic adjustment takes place in the US (Blanchard and Katz, 1992: 52). Still, we can learn from the US example, and do better.

I have already described the more general ways in which regional economies in the US are forced to adjust to the absence of local monetary policy autonomy. US states adjust to local economic challenges by way of workaway, wage/price flexibility and federal fiscal transfers. What concerns me is that Europe's capacity for federal fiscal transfers is relatively limited, so that the main burden of adjustment in Europe falls more squarely on workers.

This concern is exacerbated when we look closer at the US evidence: workaway responses to regional labour demand in the US are actually quite slow and incomplete (Blanchard and Katz, 1992; Yagan, 2014) and the cost of adjustment falls hardest on less educated workers (Bound and Holzer, 2000; Wozniak, 2010; Malamud and Wozniak, 2012; Diamond, 2016). As noted in Chapter 5, the work of David Autor and his colleagues has demonstrated how slow and ineffective regional labour market adjustments have been in response to trade shocks emanating from China (see Autor et al, 2016).

While it is relatively common to note that labour mobility in the US is higher than in the EU, it is less recognized that US labour mobility is even higher than mobility *within* European countries (Bonin et al, 2008: 4). Despite these higher levels, US labour mobility rates seem to be falling in recent years, especially after the Great Recession. In the 1950s, 7% of the US population would move from one county to another every year. In 2018, only 4% moved (Banerjee and Duflo, 2019: 43). While the apparent reduction in US workaways is encouraging, it simply means that the burden of adjustment has been shifted once again. Europe should take notice.[7]

The USCLM does not facilitate regional convergence – if anything, it does the opposite. In response to temporary regional economic shocks, workers are forced to move and many don't seem to return. This leads to permeant regional decline. As Blanchard and Katz demonstrated back in 1992, the USCLM facilitated the permanent decline of population and economies in cities (think Detroit) and states (think Michigan), through unemployment, falling wages and workaway. If the US example is relevant, Europe can expect a similar fate for its newer member states, as workers flee failed local markets, setting in motion a permanent, long-term decline.

Europe's current status lies nearest this second strategy. The problem is that Europe lags behind the US in terms of the flexibility of its workforce and its capacity to deliver significant federal fiscal transfers. We have a long way to go before we can build a stronger community in Europe.

Conclusion

I do not think that Europe can continue on its present path. I wonder how many rounds of future economic crises the EU can survive; it is simply not strong enough, nor designed appropriately, to protect European workers. When these failures pile up, Europeans will eventually stop supporting the project. In order to rebuild its democratic legitimacy and public support, the EU needs to provide its member states with more scope for governance and justice and redesign its common markets accordingly.

I have laid out two possible strategies for moving forwards. Both strategies are heavily contested, but from different directions. The first strategy aims to build a more just market by returning political power to elected officials, closer to their constituents. If allowed to vote, I suspect this strategy would prove most popular among Europeans. But Europeans are no longer allowed to vote on such important questions, as they tend to vote incorrectly (from the perspective of EU authorities). This ugly truth was revealed in the popular vetoes to the Constitution for Europe in 2004/5, and the subsequent cancellation of the remaining referendums. Worse, proponents of this approach are often portrayed as luddites, as a return to sovereignty is seen as a historical retreat from the common market. Consequently, elements of this strategy are simply not discussed in polite political company. In short, the challenge to this strategy comes from those who benefit most from the current form of integration, and they use their market power to threaten the spectre of economic collapse and to hinder popular reforms.

The second strategy continues to embrace the efficiency gains promised from greater economic integration but aims to right the resulting wrongs by creating a stronger state at the EU level. While this strategy is most favoured by Europhiles, it faces a serious challenge from below. Citizens of EU member states are hardly inclined to send more money and power to Brussels or Frankfurt. Quite simply, the EU lacks the legitimacy needed to deliver the sort of community response that is necessary in an integrated market.

A two-pronged strategy is anything but new: it is as old as the European dream. Choosing between these two strategies is hard. It has always been hard. For this reason, it has been most convenient to postpone the hard choice and to let the resulting policy fall somewhere in between these two options. But this compromise solution is unsustainable because of the standard by which we have chosen to gauge our progress. With little public discussion, policymakers have chosen to evaluate reform options in terms of a very narrow understanding of efficiency, while largely ignoring questions of justice. The result is a policy trajectory that has us chasing the US example, in hopes of creating a more perfect market.

It was not always this way and it need not remain this way. For much of Europe's postwar history, policymakers in Europe pushed for something better. Europe has held itself up as an alternative to the US, with the promise of creating a more humane form of capitalism – one which could protect and nurture its labour force. That earlier Europe embraced a different kind of ESM: a European social model, rather than a European Stability Mechanism. In the beginning, a European Community assembled a number of democratic states, each with their own system of domestic worker protections and avenues for influence, then promised to integrate them in a way that would be beneficial for all.

I have written this book in the hope that Europe can return to its original intent of creating a Community, and a market that suits the needs of that Community: a more just market.

Notes

Chapter 1

[1] See, for example, Block and Somers (2014: 30).

[2] 'Well-functioning labour and product markets ensure the efficient allocation of resources, contribute to making economies more resilient and strengthen growth potential in the long run' (European Commission 2017a: 7). See also Birindelli and Rustichelli (2007), Bonin et al (2008) and Cerf (2018).

[3] I'm using this terminology as the Great Recession was the result of several crises, layered on top of one another. After the initial financial crisis, Europe suffered from a subsequent current account and deficit crisis, which was especially pronounced in the euro area. See Moses (2017a).

[4] There is a third approach, which is much less influential, more critical and, significantly, does not have the ear of policymakers. This approach draws on the work of sociologists and labour lawyers, especially the work of Fritz Scharpf (2002, 2010). But see also Dukes (2014) and Streeck (2019). I will build on this work in subsequent chapters.

[5] This with a nod to Sir Isaiah Berlin (1958), and his concepts of negative and positive liberty. Negative liberty refers to the absence of interference with a person's sphere of action; positive liberty, by contrast, refers to an individual's effective power or mastery over her/himself or environment.

[6] This sort of work is not limited to the EU, but tends to flourish there. See, for example, Zimmermann (2009); Jileva (2002); Heinz and Ward-Warmedinger (2006); European Commission (2001); and Fertig and Schmidt (2002). Others have argued for a parallel development at the global level, myself included (Moses, 2006). See also Harris (2002) and Hayter (2004).

[7] For background, see Barslund and Busse (2014). For typical examples, see OECD (2016, especially pp. 29–31), or European Council (2019).

[8] This approach has deep roots that extend beyond the EU and back in time. There are those who cover the pre-First World War period of global immigration, for example Williamson (1995, 1996); O'Rourke et al (1996); and Chiswick and Hatton (2003). But there are also many studies that focus on migration within national and across supranational contexts: in a unified Germany, see, for example, Bonin and Zimmermann (2000); Burda and Hunt (2001); Burda (2006); Parikh and Van Leuvensteijn (2003); Gernandt and Pfeiffer (2008); and Krueger and Pischke (1995). Across the US and North America, see, for example, Gomez and Gunderson (2002); Eberts and Schweitzer (1994); Robertson (2000, 2005); and Rosenbloom (1990, 1996). In India, see, for example, From the Editors' Desk

(2009) and Collins (1999) for a study of conditions in the 19th century; an analysis of the integration of China's labour market can be found in Cai et al (2007). Finally, for studies of labour market integration in the EU, from this perspective, see, for example, Andersen et al (2000); Raines (2000); Heckmann and Schnapper (2003); ECB (2006); Kahanec (2013); and Bertelsmann Stiftung (2014). For a thorough review of expert opinion on these matters, see Krause et al (2017).

[9] The most authoritative text remains De Grauwe's (2018) *Economics of Monetary Integration*, now in its 12th edition. Mundell (1961) is the impetus for much of this work, but see also Eichengreen (1997), while Jones (2019) provides the best overall summary to date.

[10] The most common version of this argument is found in the realm of trade theory. Among economists there is a consensus about the economic gains from free trade (relative to not trading). But there is also a recognition that these larger gains to the economy come at the expense of individual workers and investors who are adversely exposed to that trade. For example, local garment producers in the US will lose their jobs in the face of cheaper imports from garment producers in Bangladesh. To ensure that the overall economy can benefit from trade, governments can provide assistance to help retrain and relocate workers who are adversely affected by foreign imports (in the US, this is referred to as 'Trade Adjustment Assistance'; similarly, Europe has its European Globalization Adjustment Fund). By transferring a portion of the overall gains to those most adversely affected, the broader economy can benefit from the gains generated by free trade.

[11] For examples, see the work of Leif Hoffmann (2008, 2011, 2014).

[12] This pattern is also evident if we narrow the focus to net migrant outflows, where the largest per mil outflows in 2017 were Luxembourg (!) (32.9); Lithuania (28.5); Romania (22.6); Croatia (20.6) and Ireland (19.5).

[13] More precisely, the correlate of variation across the EU28 falls from 0.66 in 2004 to 0.54 in 2018.

[14] These trends are revealed in the Eurostat unemployment data (une_rt_a), for workers under 25 years of age.

[15] It is somewhat unfair to focus such critical attention on economists, but it is this sort of thinking that fuels much of contemporary market reforms. Political theorists work along similar lines. Consider Plato's *Republic* as an ideal state, against which real-world polities are compared.

[16] One exception, although very general and now outdated, is Kluth (1998).

[17] See Chapter 2 for a description of the different components of labour power.

[18] I recognize that many analysts still believe there is little scope for monetary policy autonomy in Europe. This belief was probably formed prior to 2008. Since that time, it has become clear that monetary policy autonomy is one of the important differences that separated successful from unsuccessful national responses to the Great Recession. This scope for monetary policy autonomy will be further described in Chapter 6.

Chapter 2

[1] This is not just because workers need wages to survive, but also because employers are people too, and are willing to pay non-competitive wages, in exchange for loyalty. For example, research has demonstrated how employers are unwilling to cut wages during economic downturns, and often pay more than the cost of

replacement in an effort to boost morale and productivity (Ackerlof and Yellen, 1988; Bewley, 1999).

2   This distinction is most explicit in Wright (2000: 962), but the underlying understanding of labour power is shared by most power resource approaches (even as they recognize difference faces of power, and how they are to be operationalized). See, for example, Korpi (1974, 1983), Silver (2003) and Schmalz et al (2018).

3   Of course, the state puts a finger on both sides of the scale. In the original creation of national labour markets, the state played an important role in disciplining that workforce and removing any attractive alternatives to wage labour. 'The supply of labour for waged work did not arrive out of the ether or as some spontaneous evolution from feudalism, but could only be guaranteed after a protracted process of government intervention, which created a dependency on wages for subsistence' (Doogan, 2009: 103). Of course, the foundation for this argument was laid by Marx (1954 [1867]: 165) and Polanyi (2001 [1944]), and its most prominent examples come from the Frankfurt School, in the earlier work of Jürgen Habermas (1975) and Claus Offe (1972, 1984).

4   Another, related, tradition refers to constitutions, specifically labour constitutions. This tradition is inspired by the early work of Hugo Sinzheimer and Otto Kahn-Freund. See, for example, Dukes (2014).

5   The same logic applies to obligations. For example, perhaps a state has a military draft where all citizens of a given age are required to serve in the military for a fixed amount of time. This particular obligation is derived by citizenship, linked to specific political community. There are also worker-based obligations linked to territory, for example the payment of a payroll tax.

6   For economists, a reservation wage is the wage that makes a worker indifferent between working and not working. Note, however, the lack of realism in the purported trade-off: economists assume that workers can choose not to work!

7   Further evidence of the entirely human desire to remain close to home can be seen in a 2018 survey by Esther Duflo and Abhijit Banerjee. They asked 10,000 Americans whether they thought an unemployed person should be willing to chase a job that is 200 miles (about 320 km) away. Sixty-two per cent of those who responded thought that an unemployed person should move for the job. But when these people were asked if they themselves would be willing to move for a job, the respondents were less enthusiastic: only 52% said they would be willing to move, and this fell to just 32% among those who were actually unemployed (Duflo and Banerjee, 2019).

8   One very important exception is Gunnar Myrdal, whose work has been largely forgotten. Myrdal defined economic integration as 'the realization of the old Western ideal of equality of opportunity' (Myrdal, 1956: 11).

Chapter 3

1   For example, Gros and Thygesen (1998); McNamara (1998); Frieden et al (1998); Jones et al (1998); and De Grauwe (2018). Indeed, I participated in a number of these studies myself (Moses, 1998a, 1998b).

2   For example, Mundell (1961). Consider, also, the title to Meade's (1957) contribution, upon which Mundell's argument rests: 'The balance-of-payments problems of a European free-trade area'. On the importance of including fiscal policy and transfer considerations in the OCA equation, see Kenen (2019 [1969]).

For an excellent overview of the different contributions in early OCA work, see Jones (2019).

[3] For a good review, see Darvas and Szapary (2004). Much of the work in this area extends the argument originally made by Frankel and Rose (1998) and Rose (2000, 2002), linking trade integration and business cycles.

[4] There are several problems with this argument, the largest of which is that it ignores 200 plus years of American monetary history, where regional (state) economies refuse to surrender their unique characteristics, despite sharing a currency union and an otherwise highly integrated national economy (see, for example, Blanchard and Katz, 1992).

[5] This is because the US Congress secured an exclusive right to coin money back in 1788. See, for example, Rockoff (2000); Sala-i-Martin and Sachs (1991); and Inman and Rubinfeld (1991).

[6] See, for example, Eichengreen (1991) and De Grauwe (2018). Tavlas's (1993) 'critical approach', or 'new theory of OCA' contains nine such conditions: similarity of inflation rates, factor mobility, openness/size of the economy, commodity diversification, price and wage flexibility and goods market integration, fiscal integration, little need for real exchange rate variability, as well as political will. Under these conditions, Tavlas holds that there is a low prevalence of asymmetric shocks.

[7] Washington State's reliance on a single industry was stronger in the past than it is today, but the lesson still holds.

[8] From this perspective, creating a common currency union can kill two birds with one stone: it can be used to undermine/weaken labour regulations and institutions – ensuring that wages are more (downward) flexible; and it will force member states to cut back on public support services – pushing increased commodification and workaways. These sacrifices are promised to make Europe more competitive (regionally and internationally) by forcing workers to be more responsive to market conditions (often assumed to be the source of Eurosclerosis).

[9] To be clear, this option belongs more with Mundell's teacher, James Meade, than with Mundell. Mundell's piece was written in response to Meade's argument for greater local autonomy (see Chapter 4). Mundell found Meade's argument to be ridiculous, when pushed to its conclusion, as it would mean that the US would benefit from breaking up into a number of smaller currency areas. I find the argument especially attractive for that very reason. See, for example, Appelbaum (2019: 246–7).

[10] The gutting of sovereign policies is not restricted to the EU; it is part of a larger push for market fundamentalism by a number of international organizations (for example the World Trade Organization, the International Monetary Fund and the World Bank). In most cases, the promised efficiency gains from 'deregulation' are entirely insufficient to pay for the loss in democratic/sovereign autonomy. See Moses (2021).

[11] I am aware of the political difficulties associated with this proposal and address them in Chapter 10. For now, I am simply presenting an ideal market approach.

[12] There are costs to pursuing an independent monetary policy, including the threat of inflation. I do not mean to suggest this alternative is without challenges. See Moses (2017a: Ch. 2).

[13] Capital market integration is not necessary to secure the promised gains from economic integration – most of these can be secured by trade in goods. Economists know that factor price convergence can occur even in the absence of factor (labour

or capital) mobility – as the equalization of factor prices results from international specialization and the division of labour made possible by trade. The origins of this argument can be traced back to Robert Mundell's (1957) equivalence proposition and Paul Samuelson's (1948, 1949) Heckscher-Ohlin analyses. In short, to the extent that the gains of economic integration are derived from factor price convergence, it does not matter how markets are integrated – the same effect can come from labour market integration, capital market integration or trade in goods and services (Moses, 2000).

Chapter 4

[1] I am not alone in revising this journey, see, for example, Salais (2013).

[2] See Segers (2019: 63) for a recent revisiting of this 'internal-external Janus-face of stability'.

[3] Yet another example that could have been included is Gunnar Myrdal's (1956) *An International Economy*. Although Myrdal's argument is much larger than economic integration in Europe, his analysis is quite similar to the accounts surveyed in this chapter. In particular, he argued that: 'No country in Western Europe is today prepared to accept a significant increase in unemployment or even a serious scaling down of living standards in one industry as the price of economic integration, with other countries, even its closest neighbors' (Myrdal, 1956: 63). For a recent attempt to reboot Myrdal as a model for thinking about European (dis)integration, see Jones (2018).

[4] This same sort of prioritization is revealed in James Meade's seminal article on the balance of payments problem in Europe, where he noted how: 'Governments are nowadays so wedded (and, in my opinion, rightly so wedded) to the idea that it is one of their duties to preserve full employment' (1957: 385). Indeed, when push came to shove, Meade recognized that: 'Full employment is more important than free trade for Europe' (1957: 394).

[5] In the French delegation's report to that meeting, we find a little more information: it would seem that the Community believed the invisible hand was a helping hand: 'This upward equalisation must essentially be the result of the function of the common market itself, provided that the rules of competition, especially those in respect of wages, permit the economic mechanism to bring about the result' (see Ministère des Affaires étrangères, 1951: 130, my translation).

[6] Meade had also accumulated a significant amount of policy experience, working first as a member of the economics section at the League of Nations in Geneva, then as an economic adviser and director of the economic section of the British Cabinet during the Second World War. Much later, in 1977, he won the Nobel Prize in Economics, together with Bertil Ohlin (Stevenson, 1995).

[7] The GoE came about after an initial report from the first European Regional Conference of the International Labour Organization (ILO, 1955: 73ff), which prompted the Governing Body of the ILO, at its 128th session in March 1955, to appoint the Group of Experts: Maurice Byé of France; T.U. Matthew of the UK; Helmut Meinhold of Germany; Bertil Ohlin of Sweden; Pasquale Saraceno of Italy; and Petrus J. Verdoorn of the Netherlands.

[8] They also recognize the existence of what they call 'frictional unemployment' in a regime of free trade. To address this, they recognize that Europe 'will probably require a higher degree of mobility of factors of production between occupations, industries and areas' (GoE, 1956: §231).

[9] I should note that there was at least one other critical French-speaking voice at the time, who has received a little more attention, but whose work has never been translated into English. I'm referring to the report by Albert Delpérée: a Belgian academic and civil servant who chaired the Organization for European Economic Co-operation's Manpower Committee (see Delpérée, 1956). To place Delpérée's report in a broader context, visit Sapir (1996) and Dukes (2014).

[10] The Spaak Report is available in three formats: the original French version (Spaak Report, 1956); an unofficial English translation of selected parts from the ECSC High Authority (Information Service, 1956), and a more thorough English translation published in *Political and Economic Planning* (1957).

[11] At the same time, unions were increasingly split along communist/socialist lines. For example, within the World Federation of Trade Unions, socialist unions split with their communist counterparts. See, for example, Barnouin (1986: 4).

[12] Speech made to the Foreign Press Association in Paris on 13 April 1951. Quoted in Roux (1952: 290).

Chapter 5

[1] https://ec.europa.eu/eurostat/cache/bcc/bcc.html

[2] For reviews of the literature on business cycles and the euro, see Giannone et al (2009: 8–12); Bandrés et al (2017: 10–15); and De Haan et al (2008). Pisani-Ferry (2012) describes how the eurozone continues to be hit by frequent and substantial country-specific shocks.

[3] A number of recent studies have looked at how the Great Recession affected these social models. See Zwick and Syed (2017); the special 2017 issue of the *International Journal of Manpower*, 38(7); and Boeri and Jimeno (2015).

Chapter 6

[1] This is because national economic intervention, even when it is well meant and designed, *can* generate spillovers that harm other countries. This happens, for example, when one member state attracts mobile investors, at the expense of others, by exacting a lower level of corporate income tax. In many areas, some form of coordination or harmonization can be necessary in order to secure the gains from integration.

[2] There is a large and distinguished literature supporting more or less protectionist routes to economic development, but it is seldom discussed in the EU literature, except in the context of reintroducing industrial policies (see Mazzucato et al, 2015). Reinert (2017) offers an exception. Some of the headline names in this tradition include Hamilton (1791), List (1916 [1841]), Gerschenkron (1962), Prebisch (1950), Singer (1950), Reinert (2007) and Chang (2002).

[3] This clause can be found in both Article 2 of the Procurement Directive and Article 10 of the Utilities Procurement Directive.

[4] For greater detail on these cases, see Moses (2011); Zimmer (2011); and several contributions in Bücker and Warneck (2010).

[5] For further discussion on the scope of this sort of scapegoating and depoliticization, see Mitchell and Fazi (2017: 69, 108, 138–9, 145).

[6] For a more detailed discussion of the role of monetary policy in the European economy, see chapter 2, 'The political costs of monetary union' in Moses (2017a).

[7] For introductions to modern monetary theory, see Kelton (2020), Mitchell and Fazi (2017) and Wray (2015).

[8] This was, of course, controversial, and sparked a debate about the legality of capital controls in the eurozone. See Sandbu (2013).

[9] Article 63 in the TFEU bans restrictions on 'movement of capital' and 'payments' between EU member states, but subsequent treaty articles list exceptional circumstances where bans would be allowed. For example, Article 65(1b) in the TFEU allows states 'to take measures which are justified on grounds of public policy or public security'.

[10] As with monetary policy autonomy, there is some disagreement about the utility and effectiveness of autonomous fiscal policies. As Eichengreen (2014: 12) has noted: 'The debate over whether fiscal policy has real effects or crowds out private-sector spending one-for-one has a heavy ideological component and cannot be resolved here, although recent work by the IMF would seem to provide strong evidence of real effects in the European context.' See, for example, Blanchard and Leigh (2013).

[11] For overviews of these complex processes, see several contributions in Chalmers et al (2016); Savage and Verdun (2016); and Seikel (2016). For a nice historical snapshot of pre-Euro monetary history, see Janus and Stanek (2016).

[12] On the other hand, the Fiscal Compact allows for a little more fiscal flexibility over the life of the business cycle (relative to the SGP), but 'it provides neither enough flexibility nor enough credibility for the circumstances at hand' (Eichengreen, 2014: 12).

Chapter 7

[1] For general introductions to European social and labour market policies, see Mosley (1990); Rhodes (1992); Kenner (2003); Clauwaert and Schömann (2012); Schömann (2014); De la Porte and Heins (2015); Schellinger (2016); Weiss (2017); Hendrickx (2018); and several contributions in Vanhercke et al (2020).

[2] Some have argued that the ECJ has managed to introduce a social dimension in some of its verdicts (see Caporaso and Tarrow, 2009). The December 2020 ECJ decision to uphold a revised Posted Workers Directive (Directive 2018/957) provides additional grounds for optimism (ECJ, 2020), as described in Chapter 6. For the most part, however, the ECJ has not been very supportive of the EU's social dimension when it challenges the basic free-market principles laid out in the treaties (see Schapf, 2002).

[3] The OMC was first developed in the context of European employment policy. On its relationship to labour market policy, see Weiss (2017: 349); Goetschy (2005); and Kenner (2003: 424, Ch. 11).

[4] For a comprehensive empirical survey of contemporary fiscal federalism, see Cottarelli and Guerguil (2015a).

[5] A good and influential overview of the official response is provided by the Tommaso Padoa-Schioppa Group (2012). For more critical views, see also IMF (2013a, 2013b) and Henning and Kessler (2012). Not everybody agrees that greater fiscal federalism is necessary in Europe's common currency area. For example, see Jones (2016).

[6] One alternative (in theory) is to use the ECB to fund a larger EU budget by means of money/credit creation. In this way, EU spending could increase without

requiring additional contributions from strapped member states. But this type of modern monetary theory approach remains beyond the political pale in Europe (and elsewhere).

[7]   I recognize that the EU does not constitute a federal state, and that many readers may bristle at the federalist language employed here. I ask for some leeway in comparing EU responses to other large, multilevel political entities that share a common currency, and cautiously borrow the language of federalism to make this comparison.

[8]   These lessons are derived from a vast and established literature – both theoretical and empirical in nature. See Musgrave (1959); Tiebout (1956); Oates (1972, 2005); and the IMF (2009).

[9]   To avoid getting stuck in a political quagmire, this section simply assumes that these federal states are unable to issue additional money/credit to pay for these functions. In practice, of course, it is precisely these states (at the federal/central level), that enjoy fiat currencies. See, for example, Kelton (2020).

[10]   There is an extensive literature that evaluates the effects of these transfers, in terms of distribution and stabilization/risk-sharing effects (among other things). For a recent review, and comprehensive test, see Poghosyan et al (2015).

[11]   This can happen even in federal states like the US, which lack explicit equalization transfers and/or a social preference for interregional redistribution. This occurs because the US federal income tax system is mildly progressive, but the US federal expenditure programmes (social security, infrastructure spending, targeted grants, disaster relief) benefit all member states across the federation, independent of their local tax capacity. In a recent study (Poghosyan et al, 2015: 82), the impact of redistribution in three federal states ranged from 13% (in the US) to 24% (in Australia). In the US example, West Virginia, the biggest net recipient, received a median annual net fiscal transfer that was almost 20% of that state's GDP (Poghosyan et al, 2015: 71–2).

[12]   This is currently being challenged by the demands of an EU response to the COVID-19 pandemic. See the description of the COVID-19 response at the end of this chapter.

[13]   In its online FAQ, which asks if the Commission is planning to introduce direct taxes, the response is unequivocal: 'No – the Commission has never proposed this. National governments and local authorities are and will continue to be in charge of setting and collecting taxes' (European Commission, n.d.). In its 2020 *Fact Check on the EU Budget*, the Commission is a little more precise, in promising: 'The EU is not planning to introduce any type of a tax on EU citizens' (European Commission, 2020c: 3).

[14]   Useful overviews of Europe's Cohesion Policy are provided by Bachtler and Gorzelak (2007), Manzella and Mendez (2009) and Dudek (2014). A comprehensive overview of the effects of this Cohesion Policy is provided by Bachtler et al (2017).

[15]   In particular, the ERDF was also a response to British membership demands, and its realization that it would not be able to tap into the lucrative CAP benefits.

[16]   See, for example, Beetsma and Giuliodori (2010), Poghosyan et al (2015) and Furceri and Zdzienicka (2015). A less developed (and more obscure) analysis has had more political attention because it was published in the popular *Economist* weekly (*The Economist*, 2020b). Under the title, 'America's fiscal federalism is less superior than you might think', *The Economist* argued that EU spending during and after the Great Recession contributed to slightly larger euro area growth than did the effect of (aggregate) US government spending. While this may be the case

(the actual calculation method behind the results were not reported), the article does not discuss the potential regional and countercyclical effects that concern us here.

[17] See European Council (2020b). For an updated timeline of EU responses to the pandemic, see: https://www.consilium.europa.eu/en/policies/coronavirus/timeline/.

[18] The EGF became operational three months later when member states accounting for 60% of EIB capital had signed their contribution agreement (EIB, 2020b). The initial investment period of the EGF is designed to end on 31 December 2021 (EIB 2020a). As of 13 October 2020, only €2.6 billion in financing had been approved (EIB, 2020d).

[19] In practice, this programme is a spinoff from the European Unemployment Reinsurance Scheme (EURS) proposal, announced in January 2020, but not yet finalized. Still, they target different groups: EURS focuses on the unemployed, while SURE focuses on employers, employees and self-employed. In addition, the SURE programme is temporary, loan-based and not automatic, while EURS is a permanent automatic transfer mechanism.

[20] The 2014–20 MFF, when converted into 2018 prices and including the European Development Fund, amounted to €1.138 trillion (or 1.03% of EU GNI). The original plan for the 2021–27 MFF (announced in May 2018) was €1.135 billion (or 1.11% of EU GNI). See European Parliament (2020b).

[21] Under the MFF, the ceiling allocated for annual appropriations is still fixed. For payments, the limit is set at 1.40% of the GNI of all member states; for commitments it is set at 1.46% of the GNI of all member states (European Council, 2020f).

[22] As can be seen in Table 7.9 almost 90% of the total NGEU goes to the Recovery and Resilience Facility. This money (€672.5 billion) will be distributed in the form of loans (€360 billion) and grants (€312.5 billion). With regard to the grants, 70% are committed to the years 2021 and 2022, based on the following criteria: unemployment (2015–19); inverse GDP per capita and population share. The remaining 30% of these loans are to be committed by the end of 2023, based on a different set of criteria: drop in real GDP over 2020; overall drop in real GDP 2020–21; inverse GDP per capita and population share. To access this money, member states will need to prepare national recovery and resilience plans setting out their reform and investment agenda for the years 2021 to 2023. These plans will then be reviewed and adapted as necessary in 2022 to take account of the final allocation of funds for 2023 (European Council, 2020g).

Chapter 8

[1] This concept of 'cross-border' workers is derived from the way the European Union Labour Force Survey (EU LFS) is conducted: it asks respondents their 'country of place of work', and asks another question about their 'country of residence', but the survey does not inquire about the frequency or nature of the resulting cross-border exchange. Cross-border workers are defined, simply, as EU citizens who live in one EU country and work in another, regardless of their precise citizenship – and provided they are EU28 citizens (European Commission, 2020d: 115).

[2] I put this in quotation marks, in that we know that posted workers tend to be posted twice a year – this is how the Commission calculates the number of workers, relative to the number of actual posting applications. We also know that the average length of a posting in 2017 was 98 days (European Commission, 2020d: 94). When a

worker is posted abroad, on average, twice in the course of a year – corresponding to 196 days – we should be careful about assuming where the 'regular' place of employment is.

3   These growth rates are not directly compatible, as the later includes EFTA and Swiss postings, but the Commission itself (2020d: 94) makes the comparison (albeit with a different timeframe). To see the growth in number of PDs-A1 issued, over time, see De Wispelaere et al (2019: 9, Figure 1).

4   The total number of posted workers is a little more contrived in that we don't actually have a count of the number of workers. The EU collects data on the number of *posting* applications (a 'Portable Document A1' or 'PD-A1'), and recognizes that workers are, on average, posted twice a year on the same PD-A1 permit. To complicate matters more, there are different types of PD documents, corresponding to so-called 'Article 12 and 13 movers'. What matters is that there were roughly three million PDs-A1 issued in 2018, and this number was used by the Commission to estimate the 1.9 million workers in Table 8.1.

5   This indicator lacks data for the UK (2014, 2015) and Greece (2015). The EU28 share is the total number of EU28 citizens in Europe (aggregated), minus the reporting country citizens. Likewise, the non-EU28 share is the total non-EU28 citizenship population in the EU, minus the reporting country citizens.

6   While 2018 data are available from Eurostat (migr_emi1ctz, migr_imm1ctz), the data is patchier than the 2017 data provided by the European Commission (2020d).

7   Third-country nationals are residents of EU and EFTA countries who are neither EU nor EFTA citizens.

8   For a recent review of the literature, see Jauer et al (2019). For a more official analysis and interpretation, see Arpaia et al (2014) and European Commission (2011b).

9   For the former, see Arpaia et al (2016); Kahanec and Guzi (2017); and several contributions in Kahanec and Zimmerman (2016). For the latter, see Dao et al (2014); Jauer et al (2014, 2019); and Beyer and Smets (2015).

10   I should point out that this differs from Eichengreen's (2014: 10) observation that outmigration from Spain, Italy and Greece has the appearance of a brain drain, with the exodus of relatively high-skilled individuals, with more portable job credentials and knowledge of foreign job opportunities.

11   See Merler and Pisani-Ferry (2012) for details on how these systems work, and how these different components of the current account balance can be captured empirically in Europe. See also Hristov et al (2020).

12   I think it is fair to say that policymakers did this without fully appreciating the consequences of their actions. This is clearly the case with regard to ignoring the possibility that banks could propagate asymmetric shocks (and hence the need for a banking union). See, for example, several contributions in Caporaso and Rhodes (2016).

13   For example, a recent IMF report found that 'phantom investment into corporate shells with no substance and no real links to the local economy may account for almost 40 percent of global FDI' (Damgaard et al, 2019: abstract). I don't know what the number are in Europe, but this is a phenomenally large amount of corporate subterfuge, and the authors note (p 26) that most of the world's phantom FDI is found in a small group of well-known offshore centres, the largest of which were Luxembourg ($3.8 trillion) and the Netherlands ($3.3 trillion).

14   Mind you, this was not government borrowing and debt, but private debt in the form of a consumption boom, fuelled by low domestic interest rates. After all, in the years before the crisis hit, Spain and Ireland had low debt to GDP ratios and

a fiscal surplus. No one could blame the crisis these countries faced on state fiscal profligacy (the Greek case is largely an exception to the rule).

[15] See Lane (2013); Hobza and Zeugner (2014); European Commission (2015); Beck et al (2015); and Arpaia et al (2016).

[16] The 'official' flows in this figure include the sum of all bilateral and multilateral loans from the EFSF, the EFSM, the ESM, the IMF and the intra-Eurosystem liabilities (TARGET2).

Chapter 9

[1] See, for example, Gray (1996); Pierson (2001); Keating and McCrone (2013); Lavelle (2013); and Manwaring and Kennedy (2017).

[2] See IMF (2017: Ch. 3) for an overview, but see also OECD (2012b), Karabarbounis and Neiman (2014), Wood (2018) and Autor et al (2017).

[3] It is not clear what the actual mechanism may be that links market integration to reduced wage share. It may be that a larger, unified market in Europe has been more easily captured by large, 'winner takes most' firms, which are often associated with lower labour shares (Autor et al, 2017). Alternatively, the relative returns on capital in Europe may have risen (relative to labour) because market integration tends to push corporate income tax rates downwards.

[4] Some of the motivation behind these reforms was the hope of encouraging the growth of a new service sector, which might fill the jobs lost from a decline in European manufacturing. Once again, the problem was that a shared/common reform had a differential effect in Europe's varied labour markets. Whereas the nature of industrial relations in Northern Europe allowed labour market flexibility and worker security to coexist (in the form of so-called 'flexicurity'), the absence of these institutions elsewhere meant that the EU's labour market reforms often contributed to a *decrease* in worker security. For more on the relationship between labour market reforms and decreased labour power, see Schömann (2014); Rubery and Piasna (2017); and Florczak and Otto (2019).

[5] Eurostat (TPS00159, TPS00073). Here non-standard employment is defined as the share of workers, aged 15–64, in each country, who are subject to limited duration contracts, plus the share of workers employed only part time.

[6] This is not to ignore other important aspects of union mobilization (see, for example, Kelly, 1998), but to focus on easily available and roughly comparable indictors, over time.

[7] 'Whereas Article 29 of the Charter of Fundamental Rights of the EU recognizes the individual and the collective right to strike, in accordance with community law and national laws and practices, Article 137(6) of the Treaty establishing the European Community (TEC) explicitly excludes the adoption of directives that would regulate the freedom of coalition and the right to strike. Hence, although the EU recognizes these rights, it has no competence to harmonize them' (Erne, 2008: 35).

[8] This relationship is two-sided, in that European labour relies heavily on various types of support (financial and otherwise) from the European Commission (see Lind et al, 1997; Dølvik, 1997; Léonard et al, 2007). This enthusiastic support for market integration was not always shared by its member federations (at the national level), and it may be changing, as workers begin to question the utility of a market integration strategy designed to undercut their power and influence (in the name of flexibility and modernization).

9   Although trade unions had actively campaigned for increased (and transnational) participation for decades before the directive was launched, there was no actual mention of labour unions in the text of the 1994 directive (they are mentioned in the 2009 recast)! Still, Europe's trade unions extended initial (if cautious) support for EWCs, even while recognizing their many limitations.

10 This section focuses on wage bargaining, not more generalized attempts at 'social dialogue'. This is an important distinction, because the Social Protocol to the Maastricht Treaty introduced a legally defined social dialogue procedure at the EU level (see Chapter 7). At this level of generalization, European employers and policymakers are willing to accept dialogue, as long as the dialogue is not allowed to extend to a discussion of wages.

11 Indeed, it is evident that many employers and bankers supported the creation of a common monetary union because it was expected to *undermine* the power of unions in setting wages (see Erne, 2008: 54). Employers are not interested in coordinating negotiations over wages and working conditions, as they have little to gain from engaging labour at this level. As we just saw, strike levels and union power have been falling for decades. Instead, employers have been able to secure their desired adjustments in wages, welfare policies and labour laws across Europe by convincing policymakers to unleash self-regulating market forces.

12 Many trade unions remain reluctant to transfer wage negotiating power to a supranational entity, as it will force them to agree on a solidaristic wage strategy that precludes them from exploiting the wage discipline of others. See Hancké (2013).

13 In addition, see Sisson et al (1999); Crouch (2000); Sisson and Marginson (2000); Marginson and Sisson (2006); Busch and Hirschel (2011); Glassner and Pochet (2011); and Hancké (2013: Ch. 3).

14 The European Metalworkers' Federation took the lead in embarking on a transnational approach to collective bargaining. In fact, its efforts preceded the other transnational initiatives on the intersectoral, cross-national level (for example, the Doorn Group) and European levels (Glassner and Pochet, 2011: 13).

15 For an analysis of the sort of institutional, economic and social factors that limit this potential development, see Glassner and Pochet (2011).

16 In particular, Schulten and Müller (2019) use the Kaitz (1970) index, which compares the minimum wage levels to the average or median wage in a given country and sets the poverty threshold at 60%.

Chapter 10

1   See Moses (2017a: Ch. 5) for more details on the Irish case.

2   For example, it is conceivable that a local authority may spend more resources by prioritizing local procurement providers, but if the procurement is spent in the local economy, the gains can be multiplied as these costs are reinvested/spent in local economic activity and the gainful employment of local workers. This distribution of costs can be more rewarding to the local community than watching the procurement funds go to distant suppliers who spend their earnings in faraway markets.

3   See, for example, the references to modern monetary theory in Chapter 6.

4   These sorts of threats are common, but probably exaggerated. For a more sober account of how the eurozone might disintegrate, see Mosler (2017).

5   There is remarkably little written in English on the NCLM, but see Pedersen et al (2008) and Fischer and Straubhaar (1996).

6   Once again, this assumes that the ECB remains unwilling to create the requisite funds, à la modern monetary theory.

7   The pattern of this migration is also instructive: while high-skilled workers continue to move as we might expect, from poor to rich states (mostly on the coasts); low-skilled workers are moving less, and when they do move they tend to move from rich to poor states (mostly inland, where the cost of living is cheaper). As a result, the US has been ripped apart by diverging earnings, lifestyles and voting patterns, with some regions feeling like they are being left farther behind (see Banerjee and Duflo, 2019: 42–3; Bishop, 2009).

References

Ademmer, M. and Jannsen, N. (2018) 'Post-crisis business investment in the euro area and the role of monetary policy', *Applied Economics*, 50(34/35): 3787–97.

Aiginger, K. and Leoni, T. (2009) 'Typologies of social models in Europe', *Institute of Economic Research WIFO*: 2–4. Available from: http://www.socialpolitik.ovgu.de/sozialpolitik_media/papers/Aiginger_Karl_uid563_pid502.pdf [Accessed 1 December 2020].

Akerlof, G.A. and Yellen, J.L. (1988) 'Fairness and unemployment', *American Economic Review*, 78(2): 44–9.

Allard, C., Bluedorn, J., Bornhorst, F. and Furceri, D. (2015) 'Lessons from the crisis: Minimal elements for a fiscal union in the euro area', in C. Cottarelli and M. Guerguil (eds) *Designing a European Fiscal Union: Lessons from the Experience of Fiscal Federations,* London: Routledge, pp 224–52.

Alsos, K., Nergaard, K. and Van Den Heuvel, A. (2019) 'Collective bargaining as a tool to ensure a living wage: Experiences from the Nordic countries', *Transfer*, 35(3): 351–65.

AMECO (Annual Macro-Economic database of the European Commission) (2020) 'Adjusted wage share: total economy: As percentage of GDP at current prices'. Available from: https://ec.europa.eu/economy_finance/ameco/user/serie/ResultSerie.cfm [Accessed 24 May 2020].

Andersen, T.M., Haldrup, N. and Sørensen, J.R. (2000) 'Labour market implications of EU product market integration', *Economic Policy*, 15(30): 105–33.

Andor, L. (2013a) 'Developing the social dimension of a deep and genuine Economic and Monetary Union', European Policy Centre, Policy Brief, 13 September.

Andor, L. (2013b) 'Strengthening the European Social Model', speech given at conference 'Progressive paths to growth and social cohesion: A future agenda for Eastern and Central Europe', 11 November, Vilnius. Available from: https://ec.europa.eu/commission/presscorner/api/files/document/print/en/speech_13_901/SPEECH_13_901_EN.pdf [Accessed 1 March 2020].

Appelbaum, B. (2019) *The Economists' Hour: False Prophets, Free Markets, and the Fracture of Society*, New York: Little, Brown.

Arpaia, A., Kiss, A., Palvolgyi, B. and Turrini, A. (2014) 'Labour mobility and labour market adjustment in the EU', *European Economy*, Economic Papers 539, Directorate General Economic and Financial Affairs, European Commission.

Arpaia, A., Kiss, A., Palvolgyi, B. and Turrini, A. (2016) 'Labour mobility and the labour market adjustment in the EU', *IZA Journal of Migration*, 5(1): 1–21.

Aukrust, O. (1977) 'Inflation in the open economy', in L.B. Krause and W.S. Salant (eds) *Worldwide Inflation: Theory and Recent Experience*, Washington, DC: Brookings Institution, pp 107–53.

Autor D. and Duggan, M. (2003) 'The rise in disability rolls and the decline in unemployment', *Quarterly Journal of Economics*, 118(1): 157–205.

Autor, D., Dorn, D. and Hanson, G.H. (2013a) 'The China syndrome: Local labor market effects of import competition in the United States', *American Economic Review*, 103(6): 2121–68.

Autor, D., Dorn, D. and Hanson, G.H. (2013b) 'The geography of trade and technology shocks in the United States', *American Economic Review*, 103(3): 220–5.

Autor, D., Dorn, D. and Hanson, G.H. (2016) 'The China shock: Learning from labor-market adjustments to large changes in trade', *Annual Review of Economics*, 8(1): 205–40.

Autor, D., Dorn, D., Hanson, G.H. and Song, J. (2014) 'Trade adjustment: Worker level evidence', *Quarterly Journal of Economics*, 129(4):1799–860.

Autor, D., Dorn, D., Katz, L.F., Patterson, C. and van Reenen, J. (2017) 'Concentrating on the fall of the labor share', *American Economic Review: Papers & Proceedings*, 107(5): 180–5.

Bachtler, J. and Gorzelak, G. (2007) 'Reforming EU cohesion policy', *Policy Studies*, 28(4): 309–26.

Bachtler, J., Berkowitz, P., Hardy, S. and Muravska, T. (eds) (2017) *EU Cohesion Policy: Reassessing Performance and Direction*, London: Routledge.

Balanyá, B., Doherty, A., Hoedeman, O., Ma'anit, A. and Wesselius, E. (2003) *Europe Inc: Regional and Global Restructuring and the Rise of Corporate Power*, 2nd edn, London: Pluto Press.

Balsvik, R., Jensen, S. and Salvanes, K.G. (2015) 'Made in China, sold in Norway: Local labor market effects of an import shock', *Journal of Public Economics*, 127: 137–44.

Bandrés, E., Gadea Rivas, M.D. and Gómez-Loscos, A. (2017) 'Regional business cycles across Europe', Banco de Espana Occasional Paper 1702.

Banerjee, A.V. and Duflo, E. (2019) *Good Economics for Hard Times*, New York: Public Affairs.

Barkbu, B., Berkmen, S.P., Lukyantsau, P., Saksonovs, S. and Schoelermann, H. (2015) 'Investment in the Euro area: Why has it been weak?', IMF Working paper WP/15/32, February.

Barnouin, B. (1986) *The European Labour Movement and European Integration*, London: Frances Pinter.

Barro, R.J., Sala-i-Martin, X., Blanchard, O.J. and Hall, R.E. (1991) 'Convergence across states and regions', *Brookings Papers on Economic Activity*, (1): 107–82.

Barslund, M. and Busse, M. (2014) 'Making the most of EU labour mobility', Report of a CEPS Task Force. October, Brussels: CEPS.

Barslund, M. and Busse, M. (2016) 'Labour mobility in the EU: Addressing challenges and ensuring "fair mobility"', CEPS Special Report No. 139, July.

Beck, R., Georgiadis, G. and Gräb, J. (2015) 'The geography of the great rebalancing in euro area bond markets during the sovereign debt crisis', ECB Working Paper, No. 1839, Frankfurt: European Central Bank.

Beetsma, R. and Giuliodori, M. (2010) 'The macroeconomic costs and benefits of EMU and other monetary unions: An overview of recent research', *Journal of Economic Literature*, 48: 603–41.

Benedetto, G., Hix, S. and Mastrorocco, N. (2019) 'The rise and fall of social democracy, 1918–2017', Working paper. Available from: http://personal.lse.ac.uk/hix/Working_Papers/BHM_Rise_and_Fall_of_SD.pdf [Accessed 23 May 2020].

Berend, I.T. (2020) *Economic History of a Divided Europe: Four Diverse Regions in an Integrating Context*, New York: Routledge.

Berlin, I. (1958) *Two Concepts of Liberty*, Oxford: Oxford University Press.

Bernaciak, M., Gumbrell-McCormick, R. and Hyman, R. (2014) 'European trade unionism: From crisis to renewal?', Report 133, ETUI.

Bertelsmann Stiftung (2014) *Harnessing European Labour Mobility*, Gütersloh: Bertelsmann Stiftung.

Bewley, T. (1999) *Why Wages Don't Fall During a Recession*, Cambridge, MA: Harvard University Press.

Beyer, R.C.M. and Smets, F. (2015) 'Labour market adjustments and migration in Europe and the United States: How different?', *Economic Policy*, 30(84): 643–82.

Birindelli, L. and Rustichelli, E. (2007) 'Economic benefits of long distance mobility', 24 July, Eurofoundation. Available from: http://www.eurofound.europa.eu/publications/htmlfiles/ef0702.htm [Accessed 27 October 2019].

Bishop, B. (2009) *The Big Sort: Why the Clustering of Like-Minded America is Tearing Us Apart*, New York: Mariner Books.

Blanchard, O.J. and Katz, L.F. (1992) 'Regional evolutions', *Brookings Papers on Economic Activity, Economic Studies Program*, 23: 1–76.

Blanchard, O.J. and Leigh, D. (2013) 'Growth forecast errors and fiscal multipliers', *American Economic Review*, 103: 117–20.

Blinder, A. (1987) *Hard Heads, Soft Hearts*, Reading, MA: Addison-Wesley.

Block, F. (1990) *Postindustrial Possibilities: A Critique of Economic Discourse*, Berkeley: University of California Press.

Block, F. and Somers, M.R. (2014) *The Power of Market Fundamentalism: Karl Polanyi's Critique*, Cambridge, MA: Harvard University Press.

Böckerman, P. and Uusitalo, R. (2006) 'Erosion of the Ghent system and union membership decline: Lessons from Finland', *British Journal of Industrial Relations*, 44(2): 283–303.

Boeri, T. and Jimeno, J.F. (2015) 'The unbearable divergence of unemployment in Europe', Banco de Espana Working Papers No. 1534, 25 November. Available from: https://ssrn.com/abstract=2695323 [Accessed 1 December 2020].

Boeri, T. and van Ours, J. (2008) *The Economics of Imperfect Labor Markets*, Princeton: Princeton University Press.

Boeri, T., Brugiavini, A., Calmfors, L., Booth, A., Burda, M., Checchi, D., Ebbinghaus, B., Freeman, R., Garibaldi, P., Holmlund, B., Naylor, R., Schludi, M., Verdier, T. and Visser, J. (2001) 'Union membership', in T. Boeri, A. Brugiavini and L. Calmfors (eds) *The Role of Unions in the Twenty-first Century: A Report for the Fondazione Rodolfo Debenedetti*, Oxford: Oxford University Press, pp 11–46.

Bonin, H. and Zimmermann, K.F. (2000) 'The Post-Unification German Labor Market', IZA Discussion Paper No. 185, August. Available from: ftp://131.220.86.34/pub/SSRN/pdf/dp185.pdf [Accessed 3 December 2020].

Bonin, H., Eichhorst, W., Florman, C., Okkels Hansen, M., Skiöld, L., Stuhler, J., Tatsiramos, K., Thomasen, H. and Zimmermann, K.F. (2008) 'Geographic mobility in the European Union: Optimising its economic and social benefits', IZA Research Report, No. 19, July. Available from: http://www.iza.org/en/webcontent/publications/reports/report_pdfs/iza_report_19.pdf [Accessed 27 October 2019].

Bound, J. and Holzer, H.J. (2000) 'Demand shifts, population adjustments, and labor market outcomes during the 1980s', *Journal of Labor Economics*, 18(1): 20–54.

Bouvard, M. (1972) *Labor Movements in the Common Market Countries: The Growth of a European Pressure Group*, New York: Praeger.

Brennan, J. (2016) *Against Democracy*, Princeton: Princeton University Press.

Bücker, A. and Warneck, W. (eds) (2010) *Viking-Laval-Rüffert: Consequences and Policy Perspectives*, Brussels: ETUI.

Burda, M.C. (2006) 'Factor reallocation in Eastern Germany after reunification', *American Economic Review*, 96(2): 368–74.

Burda, M.C. and Hunt, J. (2001) 'From reunification to economic integration: Productivity and the labor market in Eastern Germany', *Brookings Papers on Economic Activity*, 2: 1–71.

Burke, E. (1790) *Reflections on the Revolution in France*. Available from: https://constitution.org/eb/rev_fran.htm [Accessed 28 December 2019].

Busch, K. and Hirschel, D. (2011) *Europe at the Crossroads: Ways Out of the Crisis*, Bonn: Friedrich Ebert Stiftung. Available from: https://library.fes.de/pdf-files/id/ipa/08066.pdf [Accessed 31 May 2020].

BusinessEurope (2019) 'History of the organization', 9 January. Available from: https://www.businesseurope.eu/history-organisation [Accessed 1 June 2020].

Byé, M. (1956) 'Note by Professor Maurice Byé', Dated Paris 12 March, in GoE *Report on the Social Aspects of European Economic Co-operation* (the Ohlin Report), Studies and Reports, New Series, No. 46, Geneva: ILO, pp 119–39.

Cacciatore, M. and Fiori, G. (2016) 'The macroeconomic effects of goods and labor markets deregulation', *Review of Economic Dynamics*, 20(1): 1–24.

Cai, F., Du, Y. and Zhao, C. (2007) 'Regional labour market integration since China's WTO entry: Evidence from household-level data', in R. Garnaut and L. Song (eds) *China: Linking Markets for Growth*, Canberra: Asia Pacific Press, pp 33–50.

Caporaso, J.A. and Rhodes, M. (eds) (2016) *The Political and Economic Dynamics of the Eurozone Crisis*, New York: Oxford University Press.

Caporaso, J.A. and Tarrow, S. (2009) 'Polanyi in Brussels: Supranational institutions and the transnational embedding of markets', *International Organization*, 63(4): 593–620.

CEC (Commission of the European Communities) (1973) 'Report on regional problems of the enlarged community', COM (73) 550 def., Brussels.

CEC (1987) 'Commission Communication, The Single Act: A New Frontier for Europe', COM (87) 100 final, Brussels.

CEC (1988) 'Social dimension of the internal market', SEC (88) 1148 final, Brussels, 143, September, Commission Working Paper.

CEDEFOP (European Centre for the Development of Vocational Training) (2020) 'European qualifications framework (EQF)'. Available from: https://www.cedefop.europa.eu/en/events-and-projects/projects/european-qualifications-framework-eqf [Accessed 3 June 2020].

CEO (Corporate Europe Observatory) (n.d.) 'Lobbying the EU'. Available from: https://corporateeurope.org/en/lobbying-the-eu [Accessed 29 May 2020].

Cerf, C. (2018) 'The challenge of plenty: Tackling labour shortages in the EU', Eurofound blog entry, 19 November. Available from: eurofound.link/ef18100 [Accessed 24 October 2019].

Chalmers, D., Jachtenfuchs, M. and Joerges, C. (2016) 'The retransformation of Europe', in D. Chalmers, M. Jachtenfuchs and C. Joerges (eds) *The End of the Eurocrats' Dream: Adjusting to European Diversity*, Cambridge: Cambridge University Press, pp 1–28.

Chang, H.-J. (2002) *Kicking Away the Ladder: Development Strategy in Historical Perspective*, London: Anthem Press.

Chang, H.-J. (2010) *Bad Samaritans: The Myth of Free Trade and the Secret History of Capitalism*, London: Bloomsbury.

Chetty R., Hendren, N., Kline, P. and Saez, E. (2014) 'Where is the land of opportunity? The geography of intergenerational mobility', *Quarterly Journal of Economics*, 129(4): 1553–623.

Chiswick, B. and Hatton, T.J. (2003) 'International migration and the integration of labor markets', in M.D. Bordo, A.M. Taylor and J.G. Williamson (eds) *Globalization in Historical Perspective*, Chicago: University of Chicago Press, pp 65–117.

Clauwaert, S. and Schömann, I. (2012) 'The crisis and national labour law reforms: A mapping exercise', ETUI Working Paper 2012.04.

Clover, J. (2016) *Riot. Strike. Riot: The New Era of Uprisings*, London: Verso.

Cochet, A. (2002) 'Strengthening the Doorn process', *AGORA, Quarterly Newsletter of the Education Institution of the European Trade Union Confederation*, June: 3.

Collins, W.J. (1999) 'Labor mobility, market integration, and wage convergence in late 19th century India', *Explorations in Economic History*, 36(3): 246–77.

Cottarelli, C. (2016) 'A European fiscal union: The case for a larger central budget', *Economia Politica*, 33: 1–8.

Cottarelli, C. and Guerguil, M. (eds) (2015a) *Designing a European Fiscal Union: Lessons from the Experience of Fiscal Federations*, London: Routledge.

Cottarelli, C. and Guerguil, M. (2015b) 'Introduction and overview', in C. Cottarelli and M. Guerguil (eds) *Designing a European Fiscal Union: Lessons from the Experience of Fiscal Federations*, London: Routledge, pp 1–12.

Crouch, C. (1993) *Industrial Relations and European State Traditions*, Oxford: Clarendon Press.

Crouch, C. (2000) 'National wage determination and the European monetary union', in C. Crouch (ed) *After the Euro: Shaping Institutions for Governance in the Wake of European Monetary Union*, Oxford: Oxford University Press, pp 203–27.

Damgaard, J., Elkjaer, T. and Johannesen, N. (2019) 'What is real and what is not in the Global FDI Network?', World Bank Working Paper 19/274. Available from: https://www.imf.org/en/Publications/WP/Issues/2019/12/11/what-is-real-and-what-is-not-in-the-global-fdi-network [Accessed 3 March 2020].

Dao, M., Furceri, D. and Loungani, P. (2014) 'Regional labor market adjustments in the United States and Europe', IMF Working Paper WP/14/26.

Darvas, Z. and Szapary, G. (2004) 'Business cycle synchronization in the englarged EU: Co-movements in the new and old members', February, Magyar Nemzeti Bank Working Paper No. 2004–1. Available from: https://ssrn.com/abstract=508564 [Accessed 15 November 2020].

Dauth, W., Findeisen, S. and Suedekum, J. (2014) 'The rise of the East and the Far East: German labor markets and trade integration', *Journal of the European Economic Association*, 12(6): 1643–75.

De Grauwe, P. (2018) *Economics of Monetary Integration*, 12th edn, New York: Oxford University Press.

Degryse, C. and Pochet, P. (2018) 'European social dynamics: A quantitive approach', Working Paper 2018.02, European Trade Union Institute.

De Haan, J., Inklaar, R. and Jona-A-Pin, R. (2008) 'Will business cycles in the euro area converge? A critical survey of empirical research', *Journal of Economic Surveys*, 22(2): 234–73.

Delamaide, D. (1994) *The New Superregions of Europe*, London: Dutton/Penguin.

De la Porte, C. and Heins, E. (2015) 'A new era of European integration? Governance of labour market and social policy since the sovereign debt crisis', *Comparative European Politics*, 13(1): 8–28.

Delpérée, A. (1956) *Politique sociale et integration economique*, Liège: Georges Thone.

De Wispelaere, F. and Pacolet, J. (2018) 'Posting of workers', Report on A1 Portable Documents issued in 2017, October, Brussels: European Commission, Directorate-General for Employment, Social Affairs and Inclusion Unit D/2.

De Wispelaere, F., De Smedt, L. and Pacolet, J. (2019) 'Posting of workers', Report on A1 Portable Documents issued in 2018, October, Brussels: European Commission.

Diamond, R. (2016) 'The determinants and welfare implications of US workers' diverging location choices by skill: 1980–2000', *American Economic Review*, 106(3): 479–524.

Dølvik, J.E. (1997) *Redrawing the Boundaries of Solidarity? ETUC, Social Dialogue and the Europeanisation of Trade Unions in the 1990s*, Oslo: ARENA and FAFO.

Donoso, V., Martín, V. and Minondo, A. (2014) 'Do differences in exposure to Chinese imports lead to differences in local labour market outcomes? An analysis for Spanish provinces', *Regional Studies*, 49: 46–64.

Doogan, K. (2009) *New Capitalism? The Transformation of Work*, Cambridge: Polity.

Dow, G.K. (2003) *Governing the Firm: Workers' Control in Theory and Practice*, Cambridge: Cambridge University Press.

Dribbusch, H. and Vandaele, K. (2016) 'Comparing official strike data in Europe: Dealing with varieties of strike recording', *Transfer*, 22(3): 413–8.

Dudek, C.M. (2014) 'The history and challenges of cohesion policy', Jean Monnet/Robert Schuman Paper Series, 14(2), Miami-Florida European Union Center.

Duflo, E. and Banerjee, A. (2019) 'Economic incentives don't always do what we want them to', *New York Times*, 26 October. Available from: https://www.nytimes.com/2019/10/26/opinion/sunday/duflo-banerjee-economic-incentives.html?searchResultPosition=3 [Accessed 27 October 2019].

Dukes, R. (2014) *The Labour Constitution: The Enduring Idea of Labour Law*, Oxford: Oxford University Press.

Eberts, R.W. and Schweitzer, M.E. (1994) 'Regional wage convergence and divergence: Adjusting wages for cost-of-living differences', *Federal Reserve Bank of Cleveland Economic Review*, 30: 26–37.

ECB (European Central Bank) (2006) 'Cross-border labour mobility within an enlarged EU', Occasional Paper Series, No. 52.

ECB (2020) 'Monetary policy decisions', Press Release, 4 June. Available from: https://www.ecb.europa.eu/press/pr/date/2020/html/ecb. mp200604~a307d3429c.en.html [Accessed 3 December 2020].

ECFTUC (European Consortium of Free Trade Unions) (1969) *First Congress of the ECFTUC: Premier Congrès: Discours, decisions, resolutions*, April, Brussels: ECFTUC.

ECJ (European Court of Justice) (2020) 'Judgments of the Court of Justice in Cases C-620/18, C-626/18 Hungary v Parliament and Council', N° 155/2020, 8 December. Available from: https://curia. europa.eu/jcms/upload/docs/application/pdf/2020-12/cp200155en. pdf [Accessed 15 December 2020].

Economist, The (2020a) 'What's American for Mitbestimmung? Most of the world has yet to embrce co-determination', 1 February. Available from: https://www.economist.com/business/2020/02/01/ most-of-the-world-has-yet-to-embrace-co-determination [Accessed 19 October 2020].

Economist, The (2020b) 'America's fiscal federalism is less superior than you might think: Europe's federation has been surprisingly effective', 20 August. Available from: https://www.economist.com/ finance-and-economics/2020/08/20/americas-fiscal-federalism-is-less-superior-than-you-might-think [Accessed 19 October 2020].

EEC (European Economic Community) (1959) 'Second general report on the activities of the community (18 Sept 1958–20 March 1959)', 31 March, Brussels: European Economic Community Commission. Available from: http://aei.pitt.edu/30805/1/67680_EEC_2nd.pdf [Accessed 15 February 2020].

EEC (1960) 'Third general report on the activities of the community (21 March 1959–15 May 1960)', May. Available from: http://aei.pitt. edu/30806/1/67367_EEC_3rd.pdf [Accessed 15 February 2020].

EIB (European Investment Bank) (2020a) 'Fact sheet: The Pan-European Guarantee Fund in response to COVID-19'. Available from: https://www.eib.org/attachments/press/covid19-paneuropean-guarantee-fund-factsheet-en.pdf [Accessed 3 December 2020].

EIB (2020b) 'Coronavirus outbreak: EIB Group's response'. Available from: https://www.eib.org/en/about/initiatives/covid-19-response/index.htm [Accessed on 3 December 2020].

EIB (2020c) 'EIB Board approves 25 billion Pan-European Guarantee Fund in response to COVID-19 Crisis', 26 May. Available from: https://www.eib.org/en/press/all/2020-126-eib-board-approves-eur-25-billion-pan-european-guarantee-fund-to-respond-to-covid-19-crisis [Accessed on 3 December 2020].

EIB (2020d) 'European Guarantee Fund'. Available from: https://www.eib.org/en/products/egf/index.htm [Accessed 13 November 2020].

Eichengreen, B. (1991) 'Is Europe an optimum currency area?', No. w3579, National Bureau of Economic Research.

Eichengreen, B. (1997) *European Monetary Unification: Theory, Practice and Analysis*, Cambridge, MA: MIT Press.

Eichengreen, B. (2012) 'Throwing out the baby with the bathwater? Implications of the euro crisis for Asian monetary integration', *Journal of Economic Integration*, 27(2): 291–311.

Eichengreen, B. (2014) 'The Eurozone crisis: The theory of optimum currency areas bites back', Notenstein Academy White Paper Series, March. Available from: http://citeseerx.ist.psu.edu/viewdoc/download?doi=10.1.1.669.5131&rep=rep1&type=pdf [Accessed 18 April 2020].

Erne, R. (2008) *European Unions: Labor's Quest for a Transnational Democracy*, Ithaca: Cornell University Press.

Erne, R. (2015) 'A supranational regime that nationalizes social conflict: Explaining European trade unions' difficulties in politicizing European economic governance', *Labor History*, 56(3): 345–68.

Escolano, J., Benedek, D., Jin, H., Granados, C.M., Nozaki, M., Pereira, J., Graziosi, G.R., Sinn, L. and Torres, J. (2015) 'Distribution of fiscal responsibility in federations', in C. Cottarelli and M. Guerguil (eds) *Designing a European Fiscal Union: Lessons from the Experience of Fiscal Federations*, London: Routledge, pp 13–59.

Esping-Andersen, G. (1985) *Politics Against Markets*, Princeton: Princeton University Press.

Esping-Andersen, G. (1990) *Three Worlds of Welfare Capitalism*, Cambridge: Polity Press.

ETUC (European Trade Union Confederation) (2020) 'ETUC staff list'. Available from: https://www.etuc.org/en/staff-list [Accessed 1 June 2020].

ETUI (European Trade Union Institute) (2016) 'Facts and figures'. Available from: https://www.worker-participation.eu/European-Works-Councils/Facts-Figures [Accessed 29 May 2020].

ETUI (2019) 'Benchmarking Working Europe 2019', 7 April. Available from: https://www.etui.org/Publications2/Books/Benchmarking-Working-Europe-2019 [Accessed 29 May 2020].

ETUI (2020) 'EU strike map of Europe: EU-28', 7 April. Available from: https://www.etui.org/Services/Strikes-Map-of-Europe/EU-28 [Accessed 21 May 2020].

Eurobarometer (2007) *Eurobarometer 67: Public Opinion in the European Union*. Available from: http://ec.europa.eu/public_opinion/archives/eb/eb67/eb67_en.htm [Accessed 29 October 2020].

Eurobarometer (2010) *Special Eurobarometer 337: Geographical and Labour Market Mobility*. Available from: http://ec.europa.eucommfrontoffice/publicopinion/archives/ebs/ebs_337_en.pdf [Accessed 29 October 2020].

Eurofound (2014) *Labour Migration in the EU: Recent Trends and Policies*, Cornell University ILR School: European Foundation for the Improvement of Living and Working Conditions.

Eurofound (2017) *Estimating Labour Market Slack in the European Union*, Luxembourg: Publications Office of the European Union.

Eurofound (2018) *Non-standard Forms of Employment: Recent Trends and Future Prospects*, author D. Storrie, Dublin: Eurofound.

European Commission (n.d.) Fact check on the EU budget. Available from: https://ec.europa.eu/info/strategy/eu-budget/how-it-works/fact-check_en#doesthebudgetfundonlyusefulprojects [Accessed 2 May 2020].

European Commission (1993) *Growth, Competitiveness, Employment: The Challenges and Ways Forward into the 21st Century*, White Paper, 5 December, Parts A and B. COM (93) 700 final/A and B, Bulletin of the European Communities, Supplement 6/93.

European Commission (1994) *European Social Policy: A Way Forward for the Union. A White Paper*, 27 July, Part A. COM (94) 333 final.

European Commission (2001) *High Level Task Force on Skills and Mobility: Final Report*, December, Directorate-General for Employment and Social Affairs, Unit EMPL/A.3.

European Commission (2006) *Green Paper: Modernising Labour Law to Meet the Challenges of the 21st Century*, 22 November, COM(2006) 708 final.

European Commission (2008) *EU Budget 2007: Financial Report*, Luxembourg: Office for Official Publications of the European Communities.

European Commission (2011a) 'Proposal for a council directive on a common system of financial transaction tax and amending Directive 2008/7/EC', 28 September, COM 594 final, 2011/0261(CNS). Brussels.

European Commission (2011b) 'Adjustment via migration', *Quarterly Report on the Euro Area*, 10(3), Section II.2: 32–3.

European Commission (2012a) 'Reforming EURES to meet the goals of Europe 2020: Towards a job-rich recovery', 18 April, Commission Staff Working Document, Strasbourg. Available from: http://ec.europa.eu/social/BlobServlet?docId=7624&langId=en [Accessed 24 October 2019].

European Commission (2012b) 'Delivering for consumers: EU institutions and competition policy', 16 April. Available from: https://ec.europa.eu/competition/consumers/institutions_en.html [Accessed 14 April 2020].

European Commission (2012c) 'A blueprint for a deep and genuine economic and monetary union: Launching the debate', Press Release, 30 November. Available from: https://ec.europa.eu/commission/presscorner/detail/en/IP_12_1272 [Accessed 3 December 2020].

European Commission (2012d) 'Labour market developments in Europe 2012', *European Economy*, No. 5, Brussels, Directorate-General for Economic and Financial Affairs. Available from: http://ec.europa.eu/economy_finance/publications/european_economy/2012/pdf/ee-2012-5_en.pdf [Accessed 3 December 2020].

European Commission (2014a) 'State aid: Compilation of state aid rules in force', 15 April. Available from: https://ec.europa.eu/competition/state_aid/legislation/compilation/index_en.html [Accessed 14 April 2020].

European Commission (2014b) *EU Competition Law: Rules Applicable to State Aid*. Available from: https://ec.europa.eu/competition/state_aid/legislation/compilation/state_aid_15_04_14_en.pdf [Accessed 9 April 2020].

European Commission (2015) *Quarterly Report on the Euro Area*, 14(1), Directorate-General for Economic and Financial Affairs.

European Commission (2016) 'Proposal for a council directive on a common corporate tax base', 25 October, COM(2016) 685 final. 2016/0337(CNS). Strasbourg.

European Commission (2017a) *Quarterly Report on the Euro Area*, 16(2), European Economy Institutional Paper 060, Director-General for Economic and Financial Affairs.

European Commission (2017b) *My Region, My Europe, Our Future: The Seventh Report on Economic, Social and Territorial Cohesion*, Brussels: Directorate-General for Regional and Urban Policy.

European Commission (2018a) *2018 Annual Report on Intra-EU Labour Mobility*, Luxembourg: Publications Office of the European Union.

European Commission (2018b) *Regulation (Eu, Euratom) 2018/1046 of the European Parliament and of the Council: On the Financial Rules applicable to the general budget of the Union*, 18 July, Luxembourg: Publications Office of the European Union.

European Commission (2018c) *Labour Market and Wage Developments in Europe: Annual Review 2018*, Luxembourg: Publications Office of the European Union.

European Commission (2018d) 'Evaluation accompanying the document report from the Commission to the European Parliament, the Council and the European Economic and Social Committee Report on the implementation by Member States of Directive 2009/38/EC on the establishment of a European Works Council or a procedure in Community-scale undertakings and Community-scale groups of undertakings for the purposes of informing and consulting employees (Recast)', 14 May, SWD 187 final.

European Commission (2019a) *EU Budget 2018: Financial Report*, Luxembourg: Publications Office of the European Union.

European Commission (2019b) *Quarterly Report on the Euro Area*, 18(2), November, Institutional Paper No. 119, Directorate-General for Economic and Financial Affairs.

European Commission (2020a) 'State aid: Commission adopts temporary framework to enable Member States to further support the economy in the COVID-19 outbreak', Press Release, 19 March. Available from: https://ec.europa.eu/commission/presscorner/detail/en/ip_20_496 [Accessed 11 April 2020].

European Commission (2020b) 'Coronavirus: Commission proposes to activate fiscal framework's general escape clause to respond to pandemic', Press Release, 20 March. Available from: https://ec.europa.eu/commission/presscorner/detail/en/ip_20_499 [Accessed 11 April 2020].

European Commission (2020c) *Fact Check on the EU Budget*, doi:10.2761/25800.

European Commission (2020d) *2019 Annual Report on Intra-EU Labour Mobility*, Luxembourg: Publications Office of the European Union.

European Commission (2020e) 'Professionals moving abroad (establishment): Ranking – the most mobile professions', Regulated Professions Database. Available from: https://ec.europa.eu/growth/tools-databases/regprof/index.cfm [Accessed 18 March 2020].

European Commission (2020f) 'Statistics – Temporary Mobility', Regulated Professions Database. Available from: https://ec.europa.eu/growth/tools-databases/regprof/index.cfm [Accessed 17 March 2020].

European Commission (2020g) *Recovery Plan for Europe*. Available from: https://ec.europa.eu/info/live-work-travel-eu/health/coronavirus-response/recovery-plan-europe_en [Accessed 7 August 2020].

European Commission (2020h) 'Temporary framework for state aid measures to support the economy in the current COVID-19 outbreak', 19 March, Communication from the Commission, C(2020) 1863 final. Available from: https://ec.europa.eu/competition/state_aid/what_is_new/sa_covid19_temporary-framework.pdf [Accessed 3 December 2020].

European Commission (2020i) 'Coronavirus response investment initiative adopted', 30 March. Available from: https://ec.europa.eu/social/main.jsp?langId=en&catId=89&newsId=9585&furtherNews=yes [Accessed 3 December 2020].

European Commission (2020j) 'Proposal for a Council Regulation on the establishment of a European instrument for temporary support to mitigate unemployment risks in an emergency (SURE) following the COVID-19 outbreak', 2 April, 2020/0057 (NLE) COM(2020) 139 final. Available from: https://ec.europa.eu/info/sites/info/files/economy-finance/sure_regulation.pdf [Accessed 3 December 2020].

European Commission (2020k) 'EU budget: European Commission welcomes agreement on €1.8 trillion package to help build greener, more digital and more resilient Europe', Press Release, 10 November. Available from: https://ec.europa.eu/commission/presscorner/detail/en/ip_20_2073 [Accessed 3 December 2020].

European Council (2012a) *Towards a Genuine Economic and Monetary Union*, 5 December, Report by the President of the European Council, in collaboration with the Presidents of the Commission, the Eurogroup and the ECB.

European Council (2012b) *Conclusions*, European Council Meeting 28/29 June, EUCO 76/12, Brussels.

European Council (2014) 'Council Decision of 26 May 2014 on the system of own resources of the European Union', 7 June, 2014/335/EU, Euratom. Available from: https://eur-lex.europa.eu/legal-content/en/TXT/?uri=celex%3A32014D0335 [Accessed 3 December 2020].

European Council (2019) 'European Labour mobility', Infographic. Available from: https://www.consilium.europa.eu/en/infographics/eu-labour-mobility/ [Accessed 29 October, 2019].

European Council (2020a) 'EU's Revenue: Own resources', 4 March. Available from: https://www.consilium.europa.eu/en/policies/eu-budgetary-system/eu-revenue-own-resources/ [Accessed on 6 May 2020].

European Council (2020b) 'Report on the comprehensive economic policy response to the COVID-19 pandemic', Press Release, 9 April. Available from: https://www.consilium.europa.eu/en/press/press-releases/2020/04/09/report-on-the-comprehensive-economic-policy-response-to-the-covid-19-pandemic/ [Accessed 3 December 2020].

European Council (2020c) 'The EU's emergency response to the COVID-19 pandemic'. Available from: https://www.consilium.europa.eu/en/infographics/covid-19-eu-emergency-response/# [Accessed 3 December 2020].

European Council (2020d) 'Eurogroup statement on the pandemic crisis support', Press Release, 8 May. Available from: https://www.consilium.europa.eu/en/press/press-releases/2020/05/08/eurogroup-statement-on-the-pandemic-crisis-support/ [Accessed 3 December 2020].

European Council (2020e) 'COVID-19: The EU's response to the economic fallout', 4 November. Available from: https://www.consilium.europa.eu/en/policies/coronavirus/covid-19-economy/ [Accessed 13 November 2020].

European Council (2020f) 'Special European Council, 17–21 July 2020'. Available from: https://www.consilium.europa.eu/en/meetings/european-council/2020/07/17-21/ [Accessed 3 December 2020].

European Council (2020g) *A Recovery Plan for Europe: Introduction*, 19 November. Available from: https://www.consilium.europa.eu/en/policies/eu-recovery-plan/ [Accessed 3 December 2020].

European Parliament (2020a) 'The ESM Pandemic Crisis Support', briefing. Available from: https://www.europarl.europa.eu/RegData/etudes/BRIE/2020/651350/IPOL_BRI(2020)651350_EN.pdf [Accessed 3 December 2020].

European Parliament (2020b) 'Multiannual Financial Framework 2021–2027: Commission proposal, initial comparison with the current MFF', May 2018. Available from: https://www.europarl.europa.eu/RegData/etudes/BRIE/2018/621864/EPRS_BRI(2018)621864_EN.pdf [Accessed 3 December 2020].

Eurostat (n.d.) 'Background'. Available from: https://ec.europa.eu/eurostat/web/nuts/background [Accessed 9 June 2020].

Eurostat (2017) 'GDP per inhabitant, 2017'. Available from: https://ec.europa.eu/eurostat/statistics-explained/index.php?title=File:GDP_per_inhabitant,_2017_ [Accessed 1 March 2020].

Eurostat (2018) 'Income inequality in the EU', 26 April. Available from: https://ec.europa.eu/eurostat/web/products-eurostat-news/-/EDN-20180426-1 [Accessed 1 November 2019].

Eurostat (2019) 'Employment specialization, 2016', Statistical Atlas Eurostat regional yearbook 2019. Available from: https://ec.europa.eu/eurostat/statistical-atlas/gis/viewer/?config=config.json&ch=ECF,C06,C02&mids=BKGCNT,C06M03,CNTOVL&o=1,1,0.7&center=47.80719,14.16892,3&lcis=C06M03& [Accessed 3 March 2020].

Eurostat (2020) 'Business Cycle Clock'. Available from: https://ec.europa.eu/eurostat/cache/bcc/bcc.html [Accessed 4 March 2020].

Ferrera, M. (1996) 'The "southern model" of welfare in social Europe', *Journal of European Social Policy*, 6(1): 17–37.

Fertig, M. and Schmidt, C.M. (2002) 'Mobility within Europe: What do we (still not) know?', IZA discussion paper No. 447.

Fischer, P.A. and Straubhaar, T. (1996) *Migration and Economic Integration in the Nordic Common Labour Market*, Nord 1996: 2, Copenhagen: Nordic Council of Ministers.

Florczak, I. and Otto, M. (2019) 'Precarious work and labour regulation in the EU: Current reality and perspectives', in J. Kenner, I. Florczak and M. Otto (eds) *Precarious Work: The Challenge for Labour Law in Europe*, Cheltenham: Edward Elgar, pp 2–21.

Frankel, J.A. and Rose, A.K. (1998) 'The endogeneity of the optimum currency area criteria', *Economic Journal*, 108(449): 1009–25.

Frieden, J., Gros, D. and Jones, E. (eds) (1998) *The New Political Economy of EMU*, Lanham: Rowman and Littlefield.

From the Editors' Desk (2009) 'Labour market integration', *Review of Market Integration*, 1(3): 257–63.

Furceri, D. and Zdzienicka, A. (2015) 'The euro area crisis: Need for a supranational fiscal risk sharing mechanism?', *Open Economies Review*, 26: 683–710.

Genschel, P. and Jachtenfuchs, M. (2016) 'Conflict-minimising integration: How the EU achieves massive integration despite massive protest', in D. Chalmers, M. Jachtenfuchs and C. Joerges (eds) *The End of the Eurocrats' Dream: Adjusting to European Diversity*, Cambridge: Cambridge University Press, pp 166–89.

Gernandt, J. and Pfeiffer, F. (2008) 'Wage convergence and inequality after unification: (East) Germany in transition', ZEW Discussion Paper 2008–022, Mannheim: ZEW.

Gerschenkron, A. (1962) *Economic Backwardness in Historical Perspective*, Cambridge, MA: Harvard University Press.

Giannone, D., Lenza, M. and Reichlin, L. (2009) 'Business Cycles in the Euro Area', February, European Central Bank Working Paper, No. 1010.

Glassner V. and Pochet, P. (2011) 'Why trade unions seek to coordinate wages and collective bargaining in the eurozone', ETUI Working Paper 2011.03, Brussels.

GoE (Group of Experts) (1956) *Report on the Social Aspects of European Economic Co-operation* (the Ohlin Report), Studies and Reports, New Series, No. 46, Geneva: ILO.

Goetschy, J. (2005) 'The European social dialogue in the 1990s: Institutional innovations and new paradigms', *Transfer*, 11(3): 409–22.

Gomez, R. and Gunderson, M. (2002) 'The integration of labour markets in North America', in G. Hoberg (ed) *North American Integration: Economic, Cultural and Political Dimensions*, Toronto: University of Toronto Press, pp 104–27.

Gorzelak, G. (2017) 'Cohesion policy and regional development', in J. Batchler, P. Berkowitz, S. Hardy and T. Muravska (eds) *EU Cohesion Policy: Reassessing Performance and Direction*, London: Routledge, pp 33–54.

Gray, J. (1996) *After Social Democracy*, London: Demos.

Greenspan, A. (1997) 'Remarks by Chairman Alan Greenspan, At the Catholic University Leuven', 14 January, Leuven, Belgium, The Federal Reserve Board. Available from: https://www.federalreserve.gov/boarddocs/speeches/1997/19970114.htm [Accessed 3 December 2020].

Gros, D. (2014) 'A fiscal shock absorber for the Eurozone? Lessons from the economics of insurance', 19 March, VOX CEPR Policy Portal. Available from: https://voxeu.org/article/ez-fiscal-shock-absorber-lessons-insurance-economics [Accessed 20 April 2020].

Gros, D. and Thygesen, N. (1998) *European Monetary Integration*, London: Longman.

Grote, J.R. and Schmitter, P.C. (1999) 'The renaissance of national corporatism: Unintended side effect of European economic and monetary union or calculated response to the absence of European social policy?', *Transfer*, 5(1/2): 34–63.

Habermas, J. (1975) *Legitimation Crisis*, Boston: Beacon Press.

Hall, P. and Soskice, D. (2001) *Varieties of Capitalism: The Institutional Foundations of Comparative Advantage*, Oxford: Oxford University Press.

Hamann, K., Johnson, A. and Kelly, J. (2012) 'Unions against governments: Explaining general strikes in western Europe, 1980–2006', *Comparative Political Studies*, 46(9): 1030–57.

Hamilton, A. (1791) 'Report on the subject of manufactures', Communicated to the House of Representatives, 5 December. Available from: www.constitution.org/ah/rpt_manufactures.pdf [Accessed 8 April 2020].

Hancké, B. (2013) *Unions, Central Banks and EMU: Labour Market Institutions and Monetary Integration in Europe*, Oxford: Oxford University Press.

Hann, D., Hauptmeier, M. and Waddington, J. (2017) 'European works councils after two decades', *European Journal of Industrial Relations*, 23(3): 209–24.

Hansen, P. and Hager, S.B. (2010) *The Politics of European Citizenship*, New York: Berghahn.

Harris, N. (2002) *Thinking the Unthinkable: The Immigration Myth Exposed*, London: I.B. Tauris.

Hayter, T. (2004) *Open Borders: The Case Against Immigration Controls*, 2nd edn, London: Pluto.

Heckmann, F. and Schnapper, D. (eds) (2003) *The Integration of Immigrants in European Societies: National Differences and Trends of Convergence*, Stuttgart: Lucius & Lucius.

Heinz, F.F. and Ward-Warmedinger, M.E. (2006) 'Cross-Border Labour Mobility within an Enlarged EU', October, ECB Occasional Paper No. 52. Available from: http://papers.ssrn.com/sol3/Delivery.cfm/SSRN_ID923371_code485639.pdf?abstractid=923371&mirid=3 [Accessed 3 December 2020].

Hendrickx, F. (2018) 'The European social pillar: A first evaluation', *European Labour Law Journal*, 9(1): 3–6.

Henley, J. (2018) 'How populism swept through Europe over 20 years', *The Guardian*, 20 November. Available from: https://www.theguardian.com/world/ng-interactive/2018/nov/20/how-populism-emerged-as-electoral-force-in-europe [Accessed 1 November 2019].

Henning, C.R. and Kessler, M. (2012) 'Fiscal federalism: US history for architects of Europe's fiscal union', 10 January, Peterson Institute for International Economics Working Paper No. 2012–1. Available from: https://papers.ssrn.com/sol3/Delivery.cfm/SSRN_ID1982709_code356528.pdf?abstractid=1982709&mirid=1 [Accessed 3 December 2020].

Higgins, M. and Klitgaard, T. (2014) 'The balance of payments crisis in the euro area periphery', *Current Issues in Economics and Finance*, 20(2).

Hobza, A. and Zeugner, S. (2014) 'Current accounts and financial flows in the euro area', *Journal of International Money and Finance*, 48: 291–313.

Hoffmann, L. (2008) 'Ever closer markets: Public procurement and services in the EU and the USA', *Political Perspectives*, 2(2): 1–35.

Hoffmann, L. (2011) 'Land of the Free, Home of the (Un)Regulated: A Look at Market-Building and Liberalization in the EU and the US', PhD dissertation, Department of Political Science, University of Oregon.

Hoffmann, L. (2014) 'Can North America learn from Europe about market-building? How the EU has surpassed the US single market', September/October, paper presented to the 2014 PNWPSA Conference in Bend, Oregon.

Hristov, N., Hülsewig, O. and Wollmershäuser, T. (2020) 'Capital flows in the euro area and TARGET2 balances', *Journal of Banking and Finance*, 113: DOI: 10.1016/j.jbankfin.2020.105734.

Hyman, R. (2005) 'Trade unions and the politics of the European social model', *Economic and Industrial Democracy*, 26(1): 9–40.

ILO (International Labour Organization) (1944) 'Declaration of Philadelphia'. Available from: https://www.ilo.org/legacy/english/inwork/cb-policy-guide/declarationofPhiladelphia1944.pdf [Accessed 3 February 2020].

ILO (1955) *Minutes of the 128th Session of the Governing Body*, 1–4 March, Geneva: ILO.

IMF (International Monetary Fund) (2008) *Iceland: Request for Stand-by Arrangement*, November, IMF Country Report No. 08/362.

IMF (2009) 'Macro policy lessons for a sound design of fiscal decentralization', IMF Departmental paper 2009/072709.

IMF (2013a) 'Toward a fiscal union for the Euro area', IMF Staff Discussion Note, September, SDN/13/09.

IMF (2013b) 'Toward a fiscal union for the Euro area: Technical Background Notes', September.

IMF (2014) *External Debt Statistics: Guide for Compilers and Users*, Washington, DC: IMF.

IMF (2017) *World Economic Outlook*, April. Available from: https://www.imf.org/en/Publications/WEO/Issues/2017/04/04/world-economic-outlook-april-2017 [Accessed 3 December 2020].

Information Service (1956) 'The Brussels report on the general common market', unofficial translation of the Spaak Report, June, Luxembourg: High Authority of the ECSC.

Inman, R.P. and Rubinfeld, D.L. (1991) 'Fiscal federalism in Europe: Lessons from the United States experience', NBER Working Paper No. 3941, December. Available from: https://www.nber.org/papers/w3941 [Accessed 24 January 2020].

Investopedia (2019) 'What is Eurosclerosis?' Available from: https://www.investopedia.com/terms/e/eurosclerosis.asp [Accessed 30 October 2019].

Issing, O. (2002) 'On macroeconomic policy coordination in EMU', *Journal of Common Market Studies*, 40(2): 345–58.

ITO (International Trade Organization) (1948) 'United Nations conference on trade and employment held at Havana, Cuba from November 21, 1947 to March 24, 1948' (the Havana Charter). Available from: https://www.wto.org/english/docs_e/legal_e/havana_e.pdf [Accessed 15 February 2020].

Iversen, T. and Soskice, D. (2013) 'A structural-institutional explanation of the Eurozone crisis', 3 June, unpublished manuscript, Cambridge, MA: Harvard University, Department of Government.

Janus, J. and Stanek, P. (2016) 'Europeanisation of monetary policy: Roots and causes', in P. Stanek and K. Wach (eds) *Macro-, Meso-, and Microeconomic Dimensions of Europeanisation*, Warsaw: Wydawnictwo Naukowe PWN SA, pp 73–88.

JASP (1991) 'Joint agreement of the social partners of 31 October 1991'. Available from: https://ec.europa.eu/social/BlobServlet?mode=dsw&docId=10480&langId=en [Accessed 24 April 2020].

Jauer, J., Liebig, T., Martin, J.P. and Puhani, P.A. (2014) 'Migration as an adjustment mechanism in the crisis? A comparison of Europe and the United States', Social, Employment and Migration working papers, Paris: OECD.

Jauer, J., Liebig, T., Martin, J.P. and Puhani, P.A. (2019) 'Migration as an adjustment mechanism in the crisis? A comparison of Europe and the United States 2006–2016', *Journal of Population Economics*, 32: 1–22.

Jileva, E. (2002) 'Visa and free movement of labour: The uneven imposition of the EU acquis on the accession states', *Journal of Ethnic and Migration Studies*, 28(4): 683–700.

Jones, E. (2016) 'Financial markets matter more than fiscal institutions for the success of the euro', *International Spectator*, 51(4): 1–11.

Jones, E. (2018) 'Towards a theory of disintegration', *Journal of European Public Policy*, 25(3): 440–51.

Jones, E. (2020) 'The politics of economic and monetary union', in F. Amtenbrink and C. Herman (eds) *The EU Law of Economic and Monetary Union*, Oxford: Oxford University Press, pp 53–96.

Jones, E., Frieden, J. and Torres, F. (eds) (1998) *Joining Europe's Monetary Club: The Challenges for Smaller Member States*, New York: St Martin's Press.

Kahanec, M. (2013) 'Labour mobility in an enlarged European Union', in A.F. Constant and K.F. Zimmermann (eds) *International Handbook on the Economics of Migration*, Cheltenham: Edward Elgar, pp 137–52.

Kahanec, M. and Guzi, M. (2017) 'How immigrants helped EU labor markets to adjust during the Great Recession', *International Journal of Manpower*, 38(7): 996–1015.

Kahanec, M. and Zimmermann, K.F. (eds) (2016) *Labor Migration, EU Enlargement, and the Great Recession*, Berlin: Springer.

Kahanec, M., Pytlikova, M. and Zimmermann, K.F. (2016) 'The free movement of workers in an enlarged European Union: Institutional underpinnings of economic adjustment', in M. Kahanec and K.F. Zimmermann (eds) *Labor Migration, EU Enlargement, and the Great Recession*, Berlin: Springer, pp 1–34.

Kaitz, H. (1970) 'Experience of the past: The national minimum', *Youth Un-employment and Minimum Wages*, Bulletin 1657, Washington, DC: US Department of Labor, pp 30–54.

Kaldor, N. (1961) 'Capital accumulation and economic growth', in F.A. Lutz and D.C. Hague (eds) *The Theory of Capital*, New York: St Martin's Press, pp 177–222.

Karabarbounis, L. and Neiman, B. (2014) 'The global decline of the labor share', *Quarterly Journal of Economics*, 129(1): 61–103.

Katzenstein, P. (1985) *Small States in World Markets*, Ithaca: Cornell University Press.

Keating, M. and McCrone, D. (eds) (2013) *The Crisis of Social Democracy in Europe*, Edinburgh: Edinburgh University Press.

Kelly, J. (1998) *Rethinking Industrial Relations: Mobilization, Collectivism and Long Waves*, London: Routledge.

Kelton, S. (2020) *The Deficit Myth*, New York: Public Affairs.

Kenen, P.B. (2019 [1969]) 'The theory of optimum currency areas: An eclectic view', in P.B. Kenen, *Essays in International Economics*, Princeton: Princeton University Press, pp 163–82.

Kenner, J. (2003) *EU Employment Law: From Rome to Amsterdam and Beyond*, Oxford: Hart Publishing.

Kluth, M.F. (1998) *The Political Economy of a Social Europe: Understanding Labour Market Integration in the European Union*, London: Macmillan.

Korpi, W. (1974) 'Conflict, power and relative deprivation', *American Political Science Review*, 68(4): 1569–78.

Korpi, W. (1983) *The Democratic Class Struggle*, New York: Routledge.

Krause, A., Rinne, U. and Zimmermann, K.F. (2017) 'European labor market integration: What the experts think', *International Journal of Manpower*, 38(7): 954–74.

Krueger, A.B. and Pischke, J.-S. (1995) 'A comparative analysis of East and West German labor markets: Before and after unification', in R.B. Freeman and L.F. Katz (eds) *Differences and Changes in Wage Structures*, Chicago: University of Chicago Press, pp 405–45.

Krugman, P. (1991a) 'Increasing returns and economic geography', *Journal of Political Economy*, 99: 483–99.

Krugman, P. (1991b) *Geography and Trade*, Cambridge, MA: MIT Press.

Krugman, P. (1999) *The Accidental Theorist*, London: Penguin Books.

Krugman, P. (2012) 'Revenge of the optimum currency area', *NBER Macroeconomics Annual*, 27(1): 439–48.

Landesmann, M.A. (2015) 'Industrial policy: Its role in the European economy', *Intereconomics*, 50(3): 133–8.

Lane, P.R. (2013) 'Capital flows in the Euro Area', *European Economy*, Economic Papers 497 (April), European Commission: Directorate-General for Economic and Financial Affairs.

Lange, G. (1999) 'Billboard reading "Will the last person leaving SEATTLE – Turn out the lights" appears near Sea-Tac International Airport on April 16, 1971'. Available from: https://www.historylink.org/File/1287 [Accessed 8 February 2020].

Lavelle, A. (2013) *The Death of Social Democracy: Political Consequences in the 21st Century*, Aldershot: Ashgate.

Leibfried, S. (2002) 'Towards a European welfare state?', in C. Jones (ed) *New Perspectives on the Welfare State in Europe*, New York: Routledge, pp 128–51.

Léonard, E., Erne, R., Marginson, P. and Smismans, S. (2007) *New Structures, Forms and Processes of Governance in European Industrial Relations*, Luxembourg: Office for Official Publications of the European Communities.

Lind, J., Waddington, J. and Hoffmann, R. (1997) 'European trade unionism in transition? A review of the issues', *Transfer*, 3(3): 464–97.

List, F. (1916 [1841]) *The National System of Political Economy*, trans. S.S. Lloyd, London: Longmans, Green.

MacDougall, D., Biehl, D., Brown, A., Forte, F., Fréville, Y,. O'Donoghue, M. and Peeters, T. (1977) *Report of the Study Group on the Role of Public Finance in European Integration*, the 'MacDougall Report', Brussels: Commission of the European Communities. Available from: http://aei.pitt.edu/36433/1/Report.study.group. A13.pdf [Accessed 21 April 2020].

McLeay, M., Radla, A. and Thomas, R. (2014) 'Money creation in the modern economy', *Quarterly Bulletin*, Q1: 14–27.

McNamara, K.R. (1998) *The Currency of Ideas: Monetary Politics in the European Union*, Ithaca: Cornell University.

Malamud, O. and Wozniak, A. (2012) 'The impact of college education on geographic mobility', *Journal of Human Resources*, 47(4): 913–50.

Manwaring, R. and Kennedy, P. (eds) (2017) *Why the Left Loses: The Decline of the Centre-left in Comparative Perspective*, London: Policy Press.

Manzella, G.P. and Mendez, C. (2009) 'The turning points of EU Cohesion policy', January. Available from: https://ec.europa.eu/ regional_policy/archive/policy/future/pdf/8_manzella_final-formatted.pdf [Accessed 15 November 2020].

Marginson, P. and Sisson, K. (2006) *European Integration and Industrial Relations: Multi-level Governance in the Making*, Basingstoke: Palgrave Macmillan.

Marshall, A. (1920 [1890]) *Principles of Economics*, 8th edn, London: Macmillan and Co. Available from: http://oll.libertyfund. org/title/1676 [Accessed 26 November 2019].

Martin, S., Hartley, K. and Cox, A. (1997) 'Public purchasing in the European Union: Some evidence from contract awards', *International Journal of Public Sector Management*, 10(4): 279–93.

Martin, A. and Ross, G. (1999) 'In the line of fire: The Europeanization of labor representation', in A. Martin and G. Ross (eds) *The Brave New World of European Labor: European Trade Unions at the Millennium*, New York: Berghahn, pp 312–67.

Marx, K. (1954 [1867]) *Capital: A Critique of Political Economy*, Vol. 1, London: Lawrence & Wishart.

MaT (Maastricht Treaty) (1992) 'Treaty on European Union', also known as the Treaty on European Union (TEU). As signed in Maastricht on 7 February 1992, Luxembourg: Office for Official Publications of the European Communities.

Mazuyer, E., Laulom, S., Teissier, C. and Claude-Emmanuel, T. (2012) 'How has the crisis affected social legislation in Europe?', ETUI Policy Brief, No. 2: 1–6.

Mazzucato, M., Cimoli, M., Dosi, G., Stiglitz, J.E., Landesmann, M.A., Pianta, M., Walz, R. and Page, T. (2015) 'Which industrial policy does Europe need?', *Intereconomics*, 50(3): 120–55.

Meade, J.E. (1953) *Problems of Economic Union*, Chicago: University of Chicago Press.

Meade, J.E. (1957) 'The balance-of-payments problems of a European free-trade area', *Economic Journal*, 67(267): 379–96.

Meidner, R. (1993) 'Why did the Swedish model fail?', in R. Miliband and L. Panitch (eds) *Socialist Register 1993: Real Problems, False Solutions*, London, Merlin Press, pp 211–28.

Menéndez, A.J. (2016) 'Neumark vindicated: The three patterns of Europeanisation of national tax systems and the future of the social and democratic Rechtstaat', in D. Chalmers, M. Jachtenfuchs and C. Joerges (eds) *The End of the Eurocrats' Dream: Adjusting to European Diversity*, Cambridge: Cambridge University Press, pp 78–126.

Merler, S. and Pisani-Ferry, J. (2012) 'Sudden stops in the Euro Area', Bruegel Policy Contribution 2012/16, March.

Ministère des Affaires étrangères (1951) *Rapport de la Délégation française sur le Traité instituant la Communauté Européenne du Charbon et de l'Acier et la Convention relative aux dispositions transitoires* (*Report of the French Delegation on the Treaty instituting the European Coal and Steel Community and on the Convention relative to transitional provisions signed in Paris 18 April 1951*), Paris, October. Available from: http://aei.pitt.edu/13817/ [Accessed 3 December 2020].

Mitchell, W. and Fazi, T. (2017) *Reclaiming the State: A Progressive Vision of Sovereignty for a Post-Neoliberal World*, London: Pluto Press.

Moses, J.W. (1998a) 'Sweden and the EMU', in E. Jones, J. Frieden and F. Torres (eds) *Joining Europe's Monetary Club: The Challenges for Smaller Member States*, London: Macmillan, pp 203–24.

Moses, J.W. (1998b) 'Finland and the EMU', in E. Jones, J. Frieden and F. Torres (eds) *Joining Europe's Monetary Club: The Challenges for Smaller Member States*, London: Macmillan, pp 83–104.

Moses, J.W. (2006) *International Migration: Globalization's Last Frontier*, London: Zed Books.

Moses, J.W. (2011) 'Is constitutional symmetry enough? Social models and market integration in the US and Europe', *Journal of Common Market Studies*, 49(4): 823–43.

Moses, J.W. (2017a) *Eurobondage: The Political Costs of Monetary Union in Europe*, Colchester: ECPR Press.

Moses, J.W. (2017b) 'Sparrows of despair: Migration as a signalling device for dysfunctional states in Europe', *Government and Opposition*, 52(2): 295–328.

Moses, J.W. (2021) 'Belaboured markets: Imagining a more democratic global economic order', in A. Fishwick and N. Kiersey (eds) *Postcapitalist Futures: Political Economy Beyond Crisis and Hope*, London: Pluto Press.

Mosler, W. (2017) 'How could euro nations start a new currency?', 13 October. Available from: https://www.youtube.com/watch?v=V2iBD1x5ofw [Accessed 7 August 2020].

Mosley, H.G. (1990) 'The social dimension of European integration', *International Labour Review*, 129(2): 147–64.

Müller, T., Vandaele, K. and Waddington, J. (2019) 'Conclusion: Towards an endgame', in T. Müller, K. Vandaele and J. Waddington (eds) *Collective Bargaining in Europe*, Vol. 3, Brussels: ETUI, pp 625–68. Available from: https://www.etui.org/Publications2/Books/Collective-bargaining-in-Europe-towards-an-endgame.-Volume-I-II-III-and-IV [Accessed 10 June 2020].

Mundell, R.A. (1957) 'International trade and factor mobility', *American Economic Review*, 67: 321–35.

Mundell, R.A. (1961) 'A theory of optimum currency areas', *American Economic Review*, 51: 657–65.

Musgrave, R.A. (1959) *The Theory of Public Finance: A Study in Public Economy*, New York: McGraw-Hill.

Myrdal, G. (1956) *An International Economy: Problems and Prospects*, New York: Harper and Brothers.

Naz, A., Ahmad, N. and Naveed, A. (2017) 'Wage convergence across European regions: Do international borders matter?', *Journal of Economic Integration*, 32(1): 35–64.

Nohlen, D. and Stoever, P. (eds) (2010) *Elections in Europe: A Data Handbook*, Baden-Baden: Nomos Verlagsgesellschaft.

Oates, W.E. (1972) *Fiscal Federalism*, New York: Harcourt Brace Jovanovich.

Oates, W.E. (2005) 'Toward a second-generation theory of fiscal federalism', *International Tax and Public Finance*, 12(4): 349–73.

OECD (Organization for Economic Cooperation and Development) (2012a) *Economic Surveys: European Union, 2012*, Paris: OECD Publishing.

OECD (2012b) 'Labour losing to capital: What explains the declining labour share?', in *OECD Employment Outlook*, Paris: OECD, Chapter 3.

OECD (2016) *Economic Surveys: European Union, 2016*, Paris: OECD Publishing.

OECD (2018) *OECD Employment Outlook 2018*, Paris: OECD Publishing.

OECD (2020a) 'Government expenditure by function (COFOG)', OECDStat. Available from: https://stats.oecd.org/# [Accessed 24 April 2020].

OECD (2020b) 'Gross Domestic Product (GDP), 2019 Archive'. Available from: https://stats.oecd.org/Index.aspx?datasetcode=SNA_TABLE1_ARCHIVE# [Accessed 24 April 2020].

Offe, C. (1972) *Strukturprobleme des kapitalistischen Staates: Aufsätze zur politischen Soziologie,* Frankfurt: Campus.

Offe, C. (1984) *Contradictions of the Welfare State*, ed. John Keane, London: Routledge.

Offe, C. (2015) 'Narratives of responsibility: German politics in the Eurozone crisis', Casa della Cultura. Available from: https://www.casadellacultura.it/pdfarticoli/Claus-Offe-Narratives-of-Responsibility.pdf [Accessed 16 April 2018].

Offe, C. (2016) *Europe Entrapped*, Cambridge: Polity.

Offe, C. and Wiesenthal, H. (1985) 'Two logics of collective action', in C. Offe (ed) *Disorganized Capitalism*, Cambridge: Polity, pp. 170–220.

OJEC (Official Journal of the European Communities) (2000) 'Charter of fundamental rights of the European Union', 2000/C 364/01.

O'Rourke, K.H., Taylor, A.M. and Williamson, J.G. (1996) 'Factor price convergence in the late nineteenth century', *International Economic Review*, 37(3): 499–530.

Parikh, A. and van Leuvensteijn, M. (2003) 'Interregional labour mobility, inequality and wage convergence', *Applied Economics*, 35(8): 931–41.

Pedersen, P.J., Røed, M. and Wadensjö, E. (2008) 'The Common Nordic Labour Market at 50', TemaNord 2008: 506, Copenhagen: Nordic Council of Ministers.

Perlman S. (1928) *A Theory of the Labor Movement*, New York: Macmillan.

Peterson, P.E. (1995) *The Price of Federalism*, Washington, DC: Brookings Institution.

Phillips, L. (2011a) 'EU ushers in "silent revolution" in control of national economic policies', *EU Observer*, 16 March. Available from: http://euobserver.com/institutional/31993 [Accessed 14 May 2020].

Phillips, L. (2011b) 'Trade unions "dare" EU to hold referendum on economic pact', *EU Observer*. Available from: https://euobserver.com/economic/31910 [Accessed 31 May 2020].

Pierson, C. (2001) *Hard Choices: Social Democracy in the 21st Century*, Cambridge: Polity.

Pisani-Ferry, J. (2012) 'The known unknown and unknown unknowns of EMU', Bruegel Policy Contribution, Issue 2012/18, October.

Poghosyan, T., Senhadji, A. and Cottarelli, C. (2015) 'The role of social transfers in smoothing regional shocks', in C. Cottarelli and M. Guerguil (eds) *Designing a European Fiscal Union: Lessons from the Experience of Fiscal Federations*, London: Routledge, pp 60–89.

Polanyi, K. (2001 [1944]) *The Great Transformation: The Political and Economic Origins of Our Time*, Boston: Beacon Press.

Political and Economic Planning (1957) 'The Spaak Report: A summarised translation of Part I', *Political and Economic Planning*, 23(406): 222–43.

Prebisch, R. (1950) 'The economic development of Latin America and its principal problems', Economic Commission for Latin America, Lake Success: UN Department of Economic Affairs. Available from: http://archivo.cepal.org/pdfs/cdPrebisch/002.pdf [Accessed 11 February 2015].

Przeworski, A. and Wallerstein, M. (1988) 'Structural dependence of the state on capital', *American Political Science Review*, 82(1): 11–29.

Raines, P. (2000) 'The impact of European integration on the development of national labour markets', Employment Paper 2000/2001. Available from: http://www.ilo.int/wcmsp5/groups/public/---ed_emp/documents/publication/wcms_142279.pdf [Accessed 3 December 2020].

Reinert, E.S. (2007) *How Rich Countries Got Rich ... and Why Poor Countries Stay Poor*, London: Constable.

Reinert, E.S. (2017) 'Towards a better understanding of convergence and divergence: or, how the present EU strategy – at the expense of the economic periphery – neglects the stories that once made Europe successful', Working Papers in Technology and Economic Dynamics no. 77. Available from: https://developingeconomics.files.wordpress.com/2017/11/2017111607374848-1.pdf [Accessed 12 June 2020].

Rhodes, M. (1992) 'The future of the "social dimension": Labour market regulation in post-1992 Europe', *Journal of Common Market Studies*, 30(1): 23–51.

Robertson, R. (2000) 'Wage shocks and North American labor-market integration', *American Economic Review*, 90(4): 742–64.

Robertson, R. (2005) 'Has NAFTA increased labor market integration between the United States and Mexico?', *World Bank Economic Review*, 19(3): 425–48.

Rockoff, H. (2000) 'How long did it take the United States to become an optimal currency area?', NBER Historical Working Paper No. 124, April. Available from: https://www.nber.org/papers/h0124 [Accessed 24 January 2020].

Rome Convention (1980) '1980 Rome Convention on the law applicable to contractual obligations', OJ C 27, 26.1.1998, pp 34–53. Available from: https://eur-lex.europa.eu/legal-content/EN/TXT/PDF/?uri=CELEX:41998A0126(02)&from=EN [Accessed 15 November 2020].

Romer, P. (2020) 'The dismal kingdom: Do economists have too much power?', *Foreign Affairs*, 99(2): 150–7.

Rose, A.K. (2000) 'One money, one market: Estimating the effect of common currencies on trade', *Economic Policy*, 30: 7–33.

Rose, A.K. (2002) 'The Effect of Common Currencies on International Trade: Where Do We Stand?', Monetary Authority of Singapore Occasional Paper, No. 22.

Rosenbloom, J.L. (1990) 'One market or many? Labor market integration in the late nineteenth-century United States', *Journal of Economic History*, 50(1): 85–107.

Rosenbloom, J.L. (1996) 'Was there a national labor market at the end of the nineteenth century? New evidence on earnings in manufacturing', *Journal of Economic History*, 56: 626–56.

Roux, R. (1952) 'The position of Labour under the Schuman plan', *International Labour Review*, 65: 289–320.

Rubery, J. and Piasna, A. (2017) 'Labour market segmentation and deregulation of employment protection in the EU', in M. Myant and A. Piasna (eds) *Myths of Employment Deregulation: How it Neither Creates Jobs nor Reduces Labour Market Segmentation*, Brussels: ETUI, pp 43–60. Available from: https://www.etui.org/sites/default/files/Chapter%202_3.pdf [Accessed 15 June 2020].

Ruggie, J.G. (1982) 'International regimes, transactions, and change: Embedded liberalism in the postwar economic order', *International Organization*, 36(2): 379–415.

Sala-i-Martin, X. and Sachs, J. (1991) 'Fiscal federalism and optimum currency areas: Evidence for Europe from the United States', NBER Working Paper No. 3855, October. Available from: https://www.nber.org/papers/w3855 [Accessed 24 January 2020].

Salais, R. (2013) *Le viol d'Europe: Enquête sur la disparition d'une idée*, Paris: Presses Universitaires de France.

Samuelson, P.A. (1948) 'International trade and equalisation of factor price', *Economic Journal*, 58: 163–84.

Samuelson, P.A. (1949) 'International factor-price equalisation once again', *Economic Journal*, 59: 181–97.

Sandbu, M. (2013) 'Legal debate over Cyprus capital controls', *Financial Times*, 25 March.

Sapir, A. (1996) 'Trade liberalization and the harmonization of social policies: Lessons from European integration', in J. Bhagwati and R.E. Hudec (eds) *Fair Trade and Harmonization: Prerequisites for Free Trade?* Vol. I. *Economic Analysis*, Cambridge, MA: MIT Press, pp 543–70.

Sapir, A. (2006) 'Globalization and the reform of European social models', *Journal of Common Market Studies*, 44(2): 369–90.

Savage, J.D. and Verdun, A. (2016) 'Strengthening the European Commission's budgetary and economic surveillance capacity since Greece and the euro area crisis: A study of five directorates-general', *Journal of European Public Policy*, 23(1): 101–18.

Scharpf, F.W. (1996) 'Negative and positive integration in the political economy of European welfare states', in G. Marks, F. Scharpf, P. Schmitter and W. Streeck (eds) *Governance in the European Union*, London: Sage, pp 15–39.

Scharpf, F.W. (2002) 'The European social model: Coping with the challenges of diversity', *Journal of Common Market Studies*, 40(4): 645–70.

Scharpf, F.W. (2010) 'The asymmetry of European integration, or why the EU cannot be a "social market economy"', *Socio-Economic Review*, 8(2): 211–50.

Scharpf, F.W. (2016) 'The costs of non-disintegration: The case of the European Monetary Union', in D. Chalmers, M. Jachtenfuchs and C. Joerges (eds) *The End of the Eurocrats' Dream: Adjusting to European Diversity*, Cambridge: Cambridge University Press, pp 29–49.

Schellinger, A. (2016) *EU Labor Market Policy: Ideas, Thought Communities and Policy Change*, New York, NY: Palgrave Macmillan.

Schmalz, S. and Weinmann, N. (2016) 'Between power and powerlessness: Labor unrest in Western Europe in times of crisis', *Perspectives on Global Development and Technology*, 15: 543–66.

Schmalz, S., Ludwig, C. and Webster, E. (2018) 'The power resources approach: Developments and challenges', *Global Labour Journal*, 9(1): 113–34.

Schömann, I. (2014) 'Labour law reforms in Europe: Adjusting employment protection legislation for the worse?', ETUI Working Paper 2014.02.

Schulten, T. (2002) 'A European solidaristic wage policy?', *European Journal of Industrial Relations*, 8(2): 173–96.

Schulten, T. and Lübker, M. (2019) 'WSI minimum wage report 2019', WSI-Report No. 46e, Düsseldorf: WSI. Available from: https://www.boeckler.de/pdf/p_wsi_report_46e_2019.pdf [Accessed 26 July 2019].

Schulten, T. and Müller, T. (2019) 'What's in a name? From minimum wages to living wages in Europe', *Transfer*, 25(3): 267–84.

Schumpeter, J. A. (1998 [1942]) *Capitalism, Socialism and Democracy*, London: Routledge.

Scott, J.C. (1999) *Seeing like a State: How Certain Schemes to Improve the Human Condition Have Failed*, New Haven: Yale University Press.

Scruggs, L. (2002) 'The Ghent system and union membership in Europe, 1970–1996', *Political Research Quarterly*, 55(2): 275–97.

SEA (Single European Act) (1987) 'Resolution on the Single European Act', *Official Journal of the European Communities*, Doc. A2–169/86, 12.1.87.

Segers, M. (2019) 'Eclipsing Atlantis: Trans-Atlantic multilateralism in trade and monetary affairs as a pre-history to the genesis of social market Europe (1942–1950)', *Journal of Common Market Studies*, 57(1): 60–76.

Seikel, D. (2016) 'Flexible austerity and supranational autonomy: The reformed excessive deficit procedure and the asymmetry between liberalization and social regulation in the EU', *Journal of Common Market Studies*, 54(6): 1398–416.

Silver, B.J. (2003) *Forces of Labor: Workers' Movements and Globalization since 1870*, Cambridge: Cambridge University Press.

Singer, H. (1950) 'The distribution of gains between investing and borrowing countries', *American Economic Review*, 40(2): 473–85.

Sisson, K. and Marginson, P. (2000) *The Impact of Economic and Monetary Union on Industrial Relations: A Sector and Company View*, Luxembourg: Office for Official Publications of the European Communities.

Sisson, K., Arrowsmith, J., Gilman, M. and Hall, M. (1999) *EMU and the Implications for Industrial Relations: A Select Bibliographic Review*, Dublin: European Foundation for the Improvement of Living and Working Conditions.

Solow, R.M. (1990) *The Labor Market as a Social Institution*, Cambridge: Basil Blackwell.

Spaak Report, The (1956) *Rapport de Chefs de Délégation aux Ministres des Affaires Etrangéres*, Belgium: Comité Intergouvernemental Créé par la Conférence de Messine. Available from: http://aei.pitt.edu/996/1/Spaak_report_french.pdf [Accessed 15 February 2020].

Standing, G. (2011) *The Precariat: The New Dangerous Class*, London: Bloomsbury.

Steiner, A., Steinkamp, S. and Westermann, F. (2019) 'Exit strategies, capital flight and speculative attacks: Europe's version of the trilemma', *European Journal of Political Economy*, 59: 83–96.

Stevenson, R.D. (1995) 'James E. Meade, Nobel economist, dies at 88', *New York Times*, 28 December, B9. Available from: https://www.nytimes.com/1995/12/28/world/james-e-meade-nobel-economist-dies-at-88.html [Accessed 10 February 2020].

Streeck, W. (2015) 'Why the euro divides Europe', *New Left Review*, 95: 5–26.

Streeck, W. (2019) 'Progressive regression: Metamorphoses of European social policy', *New Left Review*, 118: 117–39.

Tavlas, G.S. (1993) 'The "new" theory of optimum currency areas', *World Economy*, 16(6): 663–85.

TEC (Treaty establishing the European Community) (2002) 'European Union Consolidated Versions of the Treaty on European Union and of the Treaty Establishing the European community', Treaty of Nice, signed on 26 February 2001, *Official Journal of the European Communities*, 24.12.2002 C325/01.

TFEU (Treaty on the Functioning of the European Union) (2012) 'Consolidated version of the Treaty on the functioning of the European Union', *Official Journal of the European Union*, 26.10.2012 C326/47.

Theodoropoulou, S. (2019) 'Convergence to fair wage growth? Evidence from European countries on the link between productivity and real compensation growth, 1970–2017', Working Paper 2019.07, ETUI.

Tiebout, C. (1956) 'A pure theory of local expenditures', *Journal of Political Economy*, 65: 416–24.

ToA (Treaty of Amsterdam) (1997) *Treaty of Amsterdam Amending the Treaty on European Union, the Treaties Establishing the European Communities and Certain Related Acts*, Luxembourg: Publications Office of the European Union.

Tolbert, C.M. and Sizer, M. (1996) US commuting zones and labor market areas: A 1990 update, Staff Paper No. 9614, Rural Economic Division, Economic Research Service, US Department of Agriculture. Available from: https://ageconsearch.umn.edu/record/278812/ [Accessed 4 March 2020].

Tommaso Padoa-Schioppa Group (2012) *Completing the Euro: A Roadmap Toward Fiscal Union in Europe*, 26 June. Available from: https://www.aicgs.org/site/wp-content/uploads/2012/10/CompletingTheEuro_Report.pdf [Accessed 23 April 2020].

ToP (Treaty of Paris) (1951) *Treaty Establishing the European Coal and Steel Community*, Paris, 18 April. Available from: https://www.cvce.eu/content/publication/1997/10/13/11a21305-941e-49d7-a171-ed5be548cd58/publishable_en.pdf [Accessed 15 February 2020].

ToR (Treaty of Rome) (1957) *Treaty of Rome*, 25 March. Available from: https://ec.europa.eu/romania/sites/romania/files/tratatul_de_la_roma.pdf [Accessed 3 February 2020].

UN (United Nations) (1945) *Charter of the United Nations*, 26 June. Available from: https://www.un.org/en/charter-united-nations/index.html [Accessed 15 February 2020].

US Bureau of Labor Statistics (2020) 'Local area unemployment statistics', 4 March. Available from: https://www.bls.gov/web/laus/laumstrk.htm [Accessed 9 March 2020].

Vanhercke, B., Ghailani, D. and Spasova, S. with Pochet, P. (eds) (2020) *Social Policy in the European Union 1999–2019: The Long and Winding Road*, Brussels: European Trade Union Institute and European Social Observatory.

Van Parisj, P. (2013) 'The euro-dividend', *Social Europe Journal*, 3 July.

Varoufakis, Y., Halevi, J. and Theocarakis, N.J. (2011) *Modern Political Economics: Making Sense of the Post-2008 World*, London: Routledge.

Visser, J. (2016) 'What happened to collective bargaining during the great recession?', *IZA Journal of Labour Policy*, 5(9). Available from: https://link.springer.com/article/10.1186/s40173-016-0061-1 [Accessed 15 June 2020].

Waddington, J., Müller, T. and Vandaele, K. (2019) 'Setting the scene: Collective bargaining under neoliberalism', in T. Müller, K. Vandaele and J. Waddington (eds) *Collective Bargaining in Europe*, Vol. 1, Brussels: ETUI, pp 1–31.

Webb, S. and Webb, B. (1894) *The History of Trade Unionism*, London: Longmans, Green and Co.

Wehner, J. (2006) 'Assessing the power of the purse: An index of legislative budget institutions', *Political Studies*, 54(4): 767–85.

Weiss, M. (2017) 'The future of labour law in Europe: Rise or fall of the European social model?', *European Labour Law Journal*, 8(4): 344–56.

Werner, P., Ansiaux, H., Brouwers, G., Clappier, B., Mosca, U., Schöllhorn, J.-B., Stammati, G. and Morelli, G. (1970) *Report to the Council and the Commission on the Realization by Stages of Economic and Monetary Union in the Community*, the 'Werner Report', Luxembourg: Bulletin of the European Communities. Available from: http://aei.pitt.edu/1002/1/monetary_werner_final.pdf [Accessed 4 April 2020].

Williamson, J.G. (1995) 'The evolution of global labor markets since 1830: Background evidence and hypotheses', *Explorations in Economic History*, 32(2): 141–96.

Williamson, J.G. (1996) 'Globalization, convergence, and history', *Journal of Economic History*, 56: 277–306.

Wright, E.O. (2000) 'Working-class power, capitalist-class interests and class compromise', *American Journal of Sociology*, 105(4): 957–1002.

Wood, A. (2018) 'The 1990s trade and wages debate in retrospect', *World Economy*, 41: 975–99.

Wozniak, A. (2010) 'Are college graduates more responsive to distant labor market opportunities?', *Journal of Human Resources*, 45(4): 944–70.

Wray, L.R. (2015) *Modern Monetary Theory*, 2nd edn, New York: Palgrave Macmillan.

Wyplosz, C. (2013) 'Fiscal rules: Theoretical issues and historical experiences', in A. Alesina and F. Giavazzi (eds) *Fiscal Policy after the Financial Crisis*, Chicago: University of Chicago Press, pp 495–530.

Yagan, D. (2014) 'Moving to opportunity? Migratory insurance over the Great Recession'. Available from: https://eml.berkeley.edu/~yagan/MigratoryInsurance.pdf [Accessed 16 June 2020].

Zimmer, R. (2011) 'Labour market politics through jurisprudence: The influence of the judgements of the European Court of Justice (Viking, Laval, Rüffert, Luxembourg) on labour market policies', *German Policy Studies*, 7(1): 211–34. Available from: http://epa-journal.eu/download/8.-labour-market-politics-through-jurisprudence-the-influence-of-the-judgements-of-the-european-court-of-justice_.pdf [Accessed 9 April 2020].

Zimmermann, K.F. (2009) 'Labour mobility and the integration of European labour markets', in E. Nowotny, P. Mooslechner and D. Ritzberger-Grunwald (eds) *The Integration of European Labour Markets*, Northampton: Edward Elgar, pp 9–23.

Zwick, H. and Syed, S.A.S. (2017) 'Great Recession impact on European labor markets integration: Cluster analyses', *International Journal of Manpower*, 38(7): 1016–35.

Index